Teach® Yourself

# Get started in Turkish

Asuman Çelen Pollard

# *for Vanessa-Su Pollard*

For UK order enquiries: please contact Bookpoint Ltd,
130 Milton Park, Abingdon, Oxon OX14 4SB.
Telephone: +44 (0) 1235 827720. Fax: +44 (0) 1235 400454.
Lines are open 09.00–17.00, Monday to Saturday, with a 24-hour
message answering service. Details about our titles and how to
order are available at www.teachyourself.com

For USA order enquiries: please contact McGraw-Hill Customer
Services, PO Box 545, Blacklick, OH 43004-0545, USA.
Telephone: 1-800-722-4726. Fax: 1-614-755-5645.

For Canada order enquiries: please contact McGraw-Hill
Ryerson Ltd, 300 Water St, Whitby, Ontario L1N 9B6, Canada.
Telephone: 905 430 5000. Fax: 905 430 5020.

Long renowned as the authoritative source for self-guided
learning – with more than 50 million copies sold worldwide –
the *Teach Yourself* series includes over 500 titles in the fields of
languages, crafts, hobbies, business, computing and education.

British Library Cataloguing in Publication Data: a catalogue record
for this title is available from the British Library.

Library of Congress Catalog Card Number: on file.

First published in UK 2003 by Hodder Education, 338 Euston
Road, London NW1 3BH as *Teach Yourself Beginner's Turkish*.

First published in US 2003 by The McGraw-Hill Companies, Inc.

The **Teach Yourself** name is a registered trade mark of
Hodder Headline.

Typeset by MPS Limited, A Macmillan Company.

The publisher has used its best endeavours to ensure that the URLs
for external websites referred to in this book are correct and active
at the time of going to press. However, the publisher and the author
have no responsibility for the websites and can make no guarantee
that a site will remain live or that the content will remain relevant,
decent or appropriate.

Hodder Headline's policy is to use papers that are natural,
renewable and recyclable products and made from wood grown
in sustainable forests. The logging and manufacturing processes
are expected to conform to the environmental regulations of the
country of origin.

Impression number        10 9 8 7 6 5 4 3 2 1
Year                             2014 2013 2012 2011 2010

# Acknowledgements

I would like to thank my student, Trisha Wick, for providing assistance in writing and editing the book and Dr Cymore Argent for working alongside me from the beginning and being so perceptive and meticulous.

I would also like to say thank you to Nur and Tim Hooton for their professional support.

I am most grateful for the support of the Turkish Tourism Office in London for providing me with material essential for the completion of the book.

Thanks are also due to Vanessa-Su Pollard for her English support and photography skills.

I would also like to say thank you to Tom Wild for proofreading and editing my material.

And last, but not least, I would like to thank all the people at Hodder & Stoughton, especially Ginny Catmur and the editorial team, for being so supportive. Their professional contribution has been invaluable.

# Credits

**Front cover:** © Lynx/Iconotec.com/Photolibrary.com

**Back cover and pack:** © Jakub Semeniuk/iStockphoto.com,
© Royalty-Free/Corbis, © agencyby/iStockphoto.com, © Andy
Cook/iStockphoto.com, © Christopher Ewing/iStockphoto.com,
© zebicho – Fotolia.com, © Geoffrey Holman/iStockphoto.com,
© Photodisc/Getty Images, © James C. Pruitt/iStockphoto.com,
© Mohamed Saber – Fotolia.com

**Pack:** © Stockbyte/Getty Images

# Contents

# Meet the author

I am a linguist, language teacher and writer and have been an enthusiastic researcher of Turkish as a modern language since 1977. I live and work in Birmingham, England, and make regular visits to my homeland, Turkey.

I have expertise in teaching Turkish both as a foreign language and for specific purposes. Having also taught English as a foreign language, I have a keen interest in undertaking comparative studies between the two languages. I keep up to date with changes that take place within both languages and create materials that are intended to aid learners at all levels, from beginners to advanced.

I am interested in helping learners understand the nuances in lexis and grammar within Turkish through learner-friendly language. To do this, I draw on my many years of classroom experience, which helps me to create materials that respond to a variety of learning needs. These materials can be used in language classes, as well as in one-to-one teaching. They can also be used by the learners themselves as self-study materials.

With my teaching experience and love of all things Turkish and English, I am ideally placed to guide you on your journey through the Turkish language. As I have said elsewhere: 'This book is a chance for me to share some of the things that I believe help people to be a good language learner based on over 30 years of teaching and research experience.'

Asuman Çelen Pollard

I would like to give my grateful thanks to Trisha Wick for her invaluable help while working with me on this manuscript.

# *Only got a minute?*

## The Turkish language

Learning Turkish will allow you to speak with over 200 million people worldwide. There are many English words in Turkish but did you know that words we use frequently in English, such as kebab, yogurt, kiosk and döner, are of Turkish origin? You may be surprised to find many French, Arabic, Persian, German and, nowadays, Russian words creeping into today's Turkish.

Here are some key Turkish words to start with:

**merhaba** = *hi*

**evet** = *yes*

**hayır** = *no*

**teşekkürler** = *thanks*

**pardon** = *sorry/excuse me*

Language learning, however, is much more than the study of vocabulary or grammar. It involves learning about culture, body language and much, much more.

Greetings, ordering drinks and food, booking somewhere to stay and shopping are just a few of the situations you will be able to handle once you have completed this course:

- ▸ Language points and explanations are simple.
- ▸ Turkish, unlike English, is very logical and regular.
- ▸ You will quickly be able to read and speak Turkish.
- ▸ Standard Turkish as spoken in Istanbul is focused on in this book.

# 10 Only got ten minutes?

## The Turkish language

Why learn Turkish? Because you can, that's why! Although Turkish is noticeably different from western languages, there is some good news:

▶ Turkish is a very regular and logical language.
▶ Nouns do not have different genders, so you do not have to remember whether something is masculine or feminine as you do in, say, French or German.
▶ There are no countable or uncountable nouns to worry about. All nouns are treated as countable.
▶ Turkish grammar is very regular – learn a rule and there are (usually) no exceptions.
▶ Once you know a little vocabulary and a few rules about vocabulary building, guessing at the potential meaning of new words is a piece of cake.
▶ You may be surprised to realize how many English words are used in today's Turkish.

The most challenging side of learning Turkish is related to the fact that it is simply different from western European languages. Let's have a look at the challenging aspects:

▶ Turkish uses vowel harmony – a feature that is unknown to English speakers. This makes the language *harmonious*.
▶ Where English uses a separate word, Turkish often adds an ending to an existing word.
▶ The word order appears unusual.

The way in which Turkish works is absolutely fascinating. Yet the more you know about it, the more you will be surprised by its simplicity!

## Why learn about Turkish culture?

Well, it is all about communication. Less than 50% of communication is verbal, while the rest is cultural, expressed through body language, etc. All cultures are different from one another, but some are more different than others. I hope you will enjoy learning more about Turkish culture.

People from different cultures use language in different ways and as you start to learn Turkish, a little knowledge of cultural context will help you communicate well with Turkish people. Good communication is not always about accurate pronunciation and grammar – it is more important that you learn the manners and customs expected by native speakers of a language as then you will be received with friendship and respect. You will also find that knowing about the culture of a country and the body language used by its people helps you to understand what you see and hear around you. For example, if you listen to English speakers shopping in England you will hear them using 'please' and 'thank you' many times. This would seem a little strange to Turkish speakers, who express politeness differently when greeting shopkeepers, using different verb endings depending on the person they are addressing.

Philosophers argue whether the way in which a language works reflects the thinking of its speakers or vice versa! It is interesting to note that while English speakers wish each other just one 'Good morning' on meeting, Turkish speakers wish each other **Günaydınlar** ('many good mornings')!

Hospitality, good manners and respectful social interaction are very important in Turkish culture. Turkish has set phrases used to wish people well on many different occasions, such as when offering and receiving food, getting a haircut and wearing new clothes etc. Turks are not protective of their personal space. They are very sociable people and like doing things as a group. If you learn to use a few of these phrases, Turkish speakers will be delighted by your manners. I hope you will find the culture notes interesting, as well as useful preparation for interaction with Turkish people.

If you don't understand something just ask:

▶ **Ne demek istiyorsun?** *What do you mean?*

Or

▶ **Ne demek?** *What does it mean?*

## Body language

In Turkey, people generally shake hands when they meet and kiss each other on both cheeks. Turks are more tactile than western Europeans tend to be. Some Turkish body language is quite subtle so interpreting this is the key to understanding the people. You will find in the book and on the website some explanations of Turkish body language. Here are a few more:

▶ A shrug of the shoulders means 'I don't know'.
▶ Tut, tut! – you can say 'no' quite politely and simply by using body language. Just raise your eyebrows and give a single tutting sound.

## Features of the Turkish language

### *AGGLUTINATION*

Where English uses a number of words, Turkish often uses only one. For example, the phrase *you will be able to learn* is expressed as a single word **öğrenebileceksin.**

Where English adds meaning to the verb *to learn* by placing other words in front of it, Turkish adds meaning to the verb **öğren** by tagging endings onto it: **öğren** (*learn*), **-ebil** (*be able to*), **-ecek** (*will*), **-sin** (*you*).

The technical word for this way of doing things is *agglutination*, which means 'sticking bits together'. Turkish is an 'agglutinating language'.

### VOWEL HARMONY

When you agglutinate in Turkish, most of the endings usually have to rhyme, or harmonize, with the word you're adding them to. In order to be able to rhyme like this, the endings have a number of different forms. There are two types of ending. These are:

▶ 'e' endings that contain the letter **e**. These have two possible forms. For example, the ending **-de** can be either **-de** or **-da**.
▶ 'i' endings that contain the letter **i**. These have four possible forms. For example, the ending **-iyor** can be **-iyor**, **-ıyor**, **-uyor**, or **-üyor**.

The knack lies in knowing which of the two or four forms to use. This is explained clearly at the beginning of the book and is also summarized in the appendix.

### WORDS

A word is a single unit of language in speech or writing. In English, a word has a gap on either side of it. Turkish words take endings so they may not be separated by gaps. In Turkish, one word can be a whole sentence.

### VERBS

Verbs are also known as 'doing words' or 'action words'. For the dictionary form of an English verb, you see the main part of the verb with *to* in front of it, e.g. *to make, to do*. This is called the infinitive.

The dictionary, or infinitive, form of Turkish verbs is made by combining the stem with the ending -**mek** or -**mak**.

Sometimes the dictionary form is used as it stands and sometimes it is necessary to add an ending to make the correct form. See Unit 5.

### Verb 'to be'
*Am*, *are*, *is*, *was*, *were* are all formed from the verb *to be*. The verb *to be* is very useful as it can be used with nouns, adjectives and pronouns to describe people. Turkish, in similar fashion to many other languages, does not have an exact equivalent of the verb *to be*. In Turkish, there are not separate words for *am*, *are*, *is*, etc. Instead, each personal pronoun has its own ending. See Unit 7 for more explanations, examples and exercises.

### Tenses
The tense of a verb is the form that shows whether you are referring to past, present or future time. By the end of this book, you will be able to speak Turkish in present, past and future tenses.

## NOUNS

Words that name things (objects, ideas, people or places) are called nouns. *People*, *cinema*, *money*, *water* and *book* are all examples of nouns. In Turkish, all nouns can be either singular or plural. For an explanation of how to form the plural, see Unit 2.

### Proper nouns
These are words that have their own special name, such as people's names, city names, countries, etc. All proper nouns begin with a capital letter, e.g. *Vanessa*, *Nur*, *Tom*, *Londra*, *Istanbul*, *Turkey*.

### Pronouns
Pronouns are short words that are used instead of nouns, e.g. *I*, *you*, *he*, *she*, *it*, *we*, *they*. In Turkish, the pronouns are: **ben, sen, o, biz, siz, onlar**.

## YOU: 'SEN' AND 'SİZ'

Like a number of other languages – French, German, Russian etc. –
Turkish has two words for *you*. You use **siz** when talking to more
than one person or when addressing a single person with whom
you are being formal. You use **sen** when talking to a close friend or
a child. If in doubt about which to use, you are advised to play safe
and use **siz**.

### ADJECTIVES

An adjective is a word that describes a noun or pronoun, e.g. *good*,
*beautiful*, *young*. Turkish adjectives, like other Turkish words, take
endings.

### WORD ORDER

Although Turkish word order is relatively free and flexible, it is
best to follow the main principle that verbs go at the end of the
sentence. The basic word order in Turkish is *the learner the book
read*. The subject (the person or thing performing the action)
comes first, the verb (the action word) comes at the end and the
object (the person or thing having the action done to it) comes in
between. So the basic word order is: subject – object – verb (SOV):

**Öğrenci kitabı okudu.**      <u>literally</u>      *The learner the book read.*

Word order is described in more detail and with examples in the
book. (See Unit 7.) For now, it is enough to be aware that you
need to do a bit of juggling to work out the English equivalent of
anything in Turkish. Simple English word order is S + V + O.

### VOCABULARY BUILDING

Guessing the meaning of words can be good fun. **Gazete** means
*newspaper* and **gazeteci** means *journalist*. **Kahve** means *coffee*
while **kahveci** means *coffee-making person*. **Futbol** means *football*
and **futbolcu** means *footballer*.

Question: If **deniz** means *sea*, what is the Turkish word for *sailor*?
The answer is **denizci**. Did you guess correctly?

## MAKING QUESTIONS

▶ You can make questions using intonation.
▶ You can make questions by using the word **mi**.
▶ Or you can use question words – **ne** = *what*, **kim** = *who*,
  **nasıl** = *how*, **niçin** = *why*, **kaç lira** = *how much?*

It is also possible to ask why with your body language: hold your
open palms upwards and then simply lift your shoulders. See?
Easy, isn't it!

## NEGATIVE

▶ In Turkish, **değil** is used to make a word or phrase negative,
  e.g. **iyi değil** – *It's not nice*. (See Unit 1.)
▶ **yok** means *there is none*, *we haven't got any*, e.g. **Bira yok**
  *There's no beer, we haven't got any beer*.
▶ To tell people not to do things add -**me** or -**ma** to the end of
  the main part of the verb, e.g. **Yapma** – *don't*. (See Unit 6.)

In Turkey, it is not considered impolite to imply *no* simply by using
body language. To do this, raise your eye brows and give a single
tutting sound.

## THE ALPHABET AND PRONUNCIATION

Turkish pronunciation is very regular. Throughout the centuries
Turks have, however, used different alphabets. During the
Ottoman Empire, they used Arabic script. The Latin alphabet was
adapted by the Republic of Turkey in 1928. Nowadays, Turkish
uses the Latin script, with a small number of modifications. It
has 29 letters, eight of which are vowels, the remaining 21 being
consonants. Some vowels differ from English sounds but English
speakers can pronounce all the sounds with little difficulty. Once

you have learnt the alphabet, you will find Turkish simple and straightforward to read, because unlike English:

- ▶ you pronounce Turkish in exactly the same way as you spell it
- ▶ each Turkish letter stands for a single sound.

## Vowels
Turkish vowels are generally short. In English, we do not necessarily always pronounce every vowel. Turkish, however is different – you always pronounce all the vowels. Here are the Turkish vowels:

Aa, Iı, Oo, Uu, Ee, İi, Öö, Üü

## Consonants
Most of the Turkish consonants sound the same as they do in English. In English, we do not necessarily always pronounce some consonants. Turkish is different – you *always* pronounce *all* the consonants. If it is a double consonant, both consonants are pronounced.

## ARTICLES

*A*, *an* and *the* are known as articles. In general, articles are not used in Turkish. The equivalent of *a/an* in Turkish is either **bir** or no word at all. At this stage, don't worry about getting this aspect of the language right. People will still understand you, even if you do not use it or use it incorrectly. (See Units 1, 2 and 5.)

## ACCENT

Accents are difficult to get right in any language – even your own! You should not worry too much about acquiring the perfect Turkish accent. An accent good enough to be understood will do for most people. If you have the choice, do try to imitate the standard accent – Istanbul pronunciation – so you will be understood wherever you go!

## STRESS

Turkish words carry only a very light stress, generally on the last syllable. On the whole, compared to English, stresses are hardly noticeable. As a general rule of thumb, you should try to stress the last syllable of a word (lightly).

## RHYTHM

When we listen to someone speak, we do not just listen to and try to hear the individual words to understand the meaning, we also listen to the rhythm of the speech.

Turkish rhythm is different from English rhythm. If you use English rhythm when you speak Turkish, your listeners will find it difficult to understand you. This can happen even if you pronounce each syllable of each word correctly. Rhythm is not something that is easy to get right through conscious effort. You need exposure to it. The best way of getting the rhythm is to listen, listen, listen and copy, copy, copy. You can listen to the recording accompanying this book and Turkish television or radio via satellite or on the internet.

Do not worry about making mistakes. Everyone makes mistakes and they are an integral and important part of learning.

**Bol şanslar!**

# Introduction

Welcome to *Get started in Turkish*. This course is for anyone who wants to speak and write some basic Turkish so that they can get the most out of a visit to Turkey.

Starting with the alphabet and pronunciation, we have designed the units so that your Turkish builds gradually. We have included topics and situations which visitors to Turkey will find immediately useful. There are ten carefully graded and interlocking units.

We have assumed no previous knowledge of foreign language learning and have avoided grammatical terminology where possible. Since the book is aimed at beginners, we have tried to keep the language points and explanations as simple and straightforward as possible. The Turkish language works very differently from English, and some letters of the alphabet look different from English – but do not be put off by this. The good news is that Turkish, unlike English, is very logical and regular. With some basic knowledge, you will quickly be able to read and speak Turkish. We have focused on Turkish as spoken in Istanbul at the turn of the 21st century.

This book is intended for you to use on your own, with the support of the accompanying recordings, indicated by ◀) in your book. It can also be used for study with a teacher. Each unit contains dialogues, which are all recorded and have (natural) English translations at the back of the book, language and culture points, with plenty of examples, and all the necessary vocabulary. At the end of each unit, there are exercises for practice, including occasionally word searches to reinforce the vocabulary, and a mini-test which is also recorded, for you to check your progress. At the back of the book, you will find the answer key for the exercises and a glossary, as well as the dialogue translations.

## How to use this book

As modern Turkish is a phonetic language we have started with the Turkish alphabet and pronunciation. Look at the letters, listen to them more than once, then imitate the sounds. At this stage do not try to learn the alphabet by heart. Once you have practised it you can refer back to it if you need to. Throughout the book there is plenty of pronunciation practice. Unit 3 concentrates on the alphabet and Turkish names to give more practice.

Each unit has at least two dialogues. Most of the dialogues have very simple comprehension questions before and after. The mini-test and exercises are essential parts of each unit. For each unit you can choose whether you read each dialogue first or listen to it first. You may prefer to do both together. Whichever way you do it, listen to and read the dialogues a number of times.

Do not worry if you don't understand everything, your understanding will improve as time goes on. Don't try to learn all the items in the vocabulary box off by heart – you can go back any time you want. In real life, people do not learn lists of vocabulary – they are simply exposed to words over and over again in a context which they know, and in the end (with a little looking-up or asking) things stick.

Speak along with the dialogues as you get to know them and imitate what you hear. Don't be afraid to make mistakes.

After checking your understanding with the comprehension questions and answers, read the language points carefully and go back to the dialogue.

The practice exercises are where you can have some fun. If you want to write the answers in the book, do so in pencil. Then you can rub them out later and try again. When you have completed a couple of units, go back to the exercises in earlier units – it is very satisfying to find them easier to do than the first time!

Early on in your studies find something real to read, such as Turkish newspapers, magazines or comics. If you have access to the internet spend a few moments searching for items in Turkish – you may turn up anything from a collection of Turkish recipes to the life story of Atatürk. We have put some web addresses of general interest at the back of the book and some units have references to websites related specifically to the content of the unit.

Set yourself a routine for learning, somewhere relaxed. Look at our section called **Learning tips**. You may find some of the advice helpful, especially if you are returning to learning after a long break.

For information about Turkish lira, go to www.tcmb.gov.tr.

---

## Why learn about Turkish culture?

Throughout the book, we have included author **Insight** boxes alongside language learning points. We have done this for a number of reasons. People from different cultures use language in different ways and as you start to learn Turkish a little knowledge of the cultural context will help you communicate well with Turkish people. Good communication is not always about accurate pronunciation and grammar – if you learn the manners and customs expected by native speakers of a language, you will be received with friendship and respect. Also knowing about the culture of a country you visit helps you understand what you see and hear around you. For example, if you listen to English speakers shopping in England you will hear them using 'please' and 'thank you' many times. This would seem a little strange to Turkish speakers, who express politeness differently – in the way they greet the shopkeeper and the form of address they express through verb endings.

Philosophers argue whether the way a language works reflects the thinking of its speakers, or vice versa! This argument has a chicken and egg feel and is hard to resolve, but it is interesting to note that while English speakers wish each other just one 'Good night', Turkish speakers wish each other İyi geceler (many 'Good nights')! Hospitality, good manners and respectful social interaction are very important in Turkish culture. Turkish has set phrases to wish people well on a wide range of occasions, such as when offering and receiving food, getting a haircut and wearing new clothes. If you learn to use a few of these, Turkish speakers will be delighted by your manners.

We hope you will find the culture notes interesting, as well as useful preparation for a visit to Turkey.

### LIFE AFTER THIS BOOK

Once you have completed this book, you will be able to communicate in a variety of everyday situations and have a sound knowledge of the basic Turkish language points. What then? You can move to *Complete Turkish*.

Enjoy your learning!

### SYMBOL

◄◊ This indicates that the recording is needed.

---

## Learning tips

This book is for all kinds of people learning Turkish, for a wide range of reasons. This may be the first time you have tried to learn another language. We have planned the units to build up your Turkish gently, step by step – but once you have started, you may want to explore the book at your own pace. One of the advantages of a self-study book like this is that you can return to a section as many times as you need, working at your own speed.

Here are some tips on language learning that you may find helpful in getting the most out of this book:

**1** Be active in your learning. *Find out which ways of learning work for you. Everyone is different.*

**2** Do a little bit every day. *Don't expect to be able to learn large amounts in one sitting. Set yourself a goal of learning a certain number of new words every day, say 5–10.*

**3** Create learning habits. *Set time aside for your learning on a regular basis. Stick to a routine.*

**4** Don't wait till you can speak the language perfectly – *talk to yourself!*

**5** Be positive about your achievements. *Enjoy learning. Concentrate on what you have learnt, not on what you cannot remember.*

**6** Get a good dictionary. *When you come across a new word, try to guess the meaning first, then use a good dictionary to check. If you want to learn the word, write it down, with the definition and the word in context.*

**7** Create your own personal vocabulary book. *Group the words either in grammar type (e.g. separate sections for verbs, nouns and adjectives), or by theme (e.g. food, drink, transport, numbers), or according to the purpose they serve in conversation (e.g. how to greet people/how to shop/how to order a meal).*

**8** Don't worry too much about making mistakes. *Mistakes are a natural part of learning. Turkish speakers will be pleased that you are having a go and will appreciate anything you can say.*

**9** Revise regularly. *Use the mini-test at the end of each unit.*

**10** Listen carefully. *Listen to the recording or, if possible, a native speaker or a teacher, repeating out loud whenever possible. If you can, get some help from a Turkish speaker or find out about Turkish clubs or societies in your area.*

**11** Record yourself. *Record yourself and compare your pronunciation with a native speaker, then try again.*

**12** Make flashcards. *Write the Turkish words you are trying to learn on small cards and stick them around the house where* *you will come across them during the day. Relevant pictures could be an extra support for word meanings.*

**13** **Don't give up.** *Keep going, using little treats or rewards for your achievements along the way to keep up your motivation. Enjoy it.*

BOL ŞANSLAR!

## The alphabet and pronunciation

The Latin alphabet was adopted by the Republic of Turkey in 1928. Prior to that, Turkish was written in Arabic script. Nowadays, Turkish uses the Latin script, with a small number of modifications. It has 29 letters: eight of them (**a, ı, o, u, e, i, ö, ü**) are vowels, the remaining 21 are consonants. Some vowels differ from English sounds but English speakers can pronounce all of the sounds with little difficulty. Once you have learnt the alphabet, you will find Turkish simple and straightforward to read, because unlike English:

▶ *you pronounce Turkish in exactly the same way as you spell it*
▶ *each Turkish letter stands for a single sound.*

Here is the Turkish alphabet. This book focuses on Turkish as spoken in Istanbul at the turn of the 21st century, which is Standard Turkish.

◆ **CD1, TR 1**

Listen to the alphabet while looking at the following list of sounds, then repeat the sounds out loud as you hear them.

| Turkish letter | Letter name pronounced roughly as English | Sound pronounced roughly as English |
|---|---|---|
| Aa | *ah* | *art* |
| Bb | *bay* | *big* |
| Cc | *jay* | *John* |
| Çç | *chay* | *child* |
| Dd | *dey* | *do* |
| Ee | *ey* | *get* |
| Ff | *fey* | *far* |
| Gg | *gay* | *get* |
| Ğğ yumuşak ğ | *yumushak gay* | *this letter has no sound!* |
| Hh | *hey* | *how* |
| Iı | *uh* | *butter* |
| İi | *ee* | *it* |
| Jj | *zhe* | *pleasure* |
| Kk | *kay* | *kitten* |
| Ll | *ley* | *lovely* |
| Mm | *mey* | *man* |
| Nn | *ney* | *no* |
| Oo | *o* | *box* |
| Öö | *ur* | *dirt* |
| Pp | *pay* | *pen* |
| Rr | *ray* | *dry* |
| Ss | *say* | *sea* |
| Şş | *shay* | *show* |
| Tt | *tay* | *tea* |
| Uu | *oo* | *pull* |
| Üü | *ew* | German *ü* or French *tü* |
| Vv | *vey* | *very* |
| Yy | *ye* | *yes* |
| Zz | *zey* | *zip* |

Note the difference between İ or i with a dot and I or ı without a dot.

In English we do not always pronounce every letter. Turkish is different – you always pronounce all the letters. What you see is what you say! The only slight exception is the letter **ğ**. The letter **ğ** is called **yumuşak g**, which means *soft g*. It always comes after a vowel and turns that vowel into a long sound. You might think of it as doubling the vowel before it. Therefore, think of **ağ** as *aa* or think of **öğle** as *ööle*. There are no words beginning with soft **g** (**ğ**).

Now it's your turn to practise!

Listen to the following 29 letters of the Turkish alphabet and repeat the example words out loud as you hear them. They are all towns and cities in Turkey, except one. Listen for the odd one out!

| | | | |
|---|---|---|---|
| A | Ankara | M | Malatya |
| B | Bursa | N | Niğde |
| C | Ceyhan | O | Ordu |
| Ç | Çanakkale | Ö | Ödemiş |
| D | Denizli | P | Perşembe |
| E | Edirne | R | Rize |
| F | Fatsa | S | Samsun |
| G | Giresun | Ş | Şırnak |
| Ğ | yumuşak G | T | Tokat |
| H | Hatay | U | Urfa |
| I | Isparta | Ü | Üsküdar |
| İ | İzmir | V | Van |
| J | Japonya | Y | Yozgat |
| K | Konya | Z | Zonguldak |
| L | Lüleburgaz | | |

For more practice turn to Unit 3. Now you have learnt the sounds of Turkish you can read a newspaper even if you cannot understand it! But at this stage, knowing your sounds and letters will be very useful if you need to look at a menu or phrase book.

---

## Pronunciation practice – survival guide

As well as introducing you to Turkish pronunciation, this section will give you a kickstart in survival words and phrases. Listen to the 75 items listed while looking at how they are spelled. Repeat the words out loud as you hear them.

◀ CD1, TR 2, 00:53

### BASICS

| | |
|---|---|
| evet | *yes* |
| hayır | *no* |
| lütfen | *please* |
| sağ olun | *thank you* |
| merhaba | *hello* |
| hoşça kalın | *goodbye* |
| nasılsınız? | *how are you?* |
| iyiyim | *I'm fine* |
| pardon | *sorry, excuse me* |

### TALKING

| | |
|---|---|
| anladım | *I understand* |
| anlamadım | *I don't understand* |
| tekrar | *again* |
| yavaş | *slowly* |
| ne demek? | *what does it mean?* |
| İngilizce | *English* |
| Türkçesi ne? | *what is it in Turkish?* |

### SHOPPING

| | |
|---|---|
| kaç para? | *how much (money)?* |
| ucuz | *cheap* |
| pahalı | *expensive* |
| var | *there is some* |
| yok | *there isn't any* |
| pul | *stamp* |
| jeton | *token (formerly used in public telephones; now used for public transport)* |

### EATING

| | |
|---|---|
| bakar mısınız! | *waiter! excuse me!* |
| fiyat listesi | *price list* |
| hesap | *bill* |
| öğle yemeği | *lunch* |

### DIRECTIONS

| | |
|---|---|
| nerede? | *where?* |
| sol | *left* |
| sağ | *right* |
| düz | *straight on* |
| kaç kilometre? | *how many kilometres?* |

### TRAVELLING

| | |
|---|---|
| ne zaman? | *when?* |
| hangi otobüs? | *which bus?* |

| | |
|---|---|
| ilk | *first* |
| son | *last* |
| bilet | *ticket* |
| burada | *here* |
| inecek var | *I want to get out/off* |

◀) **CD1, TR 2, 04:10**

## ACCOMMODATION

| | |
|---|---|
| bir kişi | *one person* |
| bir gece | *one night* |
| sıcak su | *hot water* |
| devamlı su | *non-stop water* |
| kahvaltı dahil | *breakfast included* |

◀) **CD1, TR 2, 04:39**

## TIMES

| | |
|---|---|
| dakika | *minute* |
| saat | *hour* |
| hafta | *week* |
| şimdi | *now* |
| sonra | *later* |
| gün | *day* |
| dün | *yesterday* |
| bugün | *today* |
| yarın | *tomorrow* |
| önce | *earlier/ago* |

◀) **CD1, TR 2, 05:31**

## NUMBERS

| | |
|---|---|
| az | *little* |
| çok | *a lot* |
| bir | *one* |

| iki | two |
| üç | three |
| dört | four |
| beş | five |
| yüz | hundred |
| bin | thousand |
| milyon | million |
| milyar | billion |

🔊 **CD1, TR 2, 06:34**

### PLACES

| tuvalet | toilet |
| postane | post office |
| eczane | chemist's |
| otogar | bus station |
| iskele | jetty, ferry stop |
| bakkal | grocer's shop |

🔊 **CD1, TR 2, 07:16**

### TROUBLE

| imdat! | help! |
| kaza | accident |
| doktor | doctor |
| çok ayıp! | shame on you! (use this to repel unwanted advances) |

Listen to these words a number of times, each time concentrating on a different letter. Pay particular attention to:

▶ *the letters c, ç, ğ, ı, İ, j, ö, ş and ü*
▶ *how the words are stressed*
▶ *the fact that you pronounce every letter of every word.*

# 1

·····································································································

# Greetings

In this unit you will learn
- *How to say 'hello!'*
- *How to say 'goodbye!'*
- *How to say 'how are you?'*
- *Mr, Mrs, Ms*
- *Numbers (1–10)*
- *Pronunciation: a, b, c*

## Dialogues

First listen to the dialogues on the recording without looking at the book. Then listen again while reading them. Then listen and read the dialogue, pause the recording after each word and sentence and repeat out loud. Don't worry, just relax and try to copy what you hear. Keep practising till you know the words almost by heart.

Look up any words you don't know in the vocabulary box. See if you can understand the conversation for yourself. If you need more help, you can find translations of all the dialogues at the back of the book.

## Dialogue 1 Good evening

Ülkü, Doktor Bahadır Bey, Hüseyin and Banu are all at a party in a club. Ülkü is married to Bahadır, who joins them later. He is in his forties. Hüseyin approaches Ülkü and introduces himself.

| | |
|---|---|
| **Hüseyin** | İyi akşamlar, ben Hüseyin. Ya, siz? |
| **Ülkü** | İyi akşamlar, ben Ülkü. |
| **Hüseyin** | Nasılsınız, Ülkü Hanım? |
| **Ülkü** | Teşekkürler, Hüseyin Bey. İyiyim. Siz nasılsınız? |
| **Hüseyin** | Ben de iyiyim. |
| *They shake hands. Hüseyin offers Ülkü a glass of wine. She accepts.* | |
| **Hüseyin** | Şarap? |
| **Ülkü** | Evet, lütfen. |

## Question

Answer the following question based on the dialogue, then check your answer in the back of the book.

Hüseyin hanım mı? *(Is Hüseyin a lady?)*

| | |
|---|---|
| **iyi** | *good/fine* |
| **iyi akşamlar** | *good evening* |
| **ben** | *I* |

| ya, siz?/ya, sen? | and you? |
| nasılsınız?/nasılsın? | how are you? |
| **Hanım** | Miss/Mrs (after the first name only) |
| **teşekkürler** | thanks |
| **Bey** | Mr (after the first name only) |
| **iyiyim** | I am fine |
| **siz/sen** | you |
| **ben de** | me too (lit. I too) |
| **şarap** | wine |
| **evet** | yes |
| **hagir** | no |
| **lütfen** | please |

## Dialogue 2 Hi, how are you?

Then Ülkü's husband joins them.

♦ CD1, TR 3, 00:40

| **Bahadır** | Merhaba Ülkü, nasılsın? |
| **Ülkü** | İyiyim, teşekkürler. Sen nasılsın? |
| **Bahadır** | Ben de iyiyim. (*They kiss each other on both cheeks.*) |
|  | *Ülkü offers Bahadır a beer. He accepts.* |
| **Ülkü** | Bira? |
| **Bahadır** | Evet, lütfen. |

Questions
1 Ülkü nasıl? *(How is Ülkü?)*
2 Bahadır nasıl? *(How is Bahadır?)*

**merhaba/selam**   hello/hi          **bira**   beer

## Dialogue 3 It's a very nice party

Ülkü introduces herself to Banu, who is 26 years old. Later on
Bahadır joins the conversation. Banu has to leave quite early.

CD1, TR 3, 01:10

| Ülkü | İyi akşamlar, ben Ülkü. Ya, sen? |
|------|----------------------------------|
| **Banu** | İyi akşamlar, ben Banu. (*They shake hands.*) |
| **Ülkü** | Nasılsın Banu? |
| **Banu** | (*Smiles.*) Teşekkürler, iyiyim. |
| **Ülkü** | Çok güzel bir parti, değil mi? |
| **Banu** | Evet, çok güzel. |
| **Ülkü** | Banu, Dr Bahadır Bey. (*They shake hands.*) |

Question
Parti nasıl?

QUICK VOCAB

| çok | *very* |
|-----|--------|
| **güzel** | *beautiful, nice, great* |
| **bir** | *a* (see explanation later in this unit) |
| **parti** | *party* |
| **değil** | *not* |
| **değil mi?** | *isn't it?* |

---

## Dialogue 4 Goodbye

Bahadır joins them.

CD1, TR 3, 01:45

| Bahadır | İyi akşamlar. |
|---------|---------------|
| **Banu** | İyi akşamlar Bahadır Bey. |
| **Bahadır** | Nasılsın Banu? |
| **Banu** | Teşekkürler, iyiyim. Siz nasılsınız? |
| **Bahadır** | Ben de iyiyim. |

*Banu looks at her watch as she has to leave early. She says goodbye to Ülkü and, and Bahadır wishes everybody goodnight.*

| Banu | Hoşça kalın Ülkü Hanım. Hoşça kalın Bahadır Bey. İyi geceler. |
|------|---------------------------------------------------------------|
| **Ülkü and Bahadır** | Güle güle Banu. |

Question
Banu nasıl?

Listen to the words in the dialogue while looking at their spelling.
Repeat the words out loud as you hear them. Relax and enjoy
speaking Turkish!

| | |
|---|---|
| **hoşça kalın** | *goodbye* |
| **iyi geceler** | *good night* |
| **güle güle** | *goodbye* (reply to hoşça kalın) |

---

## Language points

### *USING SEN OR SİZ (YOU)*

You probably noticed that Ülkü changed the form of her language
slightly in each dialogue, although she meant the same thing.

Turkish has two ways of saying *you*, depending on how well you
know the other person. **Sen** means *you* when you are speaking to
one person whom you know well. So in the second dialogue Ülkü
asked her husband, '**Sen nasılsın?**'

If you are speaking to one person whom you do not know, **siz**
means *you*. So when meeting Hüseyin for the first time, Ülkü asked,
'**Siz nasılsınız?**' When you use **siz**, **nasılsın** changes to **nasılsınız**.
You would also use the **siz** form to show respect to someone who
is older than you, or of a higher social standing than you, such as
your boss. If you use **siz** when speaking to someone, they will think
you are polite and respectful – so if in doubt, use **siz**! For example:

| | |
|---|---|
| **Nasıl?** | *How is he/she/it?* |
| **Nasılsın?** | *How are you?* (**sen**) |
| **Nasılsınız?** | *How are you?* (**siz**) |

**Siz** also always means *you* when you are speaking to more than
one person, even if you know them very well.

If you are familiar with French, you'll notice that **sen** and **siz** work like *tu* and *vous*.

### NAMES

In Turkey, surnames are not used when greeting people. If you want to be polite, you use the person's first name with **Hanım** for a woman, and **Bey** for a man. Ülkü and Hüseyin are being courteous on first meeting, so Ülkü said, '**Teşekkürler Hüseyin Bey**', and Hüseyin referred to her as '**Ülkü Hanım**'. People's first names are used without **Hanım** or **Bey** only if you know them well and you are roughly the same age.

### DEĞİL MEANS 'NOT'

To make a word or phrase negative, e.g. *it's not*, place **değil** after the word or phrase.

**Şarap değil.**                    *It's not wine.*

**Değil mi?** changes a word or a phrase into the question, isn't it or aren't they?

**Şarap, *değil mi*?**                    *Wine, isn't it?*
**Çok güzel bir parti, *değil mi*?**    *A very good party, isn't it?*

### BİR SOMETIMES MEANS 'A'

In Turkish, there is no word that means *a* or *the*. Sometimes **bir**, which means *one*, is used to mean *a* or *an*:

**bir parti**                    *a party*

## Kissing and shaking hands

In Turkey, social kissing on both cheeks is common between people of the same sex. Young, westernized Turks shake hands when greeting each other and kiss on both cheeks. Strict Moslems do **not** kiss and shake hands with the opposite sex, only with the same sex. Kissing in public between lovers is not socially acceptable.

Remember, English people are generally more concerned with maintaining personal space than Turks who are more used to expressing warmth through physical contact. English people are usually more reserved while Turkish people are generally assertive and openly express their emotions.

## 00 = tuvalet

Have you ever noticed **00** on a door in Turkey and wondered what it meant? It simply means *toilet*! So learning your numbers may just come in very handy next time you are in Turkey. (We'll tell you more about asking for the toilet later in the book – hope you can wait!)

**Tuvalet nerede?** means *Where is the toilet?*

◆) **CD1, TR 3, 02:17**

### *SAYING 'HELLO'*

First listen to, then repeat the phrases. After that write them down and practise until you feel you have learnt them. Do not forget to revise them at regular intervals.

| Günaydın | İyi akşamlar | İyi geceler |
|---|---|---|
| (7 a.m. to midday) | (5 p.m. to 10 p.m.) | (after 10 p.m.) |

In the afternoon Turkish people usually use **merhaba**; however in more formal situations, such as talking to their boss, they would use **iyi günler**.

◀) CD1, TR 3, 02:29

### NUMBERS

First read and listen to these numbers; then pause the recording and repeat each number after the speaker. Do this many times until you feel comfortable with all the numbers. When you feel confident, test yourself. Try saying the numbers from 0 to 10 without looking at the book. Then try saying them backwards, from 10 to 0.

| | | | |
|---|---|---|---|
| 0 | sıfır | 6 | altı |
| 1 | bir | 7 | yedi |
| 2 | iki | 8 | sekiz |
| 3 | üç | 9 | dokuz |
| 4 | dört | 10 | on |
| 5 | beş | | |

## Insight
### Dialogue 3

In English, -s is added to the end of the word to make the plural, while in Turkish, the ending **-lar** is used to do this.

**akşam** *evening* (**singular**)    **akşamlar** *evenings* (**plural**)

See Unit 2.

### Dialogue 4

**Değil** means *not*.

**Bira değil.**                          *It's not beer.*

See Unit 3.

## Practice

1 How would you say 'Hello' to the following people at the time shown? More than one answer is possible.
   a To your friends.
   b To your grandmother.
   c To your boss.

2 It is late at night and you decide to go to bed. What would you say to your Turkish friends?

3 How would you say 'Goodbye' to your Turkish host?

4 What would the response be?

5 Fill in the blanks.

   a M_ _ _ _ _ _ _, ben Şafak.

   b Selam, _ _ _ Gökhan.

6 Reorder the following sentences to make a dialogue. Start with the phrase in bold. (The dialogue is between two friends.)
   a Hoşça kal.
   b İyiyim, sen nasılsın?
   c Merhaba Gülen, nasılsın?
   d Ben de iyiyim.
   e Merhaba Ali.
   f Güle güle.

7 Write down the following numbers as figures.
   a beş          e üç          i altı
   b on           f yedi        j sekiz
   c bir          g dört        k sıfır
   d dokuz        h iki

8 Do these sums:
   a dört + üç =        f dört – iki =
   b bir + bir =        g beş – iki =
   c üç + üç =          h on – bir =
   d dört + beş =       i dokuz – bir =
   e iki + altı =

**9** *In each unit you will get the opportunity to practise your pronunciation.* **Pronunciation: a, b, c.** *First, listen without looking, second, listen while looking, finally listen and repeat.*

| a | b | c |
|---|---|---|
| aaa | ba ba | can |
| aç | beş | ece |
| ad | bir | öc |
| af | bira | acı |

**10** *Look at the wordsearch. There are ten words which you have learnt. Can you find them? One has been found for you.*

| M | E | R | H | A | B | A | B | İ | R |
|---|---|---|---|---|---|---|---|---|---|
| N | R | S | A | V | E | Z | A | K | T |
| A | C | İ | N | O | Y | D | O | İ | R |
| S | L | A | I | N | P | J | S | T | V |
| I | R | C | M | P | O | U | S | E | N |
| L | F | N | O | P | Z | H | İ | B | J |
| S | A | L | T | İ | R | S | Z | J | C |
| I | B | N | T | R | P | S | O | V | J |
| N | İ | Y | İ | Y | İ | M | R | T | U |
| P | S | I | R | G | D | Ç | F | O | N |

## Role play

### GREETINGS

You are chatting with a friend. Play your part in the conversation, according to the prompts.

| Sema | Merhaba Gökhan. |
| Gökhan | *[Say hello to Sema]* |
| Sema | Nasılsın? |
| Gökhan | *[Say that you are fine and ask how Sema is]* |
| Sema | Ben de iyiyim. |
| Gökhan | *[Say goodbye to Sema]* |
| Gülen | Hoşça kal. |

## Mini-test

◀) **CD1, TR 3, 05:47**

Well done! You have reached the end of Unit 1. Let's see what you can remember. Give yourself a point if you can say the following in Turkish without looking at the **Key to the exercises**.

1 *How do you say 'hello'?*
2 *How do you say 'goodbye'?*
3 *How do you say 'goodnight'?*
4 *How do you ask your boss how she is?*
5 *How do you ask your friend how he is?*
6 *How do you say 'thank you'?*
7 *Recite the Turkish alphabet.*
8 *How do you say the numbers 1–10?*
9 *How do you introduce yourself?*
10 *How do you say, 'I'm fine, thank you. How are you?'*

*Points:_____/10*

If you get any wrong, go back through the unit and have another look before moving on to the next unit.

# Drinks

In this unit you will learn
- *How to order drinks*
- *How to call the waiter*
- *How to ask for the bill*
- *Numbers 10–100*
- *How to order snacks*
- *Basic colours*
- *Pronunciation: c, d, e*

## Dialogue 1 A glass of tea, please

Banu and Şafak are cousins. They are sitting at a table in a café in Istanbul by the Bosporus. A waiter comes to take the order.

**CD1, TR 4**

| | |
|---|---|
| **Garson** | Buyrun, efendim? |
| **Banu** | Bir bardak çay, lütfen. |
| *The waiter writes down the order and repeats it to* | |
| *check he has written it down correctly.* | |
| **Garson** | Bir bardak çay. (*The waiter turns to Şafak.*) Siz, efendim? |
| **Şafak** | Bir bira ve bir şişe su, lütfen. |
| **Garson** | Bira yok, efendim. |
| **Şafak** | İçecek ne var? |
| *The waiter hands Şafak a menu.* | |
| **Garson** | Buyrun, mönü. |

*Şafak looks at the menu.*

**Şafak**               Teşekkür. Bir Nescafé, lütfen.
**Garson**              Süt?
**Şafak**               Evet, sütlü.

*The waiter writes down the order and repeats it out loud to check that he has written it down correctly.*

**Garson**              Bir çay, bir sütlü Nescafé.
**Şafak**               Evet, tamam.

*The waiter comes back and puts the drinks on the table.*

**Garson**              Bir çay, bir Nescafé, şeker, süt.
**Banu and Şafak**      Teşekkürler.
**Garson**              Afiyet olsun, efendim.

*Şafak calls the waiter and asks for the bill.*

**Şafak**               Garson!
**Garson**              Buyrun.
**Şafak**               Hesap, lütfen.

*They pay the bill and tell the waiter to keep the change (it is usual to leave a 10% tip at cafés and restaurants).*

**Şafak**               Üstü kalsın.
**Garson**              Sağ olun, efendim.

Questions
1 *İçecek ne var?*
2 *Nescafé nasıl?*

| | |
|---|---|
| **Buyrun\*, efendim?** | *How can I help you, sir/madam?* |
| **bardak** | *glass* |
| **çay** | *tea* |
| **şişe** | *bottle* |
| **yok** | *there is none/we haven't got any* |
| **içecek** | *drink* |
| **ne** | *what* |
| **var** | *there is/are* |
| **mönü** | *menu* |
| **teşekkür** | *thank you* (alternative to **teşekkürler**) |
| **Nescafé** | *instant coffee* |
| **süt** | *milk* |

QUICK VOCAB

| | |
|---|---|
| **sütlü** | *with milk* |
| **tamam** | *OK* |
| **şeker** | *sugar* |
| **afiyet olsun** | *enjoy your drinks!/enjoy your meal!* |
| **garson** | *waiter!/waitress!* |
| **buyrun\*** | *yes, sir* |
| **hesap** | *the bill* |
| **üstü kalsın** | *keep the change* |
| **sağ olun** | *thanks* (showing respect and gratitude) |

\***Buyurun** is the correct dictionary spelling. **Buyrun** is what people say.

---

## Language points

### BİR: 'A' OR 'ONE'

The Turkish word **bir** is very useful. It means the number one, but it can also mean *a* as in *a bottle of beer* (**bir şişe bira**).

◀) **CD1, TR 4, 01:19**

### MORE NUMBERS

First read and listen to the following numbers, then pause the recording and repeat each number after the speaker. When you feel confident test yourself. To say more numbers, just put the words together: 41 = **kırk bir**. Now try saying the numbers from 10 to 20 and then the multiples of ten up to 100 without looking at the book. Next try saying them backwards.

| | | | |
|---|---|---|---|
| 10 | **on** | 18 | **on sekiz** |
| 11 | **on bir** | 19 | **on dokuz** |
| 12 | **on iki** | 20 | **yirmi** |
| 13 | **on üç** | 30 | **otuz** |
| 14 | **on dört** | 40 | **kırk** |
| 15 | **on beş** | 50 | **elli** |
| 16 | **on altı** | 60 | **altmış** |

| 17 | on yedi | 70 | yetmiş |
|---|---|---|---|
| 80 | seksen | 90 | doksan |
| 100 | yüz | | |

Note: In English, we say *one hundred*. In Turkish, we just say **yüz**.

---

## Dialogue 2 The coffee is very good here

Turkish restaurants and cafés make children very welcome.
A family is seen sitting at the next table to Banu and Şafak. They
are enjoying a day out together. The waiter approaches their table
and they order some drinks.

| | |
|---|---|
| **Garson** | Buyrun, efendim. |
| **Mother** | Bir şekerli kahve. |
| **Father** | Bana da şekersiz. |

*The mother asks the child what she would like.*

| | |
|---|---|
| **Mother** | Sen yavrum? Limonata? |

*The child looks at the menu.*

| | |
|---|---|
| **Child** | Hayır, ayran, lütfen. |
| **Mother** | Tamam. |

*The father orders for everyone and the waiter writes it down.*

| | |
|---|---|
| **Father** | İki kahve, bir şekerli, bir sade ve bir ayran. |
| **Garson** | Tabii, efendim. |

*(Contd)*

♦ CD1, TR 4, 02:33

The waiter brings the drinks, which include two glasses of water to go with the coffees (Turkish coffee is usually served with a glass of water).

| | |
|---|---|
| **Garson** | Buyrun efendim, içecekleriniz. |
| **Everyone** | Teşekkürler. |
| **Garson** | Afiyet olsun. |
| **Mother** | Kahveler çok güzel, değil mi? |
| **Father** | Evet, çok güzel. |
| **Child** | Acıktım. |
| **Mother** | Ben de. Tost? |
| **Child** | Evet, peynirli tost ve ayran. |

*Cezve*

The father calls the waiter and gives him the order.

| | |
|---|---|
| **Father** | Garson, lütfen. |
| **Garson** | Buyrun? |
| **Father** | Üç peynirli tost ve üç ayran lütfen. |

While waiting for the food, the mother enjoys the view.

| | |
|---|---|
| **Mother** | Manzara çok güzel, değil mi? |
| **Father** | Evet, çok güzel. |

## Questions

1 *Kahveler nasıl?*
2 *Manzara güzel, değil mi?*

QUICK VOCAB

| | |
|---|---|
| **şekerli** | sweet |
| **bana da** | for me too |
| **şekersiz** | without sugar |
| **yavrum** | my child (shows affection) |
| **limonata** | still lemonade |
| **ayran** | ayran (yogurt-based drink) |
| **sade** | without sugar |
| **içecekleriniz** | your drinks |
| **afiyet olsun** | enjoy your drinks |
| **acıktım** | I'm hungry |
| **tost** | toasted sandwich |
| **peynirli tost** | toasted cheese sandwich |
| **manzara** | view |

## Language points

Ordering drinks in Turkish is very easy – all you need to know are your numbers and the names of the drinks! Unlike in English, you don't change the ending of the name of the drink when ordering more than one. So *two teas* is **iki çay**. *Three beers* is **üç bira** and so on. The most difficult part is choosing what you want!

### PLURALS (MORE THAN ONE)

| Singular | Plural |
|----------|--------|
| akşam | akşamlar |
| kahve | kahveler |
| tost | tostlar |

In Turkish, all nouns (names of things, opinions and feelings, etc.) can be made plural by adding -ler or -lar. For example, **akşam** (*evening*) becomes **akşamlar** (*evenings*). Unlike English, however, Turkish has no irregular forms. The good news is you only need to learn one rule, and you can make any Turkish noun plural. You put -lar if the last vowel is one of these letters: **a, ı, o, u**; -ler if the last vowel is one of these: **e, i, ö, ü**. This follows one of the rules of vowel harmony. We call this formation of the plural an 'e-type' ending.

In Turkish, most salutations are in the plural. Here are some examples:

| | |
|---|---|
| **iyi akşamlar** | *good evening* |
| **iyi geceler** | *goodnight* |
| **selamlar** | *hello* |
| **tebrikler** | *congratulations* |
| **mutlu yillar** | *happy new year* |
| **mutlu bayramlar** | *have a happy Bayram* (see Unit 9) |
| **iyi şanslar** | *good luck* |
| **iyi yolculuklar** | *have a good journey* |
| **iyi günler** | *good day* |

**renkli rüyalar**       *sweet dreams*
**mutlu Noeller\***       *happy Christmas*

\*Noel Baba = Father Christmas

\*St Nicholas, or Father Christmas, was born around 270 AD in what is known in modern-day Turkey as Patara, in the province of Lycia. He lived as Bishop of Myra and his church in Demre can still be visited today.

---

## Dialogue 3 One red wine, please

Banu and Şafak meet in a bar later the same day.

| | |
|---|---|
| **Şafak** | İyi akşamlar. |
| **Garson** | İyi akşamlar, efendim. Buyrun? |
| **Banu** | Bir şarap, lütfen. |
| **Şafak** | Kırmızı mı, beyaz mı? |
| **Banu** | Kırmızı, lütfen. |
| **Şafak** | Bir kırmızı şarap ve bir rakı lütfen. |
| **Garson** | Tabii, efendim. Çerez? |
| **Şafak** | Evet, fıstık, biraz da karışık meyve ve beyaz peynir, lütfen. |
| **Garson** | Tabii, efendim. |

Questions
1 *Şarap ne renk?*
2 *Beyaz peynir mi?*

| | |
|---|---|
| **şarap** | *wine* |
| **kırmızı** | *red* |
| **kırmızı mı?** | *red?* |
| **beyaz** | *white* |
| **beyaz mı?** | *white?* |
| **ve** | *and* |
| **rakı** | *raki (aniseed-flavoured spirit)* |
| **çerez** | *snacks* |
| **fıstık** | *nuts* |

| | | | |
|---|---|---|---|
| **biraz da** | *and (some) also* | | |
| **karışık** | *mixed* | | |
| **meyve** | *fruit* | | |
| **peynir** | *cheese* | | |

---

## Language points

🔊 **CD1, TR 4, 04:40**

### RENKLER *COLOURS*

| | | | |
|---|---|---|---|
| **beyaz** | *white* | **pembe** | *pink* |
| **kırmızı** | *red* | **siyah** | *black* |
| **mavi** | *blue* | **gri** | *grey* |
| **yeşil** | *green* | **mor** | *purple* |
| **sarı** | *yellow* | **turuncu** | *orange* |

Can you work out what these combinations mean?

- *kahverengi*      *portakalrengi*
- *şaraprengi*      *metalrengi*
- *turkuaz mavi*      *kremrengi*

Check in the Vocabulary list at the back of the book to see if you are right!

**Koyu renk** means dark in colour and **açık renk** means light in colour and the colour of your tea shows how strong or weak it is:

**koyu çay** = *strong tea*
**açık çay** = *weak tea*

### ASKING QUESTIONS

Did you notice that the mother and the waiter turned the name of a drink into a question? E.g. **Limonata? Çerez?** This would probably sound a bit abrupt in English, but is perfectly normal in Turkish. Listen again! The mother asks her daughter if she would like some lemonade by simply saying *Limonata?*, and raising the pitch of her voice at the end of the word. This is a really easy way of making a question, isn't it. Have a go!

### *VAR AND YOK* THERE IS/ARE/NOT

**Var** means *there is* or *there are*.

| | |
|---|---|
| Ne var? | *What's there?/What have you got?* |
| Çay var. | *There is tea.* |
| Rakı var. | *There is raki.* |

**Yok** means *there isn't* or *there aren't* (any).

| | |
|---|---|
| Ne yok? | *What isn't there?/What haven't you got?* |
| Kahve yok. | *There isn't any coffee.* |
| Bira yok. | *There isn't any beer.* |

## Having a drink

Now you have learnt how to order a drink in a café, restaurant or bar. You are still left with the most difficult part: choosing what you want! All the usual European drinks are available, such as beer, cola, spirits, wine, mineral water and fruit juices. However, you'll be missing out if you don't try some of the typically Turkish drinks such as **rakı** (a strong aniseed spirit usually diluted with water), **vişne suyu** *sour cherry juice*, **ayran** (a yogurt drink), **çay** *tea* and **Türk kahvesi** *Turkish coffee*. **Çay** is served black in a tulip-shaped glass usually with sugar lumps on a saucer. The colour of the tea is all-important, as it is a guide to its quality. **Türk kahvesi** is also served black but in a small fine china cup, slightly smaller than an espresso one. Sugar, if required, is added during the making of coffee so you will need to learn the words to order coffee with sugar (**şekerli**), without sugar (**sade**) or with a little sugar (**az şekerli**). The coffee and sugar, if required, are heated up in a **cezve** (a small pot with a long handle) on a cooker. If you want an instant coffee, you need to ask for Nescafé. The preparation of both tea and coffee are real art forms.

Turks say that offering a cup of Turkish coffee invites 40 years of friendship. In other words, small acts of kindness are remembered for many years.

**Rakı**, when mixed with water, goes white and is known as **Arslan Sütü** *lion's milk* because of its strength and colour. When **rakı** is ordered in a bar it is usually served with **beyazpeynir** *white cheese*, **zeytin** *olives* and **fıstık** *nuts*.

# Insight
## Dialogue 2

Here are a few words for making questions:

| | |
|---|---|
| kim? | *who?* |
| ne? | *what?* |
| nerede?* | *where?* |
| ne zaman? | *when?* |
| nasıl? | *how?* |
| kaça? | *how much?* |

*nerede becomes **nerde** in spoken Turkish.

The ending **-li** means *with* while **-sız** means *without*:

şeker *sugar*    şekerli *sweet*    şekersiz *without sugar*

See Units 6 and 7.

## Practice

**1** *What is the Turkish for the following drinks?*

a        b        c

d        e

◀) **CD1, TR 4, 05:40**

**2** *Offer someone a drink by turning the names of the following drinks into questions by raising the tone of your voice at the end of the word. Listen to the recording to check you're right.*
Example: Şarap?

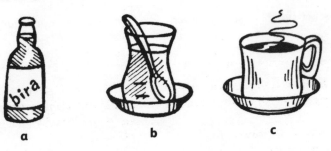

a        b        c

        **d**             **e**

◀》 **CD1, TR 4, 06:13**

**3** *Make the following words plural by giving them* **-ler** *or* **-lar** *endings as appropriate. Listen to the recording first, then write down the answers*
   **Example** *bardak → bardak<u>lar</u>.*

   **a**  *çay*          **d**  *teşekkür*
   **b**  *rakı*        **e**  *bira*
   **c**  *tost*         **f**  *içecek*

**4** *Write down what colour the following colour mixes make.*
   **a**  *mavi + sarı =*     **d**  *beyaz + kırmızı =*
   **b**  *kırmızı + sarı =*   **e**  *kırmızı + mavi =*
   **c**  *siyah + beyaz =*

◀》 **CD1, TR 4, 07:05**

**5** **Pronunciation: ç, d, e.** *First, listen without looking, then listen while looking and finally listen and repeat.*

| ç | d | e |
|------|-----|-----|
| çay | ad | ev |
| aç | de | ve |
| kaç | idi | et |
| açı | dün | kek |

**6** *Look at the following sums. Put a tick next to those that are right (***doğru***) or a cross next to those that are wrong (***yanlış***).*

                            **doğru**       **yanlış**
   **a**  *on + yirmi = kırk*
   **b**  *otuz + elli = altmış*

**c** *on beş + on beş = otuz*
**d** *seksen – kırk = kırk*
**e** *yetmiş – elli = on*

**7** Write the following numbers in figures.

  **a** *sıfır*        **e** *yirmi üç*
  **b** *elli yedi*    **f** *kırk altı*
  **c** *on bir*      **g** *altmış*
  **d** *otuz beş*

**8** Wordsearch. Find nine drinks hidden in this wordsearch. One has been done for you.

| K | A | H | V | E | Ü | J | O | C | B |
|---|---|---|---|---|---|---|---|---|---|
| R | V | A | F | Ş | E | H | Ç | T | İ |
| Ç | P | S | Ü | T | B | T | J | Ü | R |
| V | İ | Ş | N | E | S | U | Y | U | A |
| E | K | A | C | S | U | İ | Y | R | S |
| Ş | N | Y | D | R | S | J | K | I | Y |
| A | H | R | N | Ç | B | R | A | K | I |
| R | E | A | S | T | O | V | A | K | Y |
| A | K | N | O | A | Ü | Ş | I | T | Ü |
| P | E | Ç | A | P | R | O | Ç | A | Y |

## Role play

### DRINKS

You are in a café. Play your part in the conversation, according to the prompts.

| Waiter | Buyrun, efendim. |
| You | [Ask for a glass of tea] |
| Waiter | Başka. |
| You | [Ask for a toasted cheese sandwich] |
| Waiter | Tabii, efendim. |
| You | [Say thank you to the waiter] |

## Mini-test

◀) **CD1, TR 4, 09:20**

Well done – you have completed Unit 2. Now you will be able to order drinks in a café or bar. Let's see what you can remember. Give yourself a point for each of the following questions that you answer correctly in Turkish.

1 *How do you call the waiter to your table?*
2 *How do you ask for a Turkish coffee with, or without, sugar?*
3 *Ask for a white instant coffee.*
4 *How do you order a glass of tea?*
5 *Ask for a glass of red wine and a glass of white wine.*
6 *How do you ask the waiter for some snacks?*
7 *Say 'enjoy your drink/meal'.*
8 *Ask for the bill.*
9 *Tell the waiter/waitress to keep the change.*
10 *How do you say 50, 70, 90 and 100?*

*Points:_____/10*

# 3

## Accommodation

In this unit you will learn
- *How to enquire about accommodation*
- *How to choose somewhere to stay*
- *How to ask about the facilities*
- *How to check in*
- *How to fill in forms*
- *Telephone numbers*
- *Numbers – hundreds and thousands*
- *Pronunciation:* f, g, ğ

## Dialogue 1 Which hotel?

Ben and Laura are visiting Istanbul. They are brother and sister and are both in their early thirties. They are at the tourist office in **Sultan Ahmet Square** looking for accommodation. If you have the recording, listen to it a couple of times, read it through, then see if you can answer the questions.

CD1, TR 5

| | |
|---|---|
| **Ben** | Merhaba. |
| **Memur** | Merhaba efendim. |
| **Ben** | Kalacak yerler listesi var mı, lütfen? |
| **Memur** | Otel, pansiyon veya kamp? |
| **Ben** | Otel, lütfen. |
| **Memur** | Buyrun. |
| **Ben** | Hangi otel yakın? |

| | |
|---|---|
| **Memur** | 'Yeşil Ev'çok yakın. |
| **Ben** | Nasıl yazılır, lütfen? |
| **Memur** | Y – e – ş – i – l  E – v. |
| **Ben** | Teşekkürler. |
| **Memur** | İşte harita, bu 'Danışma' ve bu da 'Yeşil Ev'. |
| **Ben** | Ah! Harika, çok teşekkürler. |

*They walk towards the hotel. Ben wonders which building the hotel is.*

| | |
|---|---|
| **Ben** | Hangi bina acaba? |
| **Laura** | Şu bina galiba. |

*Ben reads the sign above the hotel.*

| | |
|---|---|
| **Ben** | Evet, o bina. |

Questions

1 *Otel listesi var mı?*
2 *Hangi otel yakın?*
3 *Yeşil Ev nasıl yazılır?*
4 *Yeşil Ev ne?*

| kalacak yer listesi | *lists of accommodation* |
|---|---|
| otel | *hotel* |
| pansiyon | *guesthouse* |
| veya | *or* |
| kamp | *campsite* |
| hangi? | *which?* |
| yakın | *near* |
| Yeşil Ev | *Green House* |
| nasıl yazılır? | *how do you spell it?* |
| çok | *very* |
| işte | *here* |
| harita | *map* |
| bu | *this* |
| danışma | *information* |
| ve | *and* |
| harika | *wonderful* |
| bina | *building* |

| | |
|---|---|
| **acaba** | *I wonder* |
| **şu** | *that* |
| **galiba** | *I think* |
| **o** | *that* (referring to something relatively far away) |

## Dialogue 2 Do you have a vacant room?

Listen to the dialogue a couple of times, then read it through.

Ben and Laura enter the hotel and are at the reception desk. (Note that **resepsiyon** is commonly used in big, international hotels.)

CD1, TR 5, 01:57

| | |
|---|---|
| **Ben** | İyi akşamlar. |
| **Receptionist** | İyi akşamlar, efendim. |
| **Ben** | Boş oda var mı? |
| **Receptionist** | Kaç kişi? |
| **Ben** | Ben ve kardeşim, tek kişilik, iki ayrı oda. |
| **Receptionist** | Maalesef, tek kişilik iki oda yok. Ama iki tek yataklı büyük bir oda var. |

*Ben and Laura are undecided, so the receptionist shows them the room.*

| | |
|---|---|
| **Receptionist** | Balkonlu ve deniz manzaralı. |
| **Laura** | Banyo ve sıcak su var mı? |
| **Receptionist** | Evet. Hem küvet hem duş var. Her zaman sıcak su var. |
| **Ben** | (*to Laura*) Bu oda güzel, değil mi? |
| **Laura** | Evet. Ne kadar? |
| **Receptionist** | 120 dolar. |
| **Laura** | Kahvaltı dahil mi? |
| **Receptionist** | Evet, kahvaltı dahil. |
| **Laura** | Evet. Tamam. |

*They go back down to reception.*

| | |
|---|---|
| **Receptionist** | Kaç gece? |
| **Ben** | Üç gece. |
| **Receptionist** | Pasaportlar, lütfen? |
| **Ben** | Tabii, işte pasaportlar. |

*They put the passports on the counter.*

| | |
|---|---|
| **Receptionist** | Teşekkürler. |

*The receptionist starts filling in the hotel forms. While doing so she repeats some of the sections of the form out loud.*

| | |
|---|---|
| **Receptionist** | Doğum yeri … doğum tarihi … milliyet … pasaport numarası … (*Turning to Ben and Laura*) Oda, 24 numara. |

*She hands them the key for room number 24.*

| | |
|---|---|
| **Receptionist** | Buyrun, anahtar. |
| **Laura** | Valizler? |
| **Receptionist** | Mehmet! (*She calls Mehmet, the porter, to carry their suitcases.*) |

Questions

1 *Boş oda var mı?*
2 *Oda nasıl?*
3 *Kaç gece?*
4 *Kahvaltı dahil mi?*

| | |
|---|---|
| **boş** | *vacant* |
| **oda** | *room* |
| **kaç kişi?** | *how many people?* |
| **kardeşim** | *my sister/my brother* |
| **tek kişilik** | *a single* |

QUICK VOCAB

| ayrı | separate |
|---|---|
| maalesef | unfortunately (a polite remark) |
| ama | but |
| tek yataklı | a single bed |
| büyük | big |
| balkonlu | with a balcony |
| deniz | sea |
| manzaralı | with a view |
| banyo | bathroom |
| sıcak | hot |
| hem … hem | both … and |
| küvet | bath |
| duş | shower |
| her zaman | always |
| ne kadar? | how much? |
| kahvaltı | breakfast |
| dahil/dahil mi? | included/is it included? |
| tamam | OK |
| pasaport | passport |
| işte | here it is |
| doğum yeri | place of birth |
| doğum tarihi | date of birth |
| milliyet | nationality |
| pasaport numarası | passport number |
| numara | number |
| anahtar | key |
| valiz | suitcase |

---

## Language points

🔊 **CD1, TR 5, 03:35**

### THE TURKISH ALPHABET: REVISION

When booking accommodation or tickets you may be asked to
spell your name or you may want to know how the name of

a hotel is spelt. If someone wants to know the spelling of a word they simply say, **'nasıl yazılır?'** Remember that an English speaker can produce the sounds of all the letters in the **Türkçe alfabe** – it just takes practice. Keep practising until you feel confident with the sounds of all the letters.

Here are the letters of the **Turkish alphabet.** Each letter is followed by a Turkish name so that you can practise the sound in context:

| A | B | C | Ç | D | E |
|---|---|---|---|---|---|
| a | be | ce | çe | de | e |
| Asu | Banu | Cengiz | Çetin | Deniz | Emel |

| F | G | Ğ[1] | H | I | İ |
|---|---|---|---|---|---|
| fe | ge | | he | ı | i |
| Fazilet | Gül | | Hatice | Işık | İnci |

| J | K | L | M | N | O |
|---|---|---|---|---|---|
| je | ke | le | me | ne | o |
| Jale | Kaya | Lale | Meral | Nesrin | Osman |

| Ö | P | R | S | Ş | T |
|---|---|---|---|---|---|
| ö | pe | re | se | şe | te |
| Ömer | Perihan | Recep | Sezgin | Şule | Timur |

| U | Ü | V | Y | Z |
|---|---|---|---|---|
| u | ü | ve | ye | ze |
| Ufuk | Ülkü | Veysel | Yeşim | Zerrin |

[1]**Ğ** has no distinct pronunciation. It makes the previous vowel longer. One example would be **sağ**, which is pronounced as 'saa'. There is no Turkish word which starts with **ğ**.

### *KAÇ?* HOW MANY? HOW MUCH?

**Kaç** is a useful little word which means *how many* or *how much*?

**Kaç lira?** *How many lira?* **Kaç kişi?** *How many people?*
**Kaç gece?** *How many nights?* **Kaç gün?** *How many days?*

## Dialogue 3 There are lots of good campsites

Banu and Şafak are at a tourist information office in İzmir enquiring about accommodation. Listen to the dialogue a couple of times, read it through then answer the questions.

| | |
|---|---|
| **Şafak** | Merhaba. |
| **Clerk** | İyi günler. |
| **Şafak** | Kalacak otel ve kamp listesi var mı? |
| **Clerk** | Var. Bu otel listesi. |

*They both look at the list.*

| | |
|---|---|
| **Banu** | Oteller biraz pahalı. |
| **Clerk** | Çok güzel kamplar var ve çok ucuz. Buyrun işte bu liste. Adresler ve telefon numaraları. |

*Banu asks politely if there is a telephone at the office.*

| | |
|---|---|
| **Banu** | Telefon var mı acaba? |
| **Clerk** | Evet. İşte orada. (*The clerk points out the telephone.*) |
| **Şafak** | Kart var mı?[2] |
| **Clerk** | Evet. 10 milyon lira.[3] |
| **Şafak** | Bir kart, lütfen. |

*The clerk gives him the telephone card. He dials the number.*

| | |
|---|---|
| **Kamp** | Alo … 752 52 06 Truva Kamping. Buyrun. |
| **Şafak** | Alo. Ben Şafak Gezer. İki kişilik çadır var mı? |
| **Kamp** | Evet, var. Kaç günlük? |
| **Şafak** | Beş gün. |
| **Kamp** | Tamam. |
| **Şafak** | Kampta neler var? Elektrik var mı? |
| **Kamp** | Tabii. Devamlı elektrik, su ve sıcak su var. Restoran, yüzme-havuzu, plaj, duşlar, çocuk oyun parkı, ilk yardım ve genel telefon da var. |
| **Şafak** | Tamam. Yarın sabah görüşürüz. |
| **Kamp** | Tamam. Adınız, lütfen? |

[2]You need a telephone card to use a public telephone in Turkey.
[3]The dialogues in this book were recorded before the currency reform of 2005, in which 6 zeroes were lopped off the old Turkish lira. You will often see the abbreviation 'TL'. It stands for 'Turkish lira'. For more information, go to www.tcmb.gov.tr.

| Şafak | Adım Şafak, soyadım Gezer. |
| Kamp | Efendim? Nasıl yazılır? |
| Şafak | Ş – a – f – a – k   G – e – z – e – r. |

## Questions

1. *Telefon var mı?*
2. *Kampta su var mı?*
3. *Kampta neler var?*

| | | |
|---|---|---|
| biraz | *a little* | |
| pahalı | *expensive* | |
| ucuz | *cheap* | |
| liste | *list* | |
| adres | *address* | |
| telefon numaraları | *telephone numbers* | |
| orada | *there* | |
| alo | *hello* (on the phone) | |
| çadır | *tent* | |
| kaç günlük? | *how many days?* | |
| kampta | *at the campsite* | |
| elektrik | *electricity* | |
| devamlı | *continuous* | |
| yüzme-havuzu | *swimming pool* | |
| ilk yardım | *first aid post* | |
| plaj | *beach* | |
| çocuk | *child* | |
| oyun parkı | *play area* | |
| genel telefon | *a public phone* | |
| da | *also* | |
| yarın | *tomorrow* | |
| sabah | *morning* | |
| görüşürüz | *see you* | |
| adınız | *your name* | |
| adım | *my name (first name)* | |
| soyadım | *my surname* | |
| efendim? | *pardon?* | |
| tekrar | *again* | |

QUICK VOCAB

## Language points

### TELEPHONE NUMBERS

Turkish telephone numbers usually have seven digits, plus an area code where appropriate. When giving a telephone number, it is usual to break it down into three digits, two digits and two digits. You learnt how to say two-digit numbers in Unit 2, and in this unit you will learn how to say three-digit numbers. Listen again to the campsite manager answering Şafak's telephone call and notice how she breaks down the number. In general, Turks answer the phone by saying '**Alo!**'.

◀) **CD1, TR 5, 07:39**

### MORE NUMBERS – HUNDREDS AND THOUSANDS

First read and listen to these numbers, then pause the recording and repeat each number after the speaker. Do this as many times as you need to, until you feel comfortable with all of the numbers. When you feel confident test yourself. Try saying the numbers from 100 to 9,000, then try saying them from 9,000 down to 100.

| | | | |
|---|---|---|---|
| 100 | yüz | 1,000 | bin |
| 200 | ikiyüz | 2,000 | ikibin |
| 300 | üçyüz | 3,000 | üçbin |
| 400 | dörtyüz | 4,000 | dörtbin |
| 500 | beşyüz | 5,000 | beşbin |
| 600 | altıyüz | 6,000 | altıbin |
| 700 | yediyüz | 7,000 | yedibin |
| 800 | sekizyüz | 8,000 | sekizbin |
| 900 | dokuzyüz | 9,000 | dokuzbin |

## Dialogue 4 This is your tent

Next day Banu and Şafak arrive at the campsite and the manageress Ayşegül meets them. Listen to the dialogue a couple of times, read it through, answer the questions and check the answers at the back of the book.

| | |
|---|---|
| **Ayşegül** | Ben Ayşegül. Hoş geldiniz. |
| **Banu** | Ben Banu. (*Points at Şafak.*) O Şafak. (*They shake hands.*) |
| **Banu and Şafak** | Hoş bulduk. |
| **Ayşegül** | Nasılsınız? |
| **Banu** | Biz iyiyiz, teşekkürler. Siz nasılsınız? |
| *Ayşegül smiles.* | |
| **Ayşegül** | Çok meşgulüz. |
| *Ayşegül shows them their tent and the facilities of the campsite.* | |
| **Ayşegül** | Bu sizin çadır, burası araba parkı, o telefon, şurası yüzme-havuzu ve şu restoran, bunlar tuvaletler, şunlar duşlar, bu bungalov ilk yardım. |
| *They hear a dog barking.* | |
| **Ayşegül** | O da bizim köpek, 'Karabaş'*. |
| *They all laugh.* | |

*Karabaş is a very common name for a dog in Turkish and literally means 'blackhead'.

hav-hav

### Questions
1 *Yüzme havuzu var mı?*
2 *Köpek var mı?*
3 *Kim meşgul?*

| | |
|---|---|
| **hoş geldiniz** | *welcome* |
| **hoş bulduk** | set reply to **hoş geldiniz** |
| **iyiyiz** | *we are well* |
| **meşgulüz** | *we are busy* |
| **sizin** | *your* |
| **burası** | *here, this place* |
| **şurası** | *there, that place* |
| **bunlar** | *these are* |
| **köpek** | *dog* |

## Language points

### PERSONAL PRONOUNS

A pronoun is a word that is used instead of a noun:

| | |
|---|---|
| **Ben** *I* | **Biz** *we* |
| **Sen** *you* | **Siz** *you* |
| **O** *he, she, it* | **Onlar** *they* |

We learnt about **sen** and **siz** in Unit 1 and now you have met some of the other personal pronouns (**ben, biz, o**). In the dialogue, Banu introduces herself, '**Ben Banu**' *I am Banu*; Banu and Şafak say '**biz iyiyiz**' *we are fine* and Ayşegül introduces the dog '**o da bizim köpek Karabaş**'. You probably noticed that Turkish is simpler than English – no words for *am*, *are* or *is* are needed!

### BU, ŞU, O THIS, THAT

Where English has two words for *this* and *that*, Turkish has three. **Bu** means *this* (*is*) as in **Bu sizin çadır** *this is your tent*, when it is very near. **Şu** means *that* (*is*), when you are referring to something fairly near. **O** means *that* (*is*), when you are referring to something further away. So when Ayşegül says, '**Şu bungalov, o telefon**' she is indicating that the bungalow is a little way off and the telephone is further away.

Again, Turkish uses fewer words than English as no words are used for *is* or *are*, e.g. **Bu çadır** *this is the tent*. However, you do need to put a plural ending on **bu, şu** or **o** if you are referring to plural nouns. As an example, Ayşegül says '**bunlar tuvaletler**' *these are the toilets*.

| Singular | Plural |
| --- | --- |
| bu | bunlar |
| şu | şunlar |
| o | onlar |

### WORD ORDER

Turkish word order is, generally speaking, flexible but note that moving the **o** can change the meaning of your sentence. For example:

| **O kim?** | *Who is that person?* |
| **Kim o?** | *Who is there?* |

### BURASI, ŞURASI, ORASI *THIS, THAT PLACE*

Three very useful words derived from **bu, şu, o** are **burası, şurası, orası** meaning *this place, that place* and *the place over there*. Listen to the recording again. You will hear Ayşegül say '**Burası araba parkı**', *this (place) is the car park*.

*Şu şişe su şişesi, şu şişe süt şişesi.*

## QUESTION WORDS

| | |
|---|---|
| hangi? | *which?* |
| ne? | *what?* |
| ne kadar? | *how much?* |
| var mı? | *is there?/have you got?* |
| nasıl? | *how?/what is it like?* |
| nasılsınız? | *how are you?* |
| kaç kişi? | *how many people?* |
| kim? | *who?* |
| kaç günlük? | *how many days?* |
| kaça? | *how much?* |

◄» CD1, TR 5, 09:25

### TONGUE TWISTER

Try this Turkish tongue twister:

Şu şişe su şişesi, şu şişe süt şişesi.

Turkey has many organized campsites for tents and caravans, and camping offers a great way to get off the beaten track and see village and country life. In pitching your tent you'd be following a long cultural tradition in Turkey – that of the nomad! Some of the medieval campsites used by ancient travellers along the historic Silk Route are being restored to their former glory – but today's travellers will find plenty of modern campsites, with good facilities, often in beautiful national parks.

## Insight
### Dialogue 1

Mi? can be used to make a question:

| | |
|---|---|
| iyi | *good* |
| iyi mi? | *(Is it) good?* |

See Unit 4.

**Dialogue 2**

**Değil** means *not*.
When it is combined with the question word **mı**, we get the meaning of 'it is not' or 'they are not':
**değil mi?** *isn't it?* or *aren't they?*

The ending **-lik** means *for*:
iki kişi                    *two people*
iki kişilik                *for two people*

What does this sign mean?

```
Dikkat
köpek
var!
```

Answer: Beware of the dog!

## Practice

◄) **CD1, TR 5, 09:35**

**1** *Read these telephone numbers out loud, then compare your version with the recording. Write down the numbers in words.*
**Example** *incekum 345 14 48 Üçyüzkırkbeş ondört kırksekiz*

| | | |
|---|---|---|
| **a** Gökova | 246 50 35 | ................................. |
| **b** Çamlıköy | 262 01 37 | ................................. |
| **c** Yat | 614 13 33 | ................................. |
| **d** V – Camp | 717 22 24 | ................................. |
| **e** Pamukcak | 896 36 36 | ................................. |
| **f** Altınkum camp | 311 48 57 | ................................. |

**2** *Write the numbers below in figures.*

**3** *Match the Turkish words on the left with the pictures on the right. The first one has been done for you.*

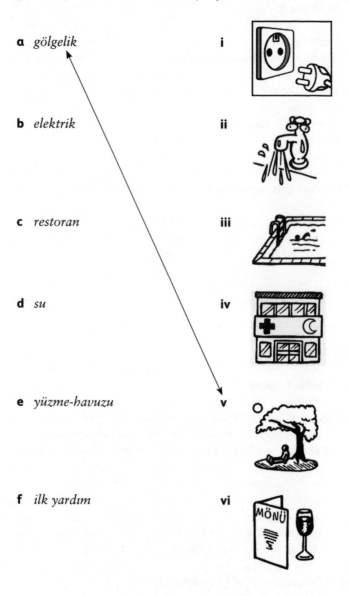

**a** *gölgelik*     **i**

**b** *elektrik*     **ii**

**c** *restoran*     **iii**

**d** *su*     **iv**

**e** *yüzme-havuzu*     **v**

**f** *ilk yardım*     **vi**

**4** Match the Turkish and the English words. The first one has been done for you.

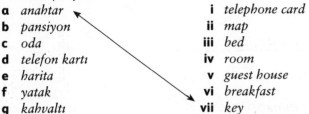

| | | | | |
|---|---|---|---|---|
| **a** | anahtar | **i** | telephone card |
| **b** | pansiyon | **ii** | map |
| **c** | oda | **iii** | bed |
| **d** | telefon kartı | **iv** | room |
| **e** | harita | **v** | guest house |
| **f** | yatak | **vi** | breakfast |
| **g** | kahvaltı | **vii** | key |

◄) CD1, TR 5, 10:35

**5** Pronunciation: f, g, ğ. First, listen to the recording, then listen while looking at the following sounds and finally listen and repeat.

| f | g | ğ |
|---|---|---|
| af | ege | sağ |
| fa | gel | dağ |
| fil | lig | ağa |

**6** Write the Turkish for the following.

| | | | |
|---|---|---|---|
| **a** | I am | **c** | it is |
| **b** | you are | **d** | we are |

**7** Wordsearch. Find ten words connected with hotels. The first has been done for you.

| A | R | O | O | T | E | L | F | G | T |
|---|---|---|---|---|---|---|---|---|---|
| D | R | A | T | Y | O | F | C | Ç | E |
| U | P | S | T | R | S | A | E | A | P |
| Ş | Z | A | N | A | H | T | A | R | E |
| M | A | N | Z | A | R | A | L | I | K |
| P | Y | A | T | A | K | F | B | R | Ü |
| B | A | L | K | O | N | L | U | O | V |
| K | O | S | Y | I | D | S | R | D | E |
| K | A | H | V | A | L | T | I | A | T |
| E | P | A | N | S | İ | Y | O | N | Z |

**8** *Letter dictation.*

___

## Role play

### *ACCOMMODATION*

You are in a hotel talking to the receptionist. Play your part in the conversation, according to the prompts.

| Receptionist | Hoş geldiniz. |
|---|---|
| **You** | *[Reply to the receptionist's welcome then ask if they have a room]* |
| Receptionist | Evet, var. |
| **You** | *[Say you want a single room]* |
| Receptionist | Tabii. |
| **You** | *[Ask if it has a shower]* |
| Receptionist | Var, efendim. Kaç gece? |
| **You** | *[Book the room for five days]* |
| Receptionist | Tabii, efendim. Pasaport, lütfen. |
| **You** | *[Thank the receptionist]* |

___

## Mini-test

Congratulations; you have now completed Unit 3. Now you will be able to choose your accommodation, make enquiries about it, book it and give your telephone number. Give yourself a point for each of the following questions that you answer correctly in Turkish.

**1** *Ask for a room with a shower.*
**2** *Ask whether the hotel has a vacant room.*

3 *Ask if breakfast is included.*
4 *Ask someone how you spell a word.*
5 *How do you say* this *and* that?
6 *How do you say* I, you, he, she, it, we, you *(plural) and* they
   in Turkish?
7 *How do you say* 'first aid' *in Turkish?*
8 *How do you say* 'welcome' *in Turkish?*
9 *How would you say* 'this place' *and* 'that place'?
10 *What do they have at the campsite?*

*Points:_____/10*

# 4

## Eating out

In this unit you will learn
- *How to order meals*
- *How to enquire what dishes there are and what's in them*
- *How to pay the bill*
- *Pronunciation:* h, ı, i

### Dialogue 1 Ordering breakfast

çay

zeytin

tereyağı

beyaz peynir

reçel

iki yumurta

şeker

Ben and Laura decide to have a typical Turkish breakfast in the hotel garden.

If you have the recording, listen to the dialogue a couple of times and see if you can answer the following questions with **doğru** *true* or **yanlış** *false* before reading the dialogue. This will help you to practise understanding spoken Turkish.

**True or false?**

1 *Çay var.*
2 *Çay çok lezzetli.*

Listen to the dialogue again, then read it through, and see if you can answer the questions at the end.

| | |
|---|---|
| **Laura** | Bahçede kahvaltı çok hoş. |
| **Ben** | Evet. Hava ne güzel! |
| **Waiter** | Günaydın, efendim. |
| **Ben** | Günaydın. Bizim için Türk kahvaltısı, lütfen. |
| **Waiter** | Tabii, efendim. |
| **Laura** | Kahvaltıda neler var? |

*The waiter brings the breakfast on a trolley.*

| | |
|---|---|
| **Waiter** | Tereyağı, bal, marmelat, reçel, peynir, zeytin, sosis. |
| **Ben** | Sucuk yok mu? |
| **Waiter** | Var, efendim. Salam, domates, salatalık, biber. Ve taze ekmek de var tabii. |
| **Ben** | Çay var mı? |
| **Waiter** | Tabii. |

*He pours their tea into tulip-shaped glasses.*

| | |
|---|---|
| **Laura** | Teşekkürler. |

*Laura has a sip of the tea.*

| | |
|---|---|
| **Laura** | Çay çok lezzetli. |
| **Waiter** | Afiyet olsun, efendim. |

*The waiter puts the breakfast on the table.*

| | |
|---|---|
| **Waiter** | Yumurta? |
| **Laura** | Hayır, teşekkürler. |
| **Ben** | Evet, bana rafadan lütfen. |
| **Waiter** | Tabii, efendim. |
| **Ben** | Sucuk da çok lezzetli. |
| **Laura** | Tuz yok mu? |
| **Ben** | İşte masada canım. |

*(Contd)*

*The waiter puts the toast on the table.*

**Waiter**    Buyrun, kızarmış ekmekler de burada. Afiyet olsun.
              Başka?

**Laura**     Yok. Teşekkürler.

Questions

  **3** *Hava nasıl?*
  **4** *Kahvaltıda neler var?*
  **5** *Kahvaltıda bal ve reçel var mı?*
  **6** *Tuz nerede?*

| | |
|---|---|
| **bahçe** | *garden* |
| **hava** | *weather* |
| **bizim çin** | *for us* |
| **Türk kahvaltısı** | *Turkish breakfast* |
| **kahvaltıda** | *at breakfast* |
| **neler?** | *what is there?* |
| **tereyağı** | *butter* |
| **bal** | *honey* |
| **marmelat** | *marmalade* |
| **reçel** | *jam* |
| **peynir** | *cheese* |
| **zeytin** | *olives* |
| **sosis** | *sausage* |
| **sucuk** | *spicy Turkish sausage* |
| **yok mu?** | *isn't there any?* |
| **salam** | *salami* |
| **domates** | *tomatoes* |
| **salatalık** | *cucumber* |
| **biber** | *pepper* |
| **taze** | *fresh* |
| **ekmek** | *bread* |
| **yumurta** | *egg* |
| **bana** | *for me* |
| **rafadan** | *soft-boiled egg* |
| **da** | *also, too* |
| **lezzetli** | *tasty* |
| **tuz** | *salt* |
| **masada** | *on the table* |

QUICK VOCAB

| kızarmış | toasted |
|----------|---------|
| **burada*** | here |
| **başka?** | anything else? |
| **yok** | no, not, there isn't, etc. |

*In spoken Turkish generally **burada** becomes **burda**.

A typical Turkish **kahvaltı** *breakfast* consists of **çay** *tea*, with **ekmek** *bread* or **kızarmış ekmek** *toast* (literally *reddened bread*), **tereyağı** *butter*, **bal** *honey* or **reçel** *jam*. **Gül reçeli** *rose petal jam*, **incir reçeli** *fig jam* and **vişne reçeli** *sour cherry jam* are worth trying. **Peynir** *cheese* and **zeytin** *olives* are usually served at breakfast, too. You can also ask for **yumurta** *eggs*, either **rafadan** *soft boiled*, **katı** *hard boiled* or **yağda** *fried*.

Every nation has its own way of cooking and eating things. Turks eat Turkish style: it has been very much influenced by the Anatolian and Mediterranean ways of cooking and eating.

## Language points

### *-DE, -DA AT, ON, IN*

In Turkish, to say *at*, *on*, or *in* you put the ending **-de**, **-da** on the noun instead of using a separate word. Here are some examples:

| Kahvaltı masada. | *Breakfast is on the table.* |
|------------------|------------------------------|
| Kahvaltıda neler var? | *What is there for breakfast.* |
| Restoranda. | *At the restaurant.* |
| Otelde. | *At the hotel.* |

To decide whether to use **-de** or **-da** on the end of a word, you simply choose the one which harmonizes best with the last vowel in that word:

▶ **da** *harmonizes best with (**a, ı, o, u**)*
▶ **de** *harmonizes best with (**e, i, ö, ü**).*

It helps if you can remember these groups but don't worry too much about it. The more you are exposed to the language (particularly the more you hear it), the easier it will become to know which ending to use. This is the same principle as with the -ler, -lar endings which we looked at in Unit 2 (the first rule of vowel harmony).

## Dialogue 2 At a fish restaurant

Ahmet and Yeşim decide to go to a **balık restoranı** *fish restaurant* with their friends Vanessa and Asuman. Yeşim makes the reservation for four people and they meet at the restaurant at 8 p.m. As they are going to have a few drinks, Ahmet does not take his car. If you have the recording, listen to it a couple of times, then answer the following questions with **doğru** *true* or **yanlış** *false*.

True or false?
1 *Çankaya var.*
2 *Su var.*

Listen to the dialogue again, then read it through and see if you can answer the questions at the end.

CD1, TR 6, 02:19

| Ahmet | Garson, lütfen. |
|---|---|
| Waiter | Buyrun, efendim. |
| Ahmet | Şarap ne var? |
| Waiter | Çankaya ve Kutman çok güzel. |
| Yeşim | Çankaya, lütfen. |
| Asuman | Bana da beyaz Çankaya, lütfen. |
| Ahmet | Ya sen, Vanessa? |
| Vanessa | Vişne suyu, lütfen. |
| *Ahmet orders the drinks first.* | |
| Ahmet | Bir büyük beyaz Çankaya. Bir küçük rakı ve bir de vişne suyu. |
| Waiter | Hemen, efendim. |
| Ahmet | Bir şişe de su tabii. |

*The waiter goes to fetch the drinks. They look at the **balık mönü** (fish menu) and are ready to order when the waiter returns.*

**Ahmet**   Bana kalkan tava ve karışık salata, lütfen.

**Asuman**   Bana levrek buğulama ve yeşil salata, lütfen.

**Vanessa**   Bana da barbunya tava ve dilimlenmiş domates, lütfen.

**Yeşim**   Lüfer ızgara ve roka, lütfen.

**Waiter**   Tabii, efendim.

*They all enjoy their meal. At the end of the meal they have **karışık meyve** (mixed fruit) followed by **Türk kahvesi** (Turkish coffee).*

**Ahmet**   Garson, hesap, lütfen.

**Waiter**   Buyrun, hesap.

*Ahmet pays the bill and leaves a tip.*

**Ahmet**   Teşekkürler. Üstü kalsın.

*The waiter is pleased with the tip.*

**Waiter**   Sağ olun, efendim.

**Ahmet**   Taksi nerede?

**Waiter**   Burada, sağda, efendim.

Questions

**3**  *Çankaya şarap mı?*

**4**  *Vanessa için vişne suyu mu?*

**5**  *Yeşim Hanım için lüfer tava mı?*

**6**  *Yeşil salata Ahmet Bey için mi?*

| | |
|---|---|
| **ya sen?** | *and you?* |
| **hemen** | *straight away* |
| **balık** | *fish* |
| **kalkan** | *turbot* |
| **karışık salata** | *mixed salad* |
| **levrek** | *bass* |
| **buğulama** | *steamed* |
| **barbunya** | *red mullet* |
| **tava** | *fried* |
| **dilimlenmiş** | *sliced* |
| **domates** | *tomatoes* |
| **lüfer** | *blue fish* |
| **ızgara** | *grilled* |
| **roka** | *rocket leaves* |

QUICK VOCAB

| | |
|---|---|
| **Üstü kalsın.** | *Keep the change.* |
| **taksi** | *taxi* |
| **nerede?** | *where?* |
| **burada** | *here* |
| **sağda** | *on the right* |

In the evenings you will find restaurants serving **sıcak ve soğuk meze** (*hot and cold hors d'oeuvres*). Restaurants often serve grilled meat or fish as a main course after the **meze**. If you want to ensure being served good, fresh fish it is best to go to a **balık lokantası** (*fish restaurant*). You can often choose the fish you want before it is cooked. Try ordering your fish in Turkish – Turks will love it if you make an effort to speak some Turkish. If in return they want to practise their English, don't give up with your Turkish!

| | | |
|---|---|---|
| **Customer** | Bu ne? | *What's this?* |
| **Waiter** | Bu mu? | *This one?* |
| **Customer** | Evet. | *Yes.* |
| **Waiter** | Lüfer | *Blue fish.* |
| **Customer** | O büyük lüfer, lütfen. | *That big blue fish, please.* |

You will often be asked how you want the fish cooked, and you can generally choose from **ızgara** *grilled*, **tava** *fried*, **buğulama** *steamed* or **kiremitte** baked on a tile in the oven.

**Rakı** *aniseed-flavoured spirit* is the normal drink with fish. Most Turks drink **rakı** with water.

## Dialogue 3 At a *köfte* restaurant

Following their visit to the Basilica cistern (a Byzantine underground reservoir) Ben and Laura are now feeling hungry. They can't decide whether to have lunch at a **köfte** restaurant

(which specializes in various types of meatball) or **muhallebici**
(shops which sell puddings and savoury pastries).

If you have the recording, listen to it a couple of times, then answer
the questions below with **doğru** *true*, or **yanlış** *false*.

True or false?
1 *The beer is cold.*
2 *The view is beautiful.*

🎧 CD1, TR 6, 04:19

| Ben | Muhallebici mi, köfteci mi? |
| Laura | Öğlen köfteci, akşam muhallebici. |
| Ben | Tamam. Hadi. |

*They go to the famous Sultan Ahmet Köftecisi, which overlooks the
Blue Mosque. They ask if the restaurant has **cız bız köfte** (grilled
meatballs.)*

| Ben | Cız bız köfte var mı? |
| Waiter | Var, efendim. Kaç porsiyon? |
| Laura | İki porsiyon, pilavlı. |
| Waiter | Tabii, efendim. |
| Laura | (*to Ben*) Bira mı, ayran mı? |
| Ben | Bira soğuk mu? |
| Waiter | Evet, çok soğuk. |
| Ben | Benim için, bir soğuk bira. |
| Laura | Bana da bir soğuk ayran, lütfen. |
| Waiter | Başka? |

*They look at the menu.*

| Ben | Piyaz var mı? |
| Waiter | Var, efendim. |
| Ben | Bana bir piyaz. |
| Laura | Bana da karışık salata. |

*The waiter brings their order to the table.*

| Waiter | Afiyet olsun. |
| Ben and Laura | Teşekkür! Teşekkürler! |
| Laura | Köfte çok lezzetli, değil mi? |
| Ben | Evet, çok. |

Listen to the dialogue again, then read through it and see if you can answer the following questions:

Questions

**3** *Kaç porsiyon köfte?*
**4** *Piyaz ne?*
**5** *Köfte güzel mi?*

QUICK VOCAB

| | |
|---|---|
| **öğlen** | *noon* |
| **hadi** | *come on* |
| **cız bız** | *sizzling/fried* |
| **porsiyon** | *portion* |
| **pilavlı** | *with cooked rice* |
| **benim için** | *for me* |
| **bana da** | *for me too* |
| **başka** | *anything else* |
| **piyaz** | *white bean salad* |

## Language points

### *MAKING QUESTIONS WITH* Mİ (MI, MU, MÜ)

In general **mı, mi, mu, mü** appear after nouns (naming words), verbs (doing words) and adjectives (describing words) to make a question. Simply choose the one which rhymes best with the last vowel in the word before:

| | |
|---|---|
| **Balık mı?** | *(Is it) fish?* |
| **Şeftalı mı?** | *(Is it) peach?* |
| **Karpuz mu?** | *(Is it) watermelon?* |
| **Üzüm mü?** | *(Are they) grapes?* |

The examples above are quite straight forward as the two vowels which need to rhyme are exactly the same. Sometimes, however, the last vowel of the preceding word may be **a, e, o** or **ö**. In such cases you use the form which sounds the closest. For example:

| Çay mi? | *Tea?* |
| Ekmek mi? | *Bread?* |
| Tost mu? | *Toasted sandwich?* |
| Likör mü? | *Liqueur?* |

- ► mı *comes after* ı, a
- ► mi *comes after* i, e
- ► mu *comes after* u, o
- ► mü *comes after* ü, ö

This follows the second rule of vowel harmony. The word **mi** is an **i**-type word.

Do not try to learn the rules of vowel harmony by heart. Whenever you hear or read Turkish, you will come across them and you will come to know which endings to use instinctively. Meanwhile, as a beginner and a foreign language learner there is little to worry about, as even if you do not harmonize your vowels correctly, it will not affect the actual meaning of what you say and people will still understand you! Everyone makes mistakes.

....................................................................

The Turks are very creative people when it comes to food. **Sebze** *vegetables*, **et** *meat*, **pilav** (cooked rice, vermicelli or cracked wheat, plain or with small pieces of vegetables or meat) and **börek** *pastry* are the main features of Turkish cuisine. Bread is served with almost everything, as is a glass of water.

Every visitor should try **börek**. These are delicious savouries made out of thin layers of pastry with minced meat, vegetable, cheese, or onion fillings. They are cooked in the oven or fried individually. You can find them at a **börekçi** *pastry shop*, **pastane** *cake shop* or **fırın** *bakery*.

Other foods to look out for include **pide**. This is a Turkish pizza made of flat baked bread. You can have **kıymalı pide** *with minced meat*, **peynirli pide** *with cheese*, **yumurtalı pide** *with egg*. You can have a takeaway or sit and eat it in a **pideci** *a Turkish pizza restaurant*. You will also find **lahmacun** served

*(Contd)*

in **pideci**. These are thin savoury pancakes baked in the oven, covered with minced meat, tomatoes and chopped onion. They are accompanied by fresh parsley and lemon. Vegetable dishes are plentiful, but strict vegetarians should ask for them to be **zeytinyağlı** *cooked with olive oil* rather than meat stock. These dishes are served cold. If you want to ask what vegetarian options are available you can say, '**Etsiz yemek ne var?**' '*What vegetarian dishes do you have?*'

In Turkish, two words are used for restaurant – **restoran** and **lokanta**. **Restoran** is more frequently used in tourist areas and big cities, and the restaurants are usually proud to display their star ratings at the entrance and on the menu: **lüks** *luxury*, **1inci sınıf** *first class*, **2nci sınıf** *second* class. **Lokanta** is more often used for local or rural restaurants and cafés.

In a restaurant the simplest way of attracting the waiter's attention is to call '**Garson**' '*Waiter*', and to order something, you can just name it. To be more polite, you can add **lütfen** *please*. You normally pay in cafés and restaurants when you're ready to leave. Restaurant prices include **KDV** *VAT*. A 10% **bahşiş** *tip* is usual and much appreciated.

## Insight
### Dialogue 2

| de | too or also |
|---|---|
| ben de | me too, I also |

### Dialogue 3

The ending **-cı** denotes a person or occupation:

| köfte | *Türkish meat balls* |
|---|---|
| köfteci | *a person who makes and sells köfte* |

## Practice

**1** *Memory game. Look at the picture of the breakfast on the table at the beginning of the unit for three minutes then turn back to this page and see how much you can remember. Write down in Turkish what was on the table. When you can't remember any more items, have another look at the picture for a further two minutes and then write down anything you missed.*

**2** *Make questions using (-mı, -mi, -mu or -mü). Use the words (-mı, -mi, -mu, -mü) to complete the following questions. You may need to use each word more than once. The first one has been done for you.*

   **a** *Kahvaltı güzel mi?*
   **b** *Karışık meyve _____?*
   **c** *Balık lezetli _____?*
   **d** *Pide ucuz _____?*
   **e** *O biber mi, tuz _____?*
   **f** *Otel lüks _____?*

**3** *Reorder the following sentences below to form a meaningful dialogue.*

   **a** *Garson.*
   **b** *Karışık meyve var mı?*
   **c** *Bir karışık meyve, lütfen.*
   **d** *Buyrun?*
   **e** *Var.*
   **f** *Tabii efendim.*

**4** *Look at the pictures and complete the accompanying sentences.*

   **a** *Bir bardak _____, lütfen.*

**b** İki porsiyon _____, lütfen.

**c** Karışık _____, lütfen.

**d** Daha _____, lütfen.

**5** Answer these questions with **evet** yes or **hayır** no. The first one has been done for you.

  **a** Yeşil Ev İstanbul'da mı?   ☺  Evet, İstanbul'da.
  **b** Rakı soğuk mu?   ☺
  **c** Döner et mi?   ☺
  **d** Karpuz ucuz mu?   ☺
  **e** Şeftali sebze mi?   ☹
  **f** Salata lezzetli mi?   ☺
  **g** Lokum alkollü mü?   ☹
  **h** Baklava tatlı mı?   ☺
  **i** Zeytin siyah mı?   ☹
  **j** Simit taze mi?   ☺

**6** *Match the Turkish words with their corresponding picture.*
*The first one has been done for you.*

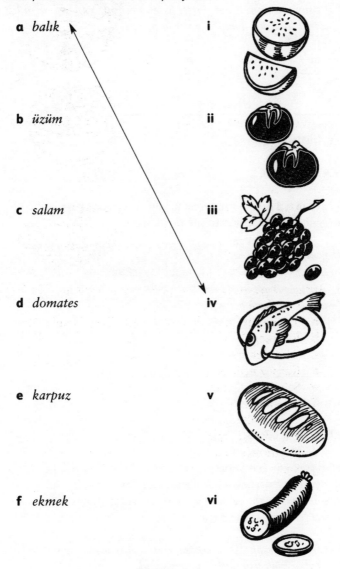

**a** *balık*　　　　　**i**

**b** *üzüm*　　　　　**ii**

**c** *salam*　　　　　**iii**

**d** *domates*　　　　**iv**

**e** *karpuz*　　　　　**v**

**f** *ekmek*　　　　　**vi**

**7** **Pronunciation: h, ı, i.** *First, listen without looking, then listen while looking. Finally listen and repeat.*

| h | ı | i |
|---|---|---|
| ah | ısı | bir |
| hey | sık | iki |

---

## Role play

### *EATING OUT*

You are in a Turkish pizza restaurant. Play your part in the conversation, according to the prompts.

| Waiter | Buyrun, efendim. |
|---|---|
| **You** | *[Ask for a minced meat pide (pizza) and a lahmacun (savoury pancake)]* |
| Waiter | Tabii, efendim. İçecek? |
| **You** | *[Ask for a yogurt drink and a cola]* |

---

## Mini-test

Well done; you have completed Unit 4. Now you will be able to order your meals, ask what dishes there are and pay the bill. Give yourself a point for each if you can say these things in Turkish without looking at the back.

**1** *Order a breakfast of coffee, butter, bread, sausages and egg.*
**2** *Order fried fish with a green salad.*
**3** *Order a large white wine.*

4 *Order two portions of meatballs with cooked rice.*
5 *Ask if the beer is cold.*
6 *Order cherry juice in Turkish.*
7 *Ask where the taxies are.*
8 *Ask for a mixed salad.*
9 *Ask for two portions of cooked rice.*
10 *How do you say 'keep the change'?*

*Points:_____/10*

# 5

## Directions

In this unit you will learn
- *How to ask for, and give, directions*
- *How to get around a new place*
- *How to ask what something means*
- *Pronunciation: j, k, l*

---

### Dialogue 1 At the airport

Dr Bahadır Bey and his wife Ülkü have just landed at Istanbul Airport. They are looking for the bank and they ask someone for directions.

First listen to the dialogue a couple of times and then read through it. See if you can understand the conversation with the aid of the words in the vocabulary box. If you need more help, look at the translation at the back of the book.

**Bahadır**    Afedersiniz, banka nerede, acaba?

**Passer-by**    Özür dilerim. Bilmiyorum. Danışmaya sorun. Danışma orada.

**Bahadır**    Çok teşekkürler.

*They ask at the information desk where the bank and the toilets are.*

**Ülkü**    Afedersiniz, banka nerede acaba?

**Clerk**    Düz gidin, pasaport kontrolü geçin ve gümrüklerden sonra sağa dönün, tekrar düz gidin, solda.

**Ülkü**    Aaa, çok teşekkürler. En yakın tuvalet nerede, acaba?

**Clerk**    Düz gidin, pasaport kontrolden önce, sağda ve solda iki tuvalet var. Pasaport kontrolden sonra iki tuvalet daha var.

**Bahadır**    Çok teşekkürler.

**Clerk**    Bir şey değil.

**Bahadır**    Taksiler nerede acaba?

**Clerk**    Kapıdan çıkın, yolu geçin, orada.

*Bahadır and Ülkü get into a taxi.*

**Driver**    Nereye, efendim?

**Bahadır**    Sultan Ahmet'e, lütfen. Sultan Ahmet uzak mı?

**Driver**    Biraz – 20 kilometre, 40 dakika falan.

## Atatürk Havalimanı/ Istanbul Havalimanı

| | | |
|---|---|---|
| A | Geliş İskelesi | Arrivals Bridge |
| B | Vize Ofisi | Visa Office |
| C | Bagaj Alım Bantı | Incoming Baggage Band |
| D | Otel Rezervasyon | Hotel Reservation |
| E | Banka | Bank |
| F | Alış Veriş Merkezi | Shopping Centre |
| G | Yemek Alanları | Food Courts |
| H | Tuvaletler | Toilets |
| I | Kayıp Bagaj | Lost Luggage |
| J | Emanet | Luggage Custody |
| K | Oto Kiralama | Rent-A-Car |
| L | VIP Salonları | VIP Lounges |
| M | Transit Yolcu Bankosu | Transit Passenger Lounge |
| N | Merdivenler | Escalators |

## Questions

Read the dialogue again and look at the plan of Istanbul Airport carefully. Were Bahadır and Ülkü given the correct directions for these places?

**1** *Banka.*
**2** *Tuvaletler.*
**3** *Taksiler.*

> Have a look at these websites: www.goturkey.com, www.tcdd.gov.tr and www.thy.com.tr.

*In spoken Turkish, **afedersiniz** has one 'f'; in written Turkish it appears as **affedersiniz**.

General information about Turkey and basic maps are available from the **turizm bürosu** *Turkish tourist offices*, abroad and in Turkey. When you need to ask something, the easiest way to attract attention is to say, '**Afedersiniz**' *'excuse me'* followed by your question. To ask where something is, say the word for what you're looking for, followed by **nerede** *where?*, e.g. **Giriş nerede?** *Where is the entrance?*, **Gişe nerede?** *Where is the ticket office?* When you're being given directions, listen out for the important bits such as whether to turn right or left, and try to repeat each bit to make sure you've understood it correctly. You can always ask the person to say it again more slowly: **bir daha lütfen** *once more, please*; **daha yavaş** *more slowly*. If you are looking for a **tuvalet** *toilet* they are sometimes labelled **baylar** *gents*, **bayanlar** *ladies* or **erkek** *men* and **kadın** *women*. They may also be marked with the sign oo.

In Istanbul, the public transport system is very convenient and provided by buses, mini-buses and the subway.

## Language points

### *VERBS*

Verbs are action words such as *go*, *do*, *walk* and, in Turkish, they generally come at the end of sentences. Verbs change according to who does the action and/or when it happens. When you look up a verb in an English dictionary you see the main part or the stem of the verb with 'to' in front of it, e.g. to mean, to ask. The dictionary form of Turkish verbs is the stem plus the ending **-mek** or **-mak**. Dictionary forms are sometimes called the infinitive. Sometimes the dictionary form is used as it stands, and sometimes you use it to make the correct form of the verb.

You will notice that some verbs have **-mek** endings while some have **-mak** endings. This is our old friend vowel harmony again!

The ending is the one which rhymes best with the last vowel in that word, so it depends on the last vowel in the stem of the verb:

- ▶ -mak *harmonizes best with* **a, ı, o, u**
- ▶ -mek *harmonizes best with* **e, i, ö, ü.**

## COMMANDS AND INSTRUCTIONS

In Turkish, you give informal commands such as **Git!** *Go!* by using the verb stem. You make the stem by taking the dictionary form of the verb and removing **-mek** or **-mak**. For example, the verb stem of **sormak** *to ask* is **sor** *ask!* and the verb stem of **dönmek** *to turn* is **dön** *turn!*

Here are some infinitives and their corresponding informal commands:

| | | | |
|---|---|---|---|
| **sormak** | *to ask* | **Sor!** | *Ask!* |
| **gitmek** | *to go* | **Git!** | *Go!* |
| **geçmek** | *to cross* | **Geç!** | *Cross!* |
| **dönmek** | *to turn* | **Dön!** | *Turn!* |
| **çıkmak** | *to come out/go up* | **Çık!** | *Come out!* |
| **girmek** | *to enter* | **Gir!** | *Enter!* |
| **bırakmak** | *to leave* | **Bırak!** | *Leave!* |

### FORMAL OR INFORMAL?

As you know, there are two ways of saying *you* (**sen** and **siz**) in Turkish, one formal and the other informal. You will, therefore, need to learn two ways of telling people what to do – one polite or formal, one friendly or informal. Here is the friendly or informal way:

| | |
|---|---|
| **Sor!** | *Ask!* |
| **Geç!** | *Cross!* |
| **Dön!** | *Turn!* |
| **Çık!** | *Come out!* |

To make the command politer use the **siz** form. Take the verb stem (which is also the friendly form of command) and add **-in, -ın, -un** or **-ün**.

On warning signs and official notices you will see a third very formal form of command, using the following endings **-ınız, -iniz, -unuz, -ünüz**. You will probably never need to use this form yourself, but you do need to recognize it.

Vowel harmony yet again determines which ending to use. Choose the one which rhymes best with the last vowel in that word, following the rules of **i**-type vowel harmony:

▶ **-ın** *and* **-ınız** *harmonizes with/comes after* **a, ı**
▶ **-un** *and* **-unuz** *harmonizes with/comes after* **u, o**
▶ **-in** *and* **-iniz** *harmonizes with/comes after* **i, e**
▶ **-ün** *and* **-ünüz** *harmonizes/comes after* **ü, ö**

| Polite commands | Very formal commands |
|---|---|
| Sorun! | Sorunuz! |
| Geçin! | Geçiniz! |
| Dönün! | Dönünüz! |
| Çıkın! | Çıkınız! |

## Dialogue 2 In Sultan Ahmet Square

Bahadır and Ülkü are in Sultan Ahmet Square. They ask for directions to some places of interest. If you have the recording, first listen to the dialogue a couple of times, then read the dialogue.

| | |
|---|---|
| **Ülkü** | Afedersiniz, Topkapı Müzesi nerede acaba? |
| **Passer-by** | Efendim? |
| **Ülkü** | Topkapı Müzesi nerede acaba? |
| **Passer-by** | Özür dilerim, bilmiyorum. |
| | *(Contd)* |

CD1, TR 7, 01:35

*They ask someone else.*

**Ülkü**        Afedersiniz, Topkapı nerede, acaba?
**Passer-by**   Düz gidin, köşeden sola dönün, tam karşıda.
**Ülkü**        Müzeler ne zaman açık?
**Passer-by**   Saat 9'dan 5'e kadar.
**Ülkü**        Teşekkürler.
**Passer-by**   Bir şey değil.
*They find the Topkapi Palace and go to the ticket office.*
**Bahadır**     İki bilet, lütfen.
**Receptionist** Buyrun. Çantaları buraya bırakın.
**Bahadır**     Teşekkürler. Harem nerede?
**Receptionist** Düz gidin. Orada işaretler var.

## Questions

Read the dialogue again and answer these questions in Turkish.

**1** *Müzeler ne zaman açık?*
**2** *Harem nerede?*

| | |
|---|---|
| müze | *museum* |
| Topkapı Müzesi* | *Topkapı Museum* |
| özür dilemek | *to apologize* |
| köşe | *corner* |
| tam | *right/exactly* |
| karşı | *opposite* |
| zaman | *time* |
| açık | *open* |
| -den ... -e kadar | *from ... to ...* |
| bilet | *ticket* |
| çanta | *bag* |
| buraya | *here* (shows movement) |
| bırakmak | *to leave* |
| Harem | *Harem* |
| işaret | *sign* |

QUICK VOCAB

*Topkapı Müzesi** is also known as **Topkapı Sarayı** meaning *Topkapi Palace.*

The Harem was the home of the imperial family. It was like a small villa with up to 500 people living there, including the sultan, his mother, wives, children and up to 300 concubines. The sultan's women were not allowed to enter the outside world and were guarded by a corps of black eunuchs who also acted as go-betweens with the outside world. The harem was a place of political intrigue. If you want to find out more about life here, *Harem: the world behind the veil* by Alev Lytle Croutlier is a very interesting read.

## Müze kartı

If you get an MK, you can use it throughout Turkey:
www.müzekart.com

## Language points

### 'THE'

There is no actual word for *the* in Turkish. But in some cases -ı, which has four variations (-ı, -i, u, ü), is used as a word ending to give the same meaning. These endings are principally used when the verb has a direct object (see next section). The -i ending follows i-type vowel harmony.

| | |
|---|---|
| Işıklar*ı* geç. | *Pass the lights.* |
| Müze*yi* geç. | *Pass the museum.* |
| Yol*u* geç. | *Cross the road.* |
| Otobüs*ü* sür. | *Drive the bus.* |

### DIRECT OBJECTS

In Turkish, it is important to spot the direct object of a verb.
A direct object is something or someone which is having an action
carried out on it, as in *Kate sees the <u>sun</u>*. There are direct objects in
these commands:

| | |
|---|---|
| **Camiyi geç.** | *Pass the mosque.* |
| **Çayı iç.** | *Drink the tea.* |
| **Üzümü ye.** | *Eat the grapes.* |

In these examples, the direct objects are the things that are to be
passed, drunk and eaten (the mosque, the tea and the grapes).

### SAYING 'THE'

Turkish does not usually distinguish between *a* and *the*. In the
case of the direct object of a verb, however, Turkish *does* make a
distinction: in this case it needs the equivalent of *the*. For direct
objects, the Turkish equivalent of *the* is the ending -**i** (-**ı**, -**u**, -**ü**)
(or -**yi** (-**ı**, -**u**, -**ü**) if the noun ends in a vowel). As we mentioned in
Unit 2, the equivalent of *a* is either **bir** or nothing.
For example:

| | |
|---|---|
| **Çay iç.** | *Drink (some) tea.* |
| **Bir çay iç.** | *Drink a (one) tea.* |
| **Çayı iç.** | *Drink the tea.* |
| **Araba sür.** | *Drive a car.* |
| **Bir araba sür.** | *Drive a car.* |
| **Arabayı sür.** | *Drive the car.* |

You use *the* in English to talk about *specific* items. Likewise in
Turkish, you use the -**i** (-**ı**, -**u**, -**ü**) ending if the direct object is a
*specific* item.

At this stage, don't worry about getting these endings right. People
will understand you. Just try to notice them when you hear or see
them. Some commands do not have direct objects:

| Git! | Go. |
|---|---|
| Çık! | Come out/Get out! |
| Dikkat et! | Watch out! Pay attention! Be careful! |

### WORD ORDER

Although Turkish word order is relatively free and flexible, it is best to follow the main principle that verbs go at the end of the sentence.

| Git. | Go. |
|---|---|
| Sen git. | You go. |
| Sen müzeye git. | You go to the museum. (lit. you museum to go.) |

The basic word order is subject (the person or thing performing the action) followed by the object (the person or thing having the action done to it), and the verb (the action word) goes at the end of the sentence. Remember this easily by SOV (subject – object – verb). Word order is described in more detail in Unit 7.

---

## Dialogue 3 Blue Cruise

Ülkü and Bahadır are at a tourist office in Bodrum, enquiring about cruises along the coast, known as 'Blue Cruises'.

| | | |
|---|---|---|
| **Ülkü** | Afedersiniz, Bodrum'dan Mavi Yolculuk var mı? | |
| **Clerk** | Var. | |
| **Ülkü** | Nereye var? | |
| **Clerk** | Birincisi, Bodrum'dan Ören'e, Ören'den Körmen'e, Körmen'den tekrar Bodrum'a. İkincisi, Bodrum'dan Karaada'ya, Karaada'dan Cedre'ye, Cedre'den Ballısu'ya, Ballısu'dan Bodrum'a. | |
| **Ülkü** | Aaa! Birinci güzel! Liman nerede? | |
| **Clerk** | Sahilde, merkezde. | |
| **Ülkü** | Teşekkürler. | |
| **Clerk** | Rica ederim. | |

CD1, TR 7, 02:42

## Questions

Read the dialogue and try to answer the following questions.

**1** *Bodrum'dan Mavi Yolculuk var mı?*
**2** *Liman nerede?*

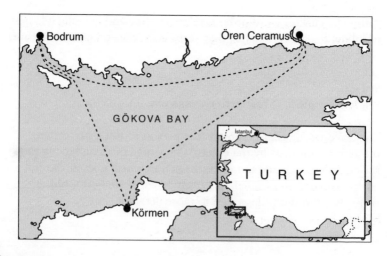

**QUICK VOCAB**

| | |
|---|---|
| **Mavi Yolculuk** | *Blue Cruise* |
| **nereye?** | *where?* (indicates movement so 'where to?') |
| **birinci\*** | *first* |
| **ikinci\*** | *second* |
| **liman** | *port* |
| **sahil** | *coast* |
| **merkez** | *centre* |
| **rica ederim** | *not at all* |

\*In the spoken language **birinci/birincisi** and **ikinci/ikincisi** are used interchangeably.

## Language points

### *ENDINGS SHOWING POSITION OR MOVEMENT*

**-de**, **-da** *at/on/in*
Remember we covered the Turkish noun ending **-de** in Unit 4.
It has two variations (**-de** and **-da**) and shows there is no movement
to, or from, and it means *at*, *on* or *in*.

**-e**, **-a** *to*
The ending **-e**, which has two variations (**-e** and **-a**) and indicates
there is movement towards, and means *to*. The endings follow the
same principle as **-de** and **-da**.

- ▶ **-a** *harmonizes best with* **a, ı, o, u**
- ▶ **-e** *harmonizes best with* **e, i, ö, ü**

Here are some examples:

| | |
|---|---|
| **İstanbul'***a* | *to Istanbul* |
| **Türkiye'***ye* | *to Turkey* |
| **Ankara'***ya* | *to Ankara* |
| **Müzeye** | *to the museum* |

Connecting *y*
In Turkish, you cannot put two vowels next to each other within
a word as it makes pronunciation difficult. If a word ends in a
vowel and the ending starts with a vowel, insert the consonant **-y-**
between them, e.g. not **müzee** but **müzeye**. This makes the word
more pronounceable.

**-den**, **-dan** *from*
The ending **-den**, which has two variations (**-den** and **-dan**) means
*from*, in the sense of movement away from.

| | |
|---|---|
| **İngiltere'den** | *from England* |
| **Amerika'dan** | *from America* |

| Saraydan camiye | *from the palace to the mosque* |
| Müzeden meydana | *from the museum to the square* |

Remember, most proper nouns (names of places and people) have
an apostrophe before the ending.

Istanbul is the only city in the world built on two continents –
Europe and Asia. It stands on the shore of the **Istanbul Boğazı**
*Bosporus* where the waters of the **Karadeniz** *Black Sea* merge
with those of the **Marmara Denizi** *Sea of Marmara* and **Haliç**
*the Golden Horn*. Here on this splendid site Istanbul guards
the precious relics of the three empires of which she has
been the capital; a unique link between East and West, past
and present.

Istanbul has infinite variety: **müzeler** *museums*, **tarihi kiliseler**
*ancient churches*, **saraylar** *palaces*, **muhteşem camiler** *great
mosques*, **Kapalı Çarşı** *covered market* and the **Istanbul
Boğazı** *Bosporus*.

A stay in Istanbul is not complete without the traditional and
unforgettable excursion by boat along the Bosporus. The
shore is lined with modern hotels, **yalılar** *old wooden villas*,
**mermer saraylar** *marble palaces*, **hisarlar** *fortresses*, and
**küçük balıkçı köyleri** *small fishing villages*. The best and most
relaxing way to see the Bosporus is to board one of the **yolcu
vapuru** *passenger boats* that regularly zigzag along the shores
starting from **Eminönü** and stopping alternately on the **Asya**
*Asian* and **Avrupa** *European* sides. **Gidiş-Dönüş** *the round
trip* takes about six hours and the fare is very reasonable.

In 21st-century Turkish 'Istanbul' can be spelled in two
different ways: **İstanbul** (dotted capital 'I') and **Istanbul**
(undotted capital 'I'). Both forms are correct, but in this book
we've chosen to use the spelling with the dotted 'I' whenever
we refer to the name of the city in Turkish.

## Insight

### Dialogue 1

**en** means *most*. It can be placed before an adjective to make the superlative (in English this is made by adding -est to the end of an adjective):

| | |
|---|---|
| **yakın** | *near* |
| **en yakın** | *nearest* |

**daha** means *more*. See Unit 6.

### Dialogue 2

**bilmek** is *to know*:

| | |
|---|---|
| **biliyorum** | *I know (lit. I am knowing)* |
| **bilmiyorum** | *I don't know* |

.................................................................................

## Practice

**1** *Can you match the following traffic signs with what they mean?*

**a**

**i** *Sola dön.*

**b**

**ii** *Dur.*

**c**     **iii** *Düz git.*

**d**    **iv** *Sağa dön.*

**2** Match the following questions with their answers.

| | | | |
|---|---|---|---|
| **a** | *İçkiler kimden?* | **i** | *Evet, Sultan Ahmet Meydanı'nda.* |
| **b** | *Kahveler senden mi?* | **ii** | *Vanessa'dan.* |
| **c** | *Posta kartı kimden?* | **iii** | *Benden.* |
| **d** | *Istanbul nerede?* | **iv** | *Türkiye'de.* |
| **e** | *Ayasofya Istanbul'da mı?* | **v** | *Hayır, senden.* |

**3** Write down the meanings of the following Turkish phrases.

| | | | |
|---|---|---|---|
| **a** | *Buyurun.* | **e** | *Özür dilerim.* |
| **b** | *Benden.* | **f** | *Bilmiyorum.* |
| **c** | *Rahatsız etmeyin!* | **g** | *Teşekkürler.* |
| **d** | *Afedersiniz.* | **h** | *Rica ederim.* |

**4** Here are some public signs with formal endings. Where would you see them?

| | | | |
|---|---|---|---|
| **a** | *İtiniz.* | **i** | on a door |
| **b** | *Çekiniz.* | **ii** | on an escalator |
| **c** | *Kart kullanınız.* | **iii** | on a door |
| **d** | *İstanbul'a Hoş Geldiniz.* | **iv** | on a road sign |
| **e** | *Yavaş sürünüz.* | **v** | on a public telephone |
| **f** | *Sağı takip ediniz.* | **vi** | approaching Istanbul |

◆) **CD1, TR 7, 03:44**

**5** Look at the map of Turkey showing the distances from Istanbul to other cities in Turkey. Write the answers first,

*then listen and repeat them. For help with the numbers,
see Units 2 and 3.*

**a** *İstanbul'dan Ankara'ya kaç km?*
**b** *İstanbul'dan Bodrum'a kaç km?*
**c** *İstanbul'dan Çanakkale'ye kaç km?*
**d** *İstanbul'dan Safranbolu'ya kaç km?*
**e** *İstanbul'dan Pamukkale'ye kaç km?*
**f** *İstanbul'dan Marmaris'e kaç km?*
**g** *İstanbul'dan Göreme'ye kaç km?*
**h** *İstanbul'dan İzmir'e kaç km?*
**i** *İstanbul'dan Trabzon'a kaç km?*
**j** *İstanbul'dan Fethiye'ye kaç km?*

**6** *Translate these sentences into English. Look up the vocabulary
in this unit or use your dictionary.*

   **a** *Danışma nerede?*
   **b** *Işıkları geçin.*
   **c** *Düz gidin, sağdan birinci yola dönün.*
   **d** *Düz gidin, solda, köşede.*

**7** Listen to the recording of the routes of the Blue Cruises and stops while looking at the map. Then put the necessary endings on the following place names e.g. **-den, -dan** (from), **-e, -a** (to).

| | | |
|---|---|---|
| **a** | *Birinci gün* | *Marmaris – Çiftlik* |
| **b** | *İkinci gün* | *Çiftlik – Bozukkale* |
| **c** | *Üçüncü gün* | *Bozukkale – Aktur – Datça* |
| **d** | *Dördüncü gün* | *Datça – Knidos* |
| **e** | *Beşinci gün* | *Knidos – Bodrum* |

Note: **d** becomes **t** after these consonants: ç, f, h, k, p, s, ş, t. But don't worry too much about consonant changes at this stage.

**8** Pronunciation: j, k, l. *Don't worry about the meanings of the words, just listen to the pronunciation and then repeat.*

| j | k | l |
|---|---|---|
| jip | ak | al |
| jet | iki | el |
| jilet | kar | la |
| jeton | kim | bal |

## Role play

### *DIRECTIONS*

You are in a street, asking for directions. Play your part according to the prompts.

| | |
|---|---|
| **You** | *[Ask, politely, where the museum is]* |
| **Passer-by** | Düz gidin, sağda, PTT'den sonra. |
| **You** | *[Thank the passer-by]* |

## Mini-test

◀) **CD1, TR 7, 07:48**

Well done; you have now completed Unit 5! Now you will be able to ask for, give and understand directions in Turkish, you will be able to get around new places and clarify meanings. Give yourself a point for each of the following questions that you answer correctly in Turkish.

1 *Ask for directions to the bank.*
2 *Ask where the taxis are.*
3 *Tell a taxi driver to go straight on and turn right at the corner.*
4 *Ask when the museum is open.*
5 *Ask for one ticket.*
6 *Ask if there is a metro to Sultan Ahmet.*
7 *Ask for two tickets.*
8 *Ask if there is a Blue Cruise from Bodrum.*
9 *Ask where the port is.*
10 *Ask how far it is from Istanbul to Ankara.*

*Points:_____/10*

# 6

# I like the weather here!

In this unit you will learn
- *How to talk about the weather*
- *How to compare months and seasons*
- *How to talk about your likes and dislikes*
- *Pronunciation:* m, n, o

## Dialogue 1 At a travel agency

Anne and her partner are at a travel agency looking for a suitable holiday destination.

Listen to, or read at least twice, this dialogue about the weather.

| **Anne** | Türkiye'de nereleri sıcak? |
| **Travel agent** | Güney, ağustos ve temmuzda çok sıcak. İlkbaharda ılık, haziranda sıcak. |
| **Anne** | Biz çok sıcak seviyoruz. Yağmur sevmiyoruz. Çocuklar da denizi ve kumu seviyor. |

*The travel agent looks at the average temperatures for various places in Turkey.*

| **Travel agent** | Temmuzda Alanya 26°C, Antalya 28°C, Bodrum 27°C, Fethiye 27°C, İstanbul 23°C. Temmuzda, en sıcak Antalya. Yazın güneyde hiç yağmur yok. Hava hep güneşli. İlkbaharda daha çok bahar yağmurları ve sonra da gökkuşağı vardır. Kırlarda kır çiçekleri çok çeşitli ve güzeldir. |
| **Anne** | Evet. Antalya'ya hangi günler uçak var? |

*The travel agent looks at the computer (**bilgisayar**) flight timetable.*

| **Travel agent** | Pazartesi, çarşamba, cuma günde bir uçak. Cumartesi ve pazar günde iki uçak var. |
| **Anne** | 5 mayıs pazar günü yer var mı? |
| **Travel agent** | Evet, var. Kaç kişilik? |

---

If you want to check flight information yourself, you may find the Turkish Airlines (THY) website useful: http://www3.thy.com

## Questions

Read the dialogue and answer these questions:

**1** *Türkiye'de nereleri sıcak?*
**2** *Temmuzda en sıcak neresi?*
**3** *Antalya'ya hangi günler uçak var?*

| **Türkiye** | *Turkey* |
| **nereler?** | *what places?* |
| **sıcak** | *hot* |
| **güney** | *south* |
| **ağustos** | *August* |

| | |
|---|---|
| temmuz | *July* |
| ilkbahar | *spring* |
| ılık | *warm* |
| haziran | *June* |
| seviyoruz | *we like/love* |
| yağmur | *rain* |
| sevmiyoruz | *we do not like/love* |
| çocuklar | *children* |
| deniz | *sea* |
| kum | *sand* |
| en | *the most (-est)* |
| en sıcak | *hottest* |
| hava | *weather* |
| yaz | *summer* |
| güneşli | *sunny* |
| daha çok | *mostly* |
| daha | *more (-er)* |
| sonra | *then* |
| gökkuşağı | *rainbow* |
| kır | *countryside/wild* |
| kır çiçekleri | *wildflowers* |
| çeşitli | *various* |
| güzel | *beautiful* |
| gün | *day* |
| pazartesi | *Monday* |
| çarşamba | *Wednesday* |
| cuma | *Friday* |
| cumartesi | *Saturday* |
| pazar | *Sunday* |
| uçak | *aeroplane* |
| mayıs | *May* |
| yer | *place/seat* |
| kaç kişilik? | *for how many people?* |

## Language points

### POINTS OF THE COMPASS

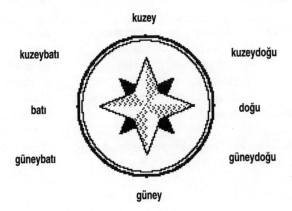

◀) CD2, TR 1, 01:50

### THE FOUR SEASONS

Listen, then repeat.

| | |
|---|---|
| ilkbahar | *spring* |
| yaz | *summer* |
| sonbahar | *autumn/fall* |
| kış | *winter* |

To say *in spring* etc.:

| | |
|---|---|
| ilkbaharda | *in spring* |
| yazın | *in summer* |
| sonbaharda | *in autumn* |
| kışın | *in winter* |

### THE MONTHS OF THE YEAR

Listen, then repeat.

| | | | |
|---|---|---|---|
| ocak | *January* | temmuz | *July* |
| şubat | *February* | ağustos | *August* |
| mart | *March* | eylül | *September* |
| nisan | *April* | ekim | *October* |
| mayıs | *May* | kasım | *November* |
| haziran | *June* | aralık | *December* |

To say *in June*, etc., you add the -de or -da ending, according to vowel harmony:

**haziranda**                     *in June*

### THE DAYS OF THE WEEK

Listen, then repeat.

| | |
|---|---|
| pazar (günü) | *Sunday* |
| pazartesi (günü) | *Monday* |
| salı (günü) | *Tuesday* |
| çarşamba (günü) | *Wednesday* |
| perşembe (günü) | *Thursday* |
| cuma (günü) | *Friday* |
| cumartesi (günü) | *Saturday* |

*On Monday*, *on Tuesday*, etc. is translated by **pazartesi günü, salı günü**.

### CAPITAL LETTERS

Unlike English, Turkish does not use capital letters for the days of the week and months of the year unless they are important dates or special days.

For example, in the sentence **her pazar çok uyuyorum** *every Sunday I sleep a lot* you can see that there is no capital letter for **pazar**. However, when writing about 1st May, which is the Spring Festival, a capital letter is used: **1 Mayıs**.

**1 Mayıs Bahar Bayramı'dır.**       *1st May is the Spring Festival.*

### DATES

Writing or saying dates is very easy. Simply say the number followed by the month:

| | |
|---|---|
| **bir mayıs** | *1 May* |
| **yirmi iki şubat** | *22 February* |

Years are said just like reading a number, so the year 2222 would be **iki bin iki yüz yirmi iki** *two thousand two hundred twenty-two*.

### -dIR (-dIR, -dUR, -dÜR): FORMAL 'iS'

There is no equivalent of the English word *is*. So the Turkish sentence **Ev kırmızı** means 'The house is red', but it actually says 'House red'. However, when people want to sound very formal, they use the ending **-dir**. You would not commonly use this ending in conversation, but you need to recognize it when you see it, usually on official notices, in official documents and in newspaper articles.

| | |
|---|---|
| **Durmak Yasaktır.** | *Stopping is forbidden.* |
| **Geçmek Yasaktır.** | *Crossing/passing is forbidden.* |
| **Türklerin dili Türkçe'dir.** | *The language of Turks is Turkish.* |

Another use of **-dir** is for describing unchanging facts:

**Güney Türkiye'de yazlar çok**     *In south Turkey summers are*
  **sıcaktır.**                      *very hot.*

You will also notice that **d** changes to **t** after **k**. For more examples, look at Unit 9. At this stage it is not important to remember to make this change but it is important to recognize it when you see it.

### MORE ABOUT WORD ENDINGS

In Turkish, certain verbs take certain endings. This is similar to the way in which some English verbs are followed by a preposition, such as *out* and *on* in *to get out*, *to get on*. Good dictionaries give these endings next to the verb. The best way of learning the endings is step by step; when you learn a new verb look at the previous word to see if there is an ending and if so, try to remember it.

Some verbs do not take any endings. At this stage just pay attention; you could make a note or highlight the ending and the verb in the book to help you to remember it. For example, **sevmek** *to love* takes the **-ı** (**-i**, **-u**, **-ü**) direct object ending:

**Biz yazı seviyoruz.**            *We love summers (i.e. We love*
                                   *the summer).*
**Biz güneşi çok seviyoruz.**      *We love the sun.*
**Biz yağmuru sevmiyoruz.**        *We do not like/love the rain.*

In these examples, *summer*, *sun* and *rain* are the objects of the verb *to love*.

When a personal pronoun (I, you, he, etc.) is the direct object of a verb, you give it an **-i** ending. This is because personal pronouns stand for *specific* things or people.

**Biz seni seviyoruz.**            *We love you.*

The following table shows the personal pronouns with -i endings.

| Personal pronoun | | with -i (-ı, -u, -ü) ending | |
|---|---|---|---|
| **ben** | *I* | **beni** | *me* |
| **sen** | *you* | **seni** | *you* |
| **o** | *he, she, it* | **onu** | *him, her, it* |
| **biz** | *we* | **bizi** | *us* |
| **siz** | *you* | **sizi** | *you* |
| **onlar** | *they* | **onları** | *them* |

## COMPARISONS

In English there are two ways to say *more* and *most*: with short words *-er* or *-est* are added (*nice, nicer, the nicest*), and with longer words *more* and *most* are used (*beautiful, more beautiful, the most beautiful*). In Turkish, you just have one system to learn.

**daha** *more (-er)*
The word **daha** is put before the adjective:

| | |
|---|---|
| **daha sıcak** | *hotter/warmer* |
| **Bugün hava daha sıcak.** | *The weather is hotter today.* (lit. *Today weather hotter.*) |
| **daha güzel** | *more beautiful* |

Then, to make the comparison, for than, you add the ending **-den, -dan, -ten, -tan** to the adjective:

| | |
|---|---|
| **Bugün hava dünden daha sıcak.** | *Today the weather is warmer than yesterday.* |
| **Temmuzda hava hazirandan daha sıcak.** | *The weather in July is warmer than in June.* (lit. *In July weather from/than June hotter.*) |
| **İstanbul, Ankara ve İzmir'den daha büyük.** | *Istanbul is bigger than Ankara and Izmir.* (lit. *Istanbul Ankara and Izmir from/than bigger.*) |

**en** *the most (-est)*

The word **en** is put before the adjective:

**en sıcak**         *the warmest (hottest)*
**Rize en yağmurlu.**  *Rize is the rainiest.* (lit. *Rize most rainy/rainiest.*)

## MAKING ADJECTIVES USING -LI (-LI, -LU, -LÜ) ENDINGS

By putting **-li** or its variations on the end of a noun it is very easy to make an adjective. Simply, the ending **-li** means *with*.

**Hava nasıl?** *What is the weather like?*

▶ **güneş** *sun*

**Bugün hava güneşli.**
*Today it is sunny.*

▶ **bulut** *cloud*

**Bugün hava bulutlu.**
*Today it is cloudy.*

▶ **yağmur** *rain*

**Bugün hava yağmurlu.**
*Today it is raining.*

▶ sis *fog*

**Bugün hava sisli.**
*Today it is foggy.*

▶ kar *snow*

**Bugün hava karlı.**
*Today it is snowy.*

▶ rüzgar *wind*

**Bugün hava rüzgarlı.**
*Today it is windy.*

### TONGUE TWISTER

Try another Turkish tongue twister:

**Şu köşe yaz köşesi, bu köşe kış köşesi.** *That corner (of the room, garden, etc.) is the summer corner, this corner is the winter corner.*

## Special days

The followings are all important dates in the Turkish calendar. Why not put the dates, days of the week and the months of the year in your diary in Turkish?

*(Contd)*

**Fixed public holidays** *Bayramlar* ☾*

| | | |
|---|---|---|
| 1 Ocak | Yılbaşı | *New Year's Day* |
| 23 Nisan | Çocuk Bayramı | *National Sovereignty and Children's Day* |
| 1 Mayıs | Bahar Bayramı | *Spring Festival* |
| 19 Mayıs | Gençlik ve Spor Bayramı | *Atatürk Commemoration and Youth and Sports Day* |
| 30 Ağustos | Zafer Bayramı | *Victory Day* |
| 29 Ekim | Cumhuriyet Bayramı | *Republic Day* |

**Moveable Islamic public holidays** ☾*

| | | |
|---|---|---|
| 14 Kasım 2004 | Ramazan/Şeker Bayramı | *Ramadan/End of the Fast* |
| 2 Şubat 2004 | Kurban Bayramı | *Helping the poor* |

**Non-holiday celebration**

| | | |
|---|---|---|
| Mayısın 2 inci pazar günü | Anneler Günü | *Mother's Day* |

During the month of **Ramazan** *Ramadan* practising Muslims do not eat or drink between sunrise and sunset. In traditional areas, you will find that restaurants will not open until sunset, but in tourist areas you will find that places to eat and drink are open as usual during daylight areas even during **Ramazan**. If you are not Muslim – don't worry, you are not expected to fast!

However, as a way of respect you may decide not to eat or drink too overtly. At sunset during **Ramazan** there is an air of celebration as people come together to break their fast. The dates of **Ramazan** change each year, as they are set by the lunar calendar. At the end of the fasting month there is a national holiday, **Şeker Bayramı**, which is a time of celebration when families get together.

## Dialogue 2 We like different things

Some young people are sitting at a seaside café in the shade of a willow tree by the sea. Listen to, or read the dialogue at least twice. Listen out for the answers to these questions:

Questions
1 *What do the boys like?*
2 *What do the girls like?*

| Cem | Ben ve Gökhan futbol, basketbol, voleybol ve tenis seviyoruz. |
|---|---|
| Gökhan | Ama en çok futbolu. |
| Vanessa | Biz denizi ve dansı, günlük gezileri seviyoruz. Yağmursuz ve rüzgarsız ne güzel bir gün! |
| Cem | Annemler de günlük gezileri, özellikle harabeleri gezmeyi seviyor. Restoranlarda yemek yemek çok keyifli. (*To a friend standing in the sun*): Orada durma, çok güneş var, gölgeye gel. (*He calls out to the waiter to order some ice cream*) Garson, bana bir çikolatalı dondurma. |
| *They all order different flavours of ice cream.* | |
| Vanessa | Bana sade dondurma. |
| Cem | Bana meyveli. |
| Çiğdem | Bana limonlu. |
| Gökhan | Bana da karışık. |
| Garson | Tamam, efendim. |

Questions
Read the dialogue again and answer the following questions.

3 *Nasıl bir gün?*
4 *Restoranlarda yemek yemek keyifli mi?*
5 *Kaç çeşit dondurma?*

QUICK VOCAB

| **futbol** | *football* |
|---|---|
| **basketbol** | *basketball* |
| **voleybol** | *volleyball* |
| **tenis** | *tennis* |
| **dans** | *dance* |
| **günlük** | *daily (day)* |
| **gezi** | *trip/journey* |
| **yağmursuz** | *without rain* |
| **rüzgarsız** | *without wind* |
| **annemler** | *my parents* (lit. *my mothers*) |
| **özellikle** | *especially* |
| **harabe** | *ruin* |
| **gezmek** | *travel/trip* |
| **yemek yemek** | *to eat food* (see **Language points**) |
| **keyifli** | *joyous, pleasurable* |
| **orada** | *there* |
| **gölge** | *shade* |
| **dondurma** | *ice cream* |
| **çikolatalı** | *chocolate flavoured/with chocolate* |
| **sade** | *plain/vanilla flavour* |
| **meyveli** | *fruit flavoured/with fruit* |
| **limonlu** | *lemon flavoured* |
| **karışık** | *mixed* |
| **bana** | *for me* |

## Language points

### *YEMEK YEMEK TO EAT FOOD*

In Turkish, there are a handful of verbs that behave in a special way. They are fairly common verbs, so it is worth taking the time to learn them! For example, in Turkish, you can't just 'eat' – you have to eat *something*, e.g. **salata yemek** *to eat salad*. If you don't want to specify what's being eaten, you have to say **yemek yemek**. These words look the same, but the first one is the noun, and the second one is the verb. Other examples include:

| | |
|---|---|
| **uyku uyumak** | *to sleep (to sleep a sleep)* |
| **yazı yazmak** | *to write (to write a writing)* |
| **oyun oynamak** | *to play (to play a game)* |

### -SİZ (-SIZ, -SUZ, -SÜZ) WITHOUT

This ending means *without* and it is the opposite of the -li ending which means *with*. You can put it on the end of nouns to make some more adjectives. (It follows i-type vowel harmony.)

| | |
|---|---|
| **güneş***siz* | *without sun* |
| **bulut***suz* | *without cloud* |
| **yağmur***suz* | *without rain* |
| **kar***sız* | *without snow* |

Now you know how to make two different adjectives from each noun!

### ANNEMLER MY PARENTS

**Anne** means *mother*. **Annemler** in plural form implies *my mother* and *my father*. **Ayşeler** means *Ayşe and her family*. This is similar to the expression *the Browns* in English. But, in Turkish, the first names, or the titles, are used instead of the surnames and this practice is informal.

### -ME, -MA DON'T

To tell people not to do things, add -me or -ma to the end of an informal command. For formal negative commands, add -in or -iniz to the informal negative (-iniz is very formal). For example:

| Infinitive | Informal negative command | Polite (formal) negative commands | |
|---|---|---|---|
| durmak *to stop* | durma *don't stop* | durmayın | durmayınız |
| geçmek *to cross* | geçme *don't cross* | geçmeyin | geçmeyiniz |

-me or -ma comes after the verbs, not after the nouns or adjectives. Remember that **değil** is used to make adjectives or nouns negative.

---

## Reading comprehension

Read the passage about the seasons and climate in Turkey. Then answer the questions at the end of the text using **doğru** *true* or **yanlış** *false*.

### TÜRKİYE'DE MEVSİMLER VE İKLİM

Türkiye'de dört mevsim vardır ve bunlar ilkbahar, yaz, sonbahar, kıştır. İklim de her bölgede çok farklıdır.

Akdeniz, Ege ve Marmara'da yazlar sıcak ve kurak, kışlar ılık ve yağmurludur. Çok yüksek dağlarda kar vardır. Türkiye'de deniz kenarları daha ılıktır. Istanbul ve Marmara'da kışlar ortalama 4°C, yazlar 27°C.

Karadeniz'de yazlar sıcaktır. Kışlar güneyden daha serindir. Ara sıra don ve her mevsimde kar vardır. Yazlar 23°C ve kışlar 7°C, dır. En çok yağmur Rize'dedir.

Orta Anadolu'da gece ve gündüz arasında sıcaklık çok farklıdır. Yazlar daha az sıcaktır. Ortalama sıcaklık yazlarda 23°C, kışlarda −2°C. Güneydoğu Anadolu'da yazlar çok sıcak, kışlar daha az soğuktur.

Doğu Anadolu'da kışlar çok soğuk, karlı ve uzundur. Yazlar yağmursuzdur. Türkiye'de en soğuk yerler kuzey doğudur.

Güney' de kumda iken Toroslar'da kar vardır.

| | |
|---|---|
| **mevsim** | *season* |
| **iklim** | *climate* |
| **bölge** | *region* |
| **farklı** | *different* |
| **Akdeniz** | *Mediterranean* |
| **Ege** | *Aegean* |
| **Marmara** | *Marmara* (the sea and region) |
| **kurak** | *dry* |
| **yüksek** | *high* |
| **dağ** | *mountain* |
| **deniz kenarları** | *seaside* |
| **ortalama** | *average* |
| **Karadeniz** | *the Black Sea* |
| **serin** | *cool* |
| **ara sıra** | *sometimes* |
| **don** | *frost* |
| **arasında** | *between* |
| **Anadolu** | *Anatolia* |
| **uzundur** | *it is long* |
| **iken** | *while/when* |

True or false?

**1** *En sıcak mevsim yazdır.*
**2** *Türkiye'de üç mevsim vardır.*
**3** *Istanbul'da kışlar ortalama 4°C.*
**4** *En çok yağmur Ankara'dadır.*
**5** *Orta Anadolu'da yazın gece ve gündüz sıcaklık farklıdır.*
**6** *Türkiye'de en sıcak yer Doğu Anadolu'dur.*

## Insight

Dialogue 1

**Hava nasıl?**    *What is the weather like?* (lit. *weather how?*)

There are no equivalents of the English words *is*, *it* and *the* in Turkish: **Hava güneşli** literally translates as *weather sunny*. A little like *Me Tarzan, you Jane*.

## Practice

◀) CD2, TR 1, 04:05

**1** *Look at the map of Turkey and write down where these places are, using the points of the compass. Then repeat what the speaker says on the recording.*

*The first one has been done for you:*
**a** *İzmir nerede?*      *Answer:* **batıda**

**a** *İzmir nerede?*
**b** *İstanbul nerede?*
**c** *Ankara nerede?*
**d** *Van nerede?*
**e** *Bodrum nerede?*
**f** *Samsun nerede?*
**g** *Mersin nerede?*
**h** *Alanya nerede?*
**i** *Marmaris nerede?*

**2** *Match the words with the corresponding pictures.*

- **a** *güneşli*
- **b** *bulutlu*
- **c** *yağmurlu*
- **d** *karlı*
- **e** *sisli*
- **f** *sicak*
- **g** *soğuk*

**i**

**ii**

**iii**

**iv**

**v**

**vi**

**vii**

**3** *Can you work out the answer to this puzzle?*

Ali, Betül'den daha uzun boylu, ama Ali Can'dan daha kısa boylu. Dursun, Betül'den daha kısa boylu. En kısa boylu kim?

**4** *Fill in the blanks to give months of the year:*

- **a** *a _ us _ _ s*
- **b** *_ yl _ l*
- **c** *_ _ i _*
- **d** *h _ zi _ _ n*
- **e** *te _ _ u _*
- **f** *_ ub _ t*

**5** Wordsearch. Find ten words connected to the weather.

| F | A | G | H | A | V | A | Y | U | P |
|---|---|---|---|---|---|---|---|---|---|
| S | İ | S | L | İ | F | H | A | O | S |
| I | B | H | P | S | E | O | Ğ | P | O |
| C | E | K | L | R | Z | G | M | O | Ğ |
| A | Ç | I | K | A | V | A | U | Y | U |
| K | A | R | L | I | G | Y | R | T | K |
| A | D | B | U | L | U | T | L | U | S |
| C | R | D | D | R | S | P | U | L | E |
| G | Ü | N | E | Ş | L | İ | S | Y | F |
| H | R | Ü | Z | G | A | R | L | I | R |

◀》 CD2, TR 1, 05:20

**6** Pronunciation: m, n, o. *First, listen without looking; second, listen while looking at the sounds below; finally listen and repeat. Do not worry about the meaning.*

| m | n | o |
|---|---|---|
| em | an | on |
| ma | no | do |
| Cem | ön | ol |
| güm | kin | çok |

◀》 CD2, TR 1, 06:00

---

## Role play

### *WE LIKE THE WEATHER HERE!*

You are at a travel agency looking for a suitable holiday destination. Play your part in the conversation, to the prompts.

| You | [Ask what the weather is like in Alanya in July] |
| --- | --- |
| **Clerk** | Sıcak, yağmursuz. Hep güneşli. |
| **You** | [Ask if there are any flights to Alanya] |
| **Clerk** | Evet, Salı, Perşembe ve Cuma günleri. |
| **You** | [Ask if there is a seat available for (a place on) Thursday] |
| **Clerk** | Evet, var. Kaç kişilik. |
| **You** | [Say 'for one person'] |

## Mini-test

◂) **CD2, TR 1, 07:02**

Well done; you have now completed Unit 6! Now you will be able to talk about the weather, seasons, months of the year, days of the week, and make comparisons. Give yourself a point for each of the following statements or questions that you can say in Turkish.

1 *Say there is no rain in summer.*
2 *Say that it rains in spring.*
3 *Say that July is hotter than February.*
4 *Say you like dancing and volleyball the most.*
5 *Ask what day there are flights to Bodrum.*
6 *Order a fruit-flavoured ice cream.*
7 *Say you love the sun.*
8 *Ask on which days there are boats to Bodrum.*
9 *Say Istanbul is bigger than Ankara and İzmir.*
10 *How would you say 'come into the shade'?*

*Points:_____/10*

# 7

........................................................................

# Talking about oneself and describing people

In this unit you will learn
- *How to talk about yourself* (I am ...)
- *How to ask other people about themselves* (are you ...?)
- *How to describe yourself and other people*
- *Hore about addressing people correctly*
- *How to increase your word power with a few simple word endings*
- *Pronunciation: ö, p, r*

_____

## Dialogue 1 Where are you from?

Two passengers on a flight to Istanbul strike up a conversation. Listen to the dialogue a couple of times and try to answer the following questions. Next, read the dialogue, listen to it again and try to answer the questions at the end of the dialogue.

Questions
 **1** *Where is she from?*
 **2** *Where is he from?*

| Woman | Merhaba. |
| Man | Merhaba. |
| Woman | Nerelisin? |
| Man | Leeds, liyim. Ya siz nerelisiniz? |
| Woman | Ben Almanım. Bonn luyum. |
| Man | Ben İngilizim ama eşim Türk, İstanbullu. *(The man holds up a book.)* Bu kitap Türkçe öğrenmek için, Teach Yourself Turkish. Ben hem Türkçe hem de Almanca, Fransızca, İspanyolca, İtalyanca ve biraz da Bulgarca biliyorum. Türkleri, Türkçe'yi ve Türkiye'yi çok seviyorum. Kızımız Vanessa da Türkçe biliyor. |
| Woman | Gerçekten mi? Çok ilginç. |
| Man | Tatillerde Türkiye'ye gitmek çok keyifli. Biz çok şanslıyız. Türkler çok samimi ve dürüst, değil mi? |
| Woman | Evet, haklısınız. |

Questions

**3** *Erkek Türk mü, İngiliz mi?*
**4** *Erkek hangi dilleri biliyor?*
**5** *Kim Türkçe biliyor?*

In recent years, people have started to use the following phrases when speaking about their nationality:

| **Türkiyeli, yim** | *I'm from Turkey* |
| **İngaltereliyim** | *I'm from England* |

QUICK VOCAB

| **Nerelisin?** | *Where are you from?* |
| **eşim** | *my wife/my husband* (my spouse) |
| **Türkçe** | *Turkish* (language) |
| **Almanca** | *German* (language) |
| **Fransızca** | *French* (language) |
| **İspanyolca** | *Spanish* (language) |
| **İtalyanca** | *Italian* (language) |
| **Bulgarca** | *Bulgarian* (language) |
| **biliyorum** | *I know* |
| **kızımız** | *our daughter* |
| **seviyorum** | *I like* |

| | |
|---|---|
| **gerçekten** | *really* |
| **ilginç** | *interesting* |
| **tatil** | *holiday* |
| **keyifli** | *enjoyable* |
| **şans** | *chance/luck* |
| **samimi** | *friendly* |
| **dürüst** | *honest* |
| **haklısınız** | *you are right* |

## Language points

### WORD POWER

You have already learnt some nouns, adjectives and verbs.
Now if you learn some more word endings you will find that your vocabulary and ability to communicate will rapidly increase!

### THE VERB 'TO BE'

The verb *to be* (*am*, *is*, *are*) is very useful. It can be used with nouns, adjectives and pronouns to describe yourself and others. In Turkish, as in many languages, the verb *to be* does not have an exact equivalent. In Turkish, there are no separate words for *am*, *is*, *are*, etc. Instead -**im**, -**sin**, -**iz**, -**siniz** and -**ler** are added to the end of adjectives, nouns or pronouns. Once you have learnt these endings you can add them to adjectives, nouns and pronouns you already know, and you will find that you can make a huge number of new sentences very easily and quickly.

| Singular | Plural |
|---|---|
| **benim** *I am* | **biziz** *we are* |
| **sensin** *you are* (informal) | **sizsiniz** *you are* (formal/plural) |
| **o** *he/she/it is* | **onlar** *they are* |

Here are some examples of adjectives of nationality with the appropriate endings, showing vowel harmony:

| | | | |
|---|---|---|---|
| **ben** | İngiliz**im** | İspanyol**um** | Türk**üm** | Alman**ım** |
| **sen** | İngiliz**sin** | İspanyol**sun** | Türk**sün** | Alman**sın** |
| **o** | İngiliz* | İspanyol* | Türk* | Alman* |
| **biz** | İngiliz**iz** | İspanyol**uz** | Türk**üz** | Alman**ız** |
| **siz** | İngiliz**siniz** | İspanyol**sunuz** | Türk**sünüz** | Alman**sınız** |
| **onlar** | İngiliz**(ler)** | İspanyol**(lar)** | Türk**(ler)** | Alman**(lar)** |

*i.e. no ending

Most adjectives follow the pattern above, but the letter y is added when the root word ends in a vowel and the personal ending starts with a vowel. This makes the word easier to pronounce. Letters inserted like this are called buffer consonants. Here is an example of 'buffer y' being used:

| | |
|---|---|
| **Amerikalıyız.** | *We are American.* |
| **Amerikalıyım.** | *I am American.* |

### COUNTRIES, NATIONALITIES AND LANGUAGES

| Kıtalar ve memleketler<br>*Continents and countries* | Milliyetler<br>*Nationalities* | Diller<br>*Languages* | Başkentler<br>*Capitals* |
|---|---|---|---|
| Almanya *Germany* | Alman | Almanca | Berlin |
| Avrupa *Europe* | Avrupalı | | |
| Asya *Asia* | Asyalı | | |
| Amerika *United States of America* | Amerikalı/ Amerikan | İngilizce | Washington |
| Avustralya *Australia* | Avustralyalı | İngilizce | Canberra |
| Büyük Britanya *Great Britain* | Britanyalı | İngilizce/ Galce | Londra |
| Belçika *Belgium* | Belçikalı | Fransızca/ Hollandaca | Brüksel |
| Fransa *France* | Fransız | Fransızca | Paris |
| İngiltere *England* | İngiliz | İngilizce | Londra |

*(Contd)*

| Kıtalar ve memleketler<br>*Continents and countries* | Milliyetler<br>*Nationalities* | Diller<br>*Languages* | Başkentler<br>*Capitals* |
|---|---|---|---|
| İrlanda *Ireland* | İrlandalı | İrlandaca | Dublin |
| İspanya *Spain* | İspanyol | İspanyolca | Madrid |
| Japonya *Japan* | Japon | Japonca | Tokyo |
| Kanada *Canada* | Kanadalı | İngilizce/<br>Fransızca | Ottawa |
| İskoçya *Scotland* | İskoç | İskoçça | Edinburg |
| Türkiye *Turkey* | Türk | Türkçe | Ankara |
| Galler *Wales* | Galli | Galce | Kardif |

## Dialogue 2 Are you Turkish?

Two young women are sitting next to each other on the coach (**otobüs**) to Ankara. They introduce themselves and begin to chat.

Listen to the dialogue a couple of times and see if you can answer the following questions. Read the dialogue, listen to it again then try to answer the questions at the end of the dialogue.

Questions
  1 *Is Ayda Turkish or American?*
  2 *Who is a model?*

| | |
|---|---|
| **Susie** | Merhaba, ben Susie. Ya sen? |
| **Ayda** | Ben Ayda. |
| **Susie** | Türk müsün? |
| **Ayda** | Evet. Ya sen? Amerikalı mısın? |
| **Susie** | Hayır. İngilizim. Londralı, yım. |
| **Ayda** | Manken misin? |
| **Susie** | Hayır, öğrenciyim. Ya sen? |
| **Ayda** | Ben doktorum. |
| **Susie** | Çok akıllısın. |
| **Ayda** | Çok akıllı değilim ama çok çalışkanım. |

**Susie** Evli misin?

**Ayda** Hayır, nişanlıyım. Sen?

**Susie** Ben bekarım, henüz 23 yaşındayım. Nişanlın yakışıklı mı?

*(Ayda takes out a photograph of her fiancé from her wallet and describes him to Susie.)*

**Ayda** Cem uzun boylu, esmer, siyah saçlı, siyah gözlü ve tabii bence çok yakışıklı. Çok akıllı ve iyi bir insan. Mühendis ve biz çok iyi arkadaşız.

Questions

**3** *Susie Amerikalı mı, İngiliz mi?*

**4** *Susie manken mi, öğrenci mi?*

**5** *Kim doktor?*

**6** *Cem yakışıklı mı? Cem nasıl?*

| | |
|---|---|
| **model** | *model* |
| **öğrenci** | *student* |
| **doktor** | *doctor* |
| **akıllı** | *clever* |
| **çalışkan** | *hard working* |
| **evli** | *married* |
| **nişanlı** | *engaged* |
| **bekar** | *single* |
| **henüz** | *only* |
| **x yaşındayım** | *I'm x years old* |
| **nişanlın** | *your fiancé* |
| **yakışıklı** | *handsome* |
| **uzun boylu** | *tall* |
| **esmer** | *dark/olive skinned* |
| **siyah saçlı** | *black haired* |
| **siyah gözlü** | *dark-brown eyed* (lit. *black eyed*) |
| **tabii** | *of course* |
| **bence** | *in my opinion* |
| **insan** | *person* |
| **mühendis** | *engineer* |
| **arkadaş** | *friend* |

## Language points

You have already seen how the verb *to be* is used with adjectives such as nationalities. The verb *to be* can also be used with nouns. In Dialogue 2, you saw the endings of the verb *to be* used with the names of jobs.

Here is an example of a noun **sekreter** *secretary* with the personal endings added:

| | |
|---|---|
| Sekreter**im**. | *I am a secretary.* |
| Sekreter**sin**. | *You are a secretary.* |
| Sekreter. | *He/she is a secretary.* |
| Sekreter**iz**. | *We are secretaries.* |
| Sekreter**siniz**. | *You are secretaries.* |
| Sekreter**ler**. | *They are secretaries.* |

The following table provides examples of some other jobs to show vowel harmony:

| | Öğretmen<br>*teacher* | Doktor<br>*doctor* | Profesör<br>*professor* | Bakkal<br>*grocer* |
|---|---|---|---|---|
| **ben** | öğretmen**im** | doktor**um** | profesör**üm** | bakkal**ım** |
| **sen** | öğretmen**sin** | doktor**sun** | profesör**sün** | bakkal**sın** |
| **o** | öğretmen | doktor | profesör | bakkal |
| **biz** | öğretmen**iz** | doktor**uz** | profesör**üz** | bakkal**ız** |
| **siz** | öğretmen**siniz** | doktor**sunuz** | profesör**sünüz** | bakkal**sınız** |
| **onlar** | öğretmen**(ler)** | doktor**(lar)** | profesör**(ler)** | bakkal**(lar)** |

All of the endings for the verb *to be*, except the *they* form (-ler ending), follow the rules of vowel harmony. At this stage, do not worry about getting the harmony right, just have a go – Turkish people will understand you, even if you make some mistakes. Making mistakes is a natural part of the language learning process! Don't wait till you know the language perfectly before trying to have a conversation – Turkish people will appreciate it if you have a go, no matter how little you know.

In Turkish, you will come across simple verbless sentences, e.g. **Doktor.** (*He or she is a doctor.*), **Çalışkan.** (*She/he/it is hard working*). You do not usually use the personal pronouns (**ben, sen,** etc.) when using the verb *to be* endings (**im, sin,** etc.) unless you want to make the point strongly. For example, **ben öğretmenim,** *I am a teacher not you.* You use the personal pronouns if you want to emphasize the point. You can see that, in Turkish, a few words can convey a great deal of meaning. You may be wondering how you will know whether **öğretmen** means *he is a teacher* or *she is a teacher*, but this will usually be clear from the context – you will normally know who you are having a conversation about!

---

## Dialogue 3 How are you?

Listen to the conversation on the recording a couple times and then read the dialogue, listen to it again and answer the questions at the end of the dialogue.

Ülkü telephones her good friend Gonca.

| | |
|---|---|
| **Ülkü** | Alo! |
| **Gonca** | Alo. Ülkü, sen misin? |
| **Ülkü** | Benim. Gonca Abla, siz misiniz? |
| **Gonca** | Benim canım. Nasılsın? |
| **Ülkü** | Teşekkür ederim, iyiyim. Siz nasılsınız? |
| **Gonca** | Ben de iyiyim. |

⊙ CD2, TR 2, 03:44

Questions
1 *Ülkü nasıl?*
2 *Gonca nasıl?*

**benim**     *it's me*     **canım**     *my dear*     QV

Social or affectionate closeness between people is expressed by using the names of family relations. If one person calls another **amca** *uncle*, **abla** *elder sister*, **abi** *elder brother*, **teyze** *auntie*, it does not necessarily mean that they are related. In Dialogue 3, you heard Ülkü refer to her friend as **Gonca Abla**, which shows affection and respect for an older person. The same family terms are used to indicate that there is no sexual motive when talking to someone of the opposite sex, that one's intentions are purely innocent and family-like. It is quite acceptable for a young man sitting on a bus to call over to an older woman **abla gel otur** *older/big sister, come and sit down*.

## Language points

### *CANIM MY DEAR*

**Canım** means literally *my soul*, but it is used as an affectionate term to mean *my dear*. You heard Gonca refer to Ülkü as **canım** in the previous dialogue. Another way of expressing the same feeling is to add the ending -**cığım** after a loved one's name or title. For example, **Canım Cemciğim** *my dear dear Cem*, **Anneciğim** *my dear Mum*.

### *BEN/BENİM; -İM I AM/MY*

When added to the end of nouns and adjectives the ending -**im** (-**ım**, -**um**, -**üm**) can mean *my*.

| | |
|---|---|
| **Tık tık.** | *Knock knock.* |
| **Kim o?** | *Who is it/that?* |
| **Benim, canım.** | *(I) It's me (my) dear.* |

When a mother cuddles her daughter she might say **canım benim** or **Benim canım** *my dear*.

| | |
|---|---|
| Ben öğretmenim. | *I am a teacher.* |
| Benim öğretmenim. | *My teacher.* |
| Ben güzelim. | *I am beautiful.* |
| Benim güzelim. | *My beauty.* |

In colloquial conversations, however, these endings are not used, e.g. **Merhaba, ben Şafak** would be used instead of **Ben Şafak'ım.**

**Ben benim, sen sensin, biz farklıyız** would be translated as *I am who I am (this is me), you are who you are (this is you), we are different.*

---

## Dialogue 4 Hello?

Listen to the recording a few times and answer the question.

Şafak telephones Banu. They are cousins and talk very informally.

| | |
|---|---|
| **Banu** | Alo? |
| **Şafak** | Merhaba, Banu, ben Şafak. |
| **Banu** | Merhaba Şafak. Nasılsın? |
| **Şafak** | İyiyim. |

CD2, TR 2, 04:30

Question
Şafak nasıl?

Although Banu and Şafak don't do it here, it is common to shorten first names in friendly, intimate situations, e.g. **Şaf** for **Şafak**, **Asu** for **Asuman** in the same way as in English *David* my be shortened to *Dave*. Sometimes you will also hear an **ş** added to the end of names to give a similar affectionate and friendly tone, e.g. **Aloş** for **Ali**, **Banuş** for **Banu**.

Unit 7 Talking about oneself and describing people    107

## Language points

### WORD POWER

Turkish takes a word and changes the meaning by adding endings. Small parts of words are used to build up meaning. At this stage in the book, you have already learnt some nouns, adjectives and verbs. If you now learn some of the word endings, which are the main building blocks of Turkish, you will find that you can use just a few nouns, adjectives and verbs to create lots of new meanings easily. You will also be able to take a good guess at the meanings of new words which you meet. Your word power will increase rapidly!

### SAYING 'I'M NOT' – NEGATIVES WITH THE VERB 'TO BE'

We have already learnt that **değil** means *not*. It can be used with a noun or adjective to make a negative sentence. For the negative of *to be*, the noun or adjective is unchanged and the personal endings are added to the word **değil**, which goes at the end of the sentence.

| Değil-**im** | Ben bakkal değil<u>im</u>. | *I am not a grocer.* |
| Değil-**sin** | Sen bakkal değil<u>sin</u>. | *You are not a grocer.* |
| Değil | O bakkal değil. | *He/She is not a grocer.* |
| Değil-**iz** | Biz bakkal değil<u>iz</u>. | *We are not grocers.* |
| Değil-**siniz** | Siz bakkal değil<u>siniz</u>. | *You are not grocers.* |
| Değil-<u>**ler**</u> | Onlar bakkal değil(<u>ler</u>) | *They are not grocers.* |

### ASKING 'AM I ...?' 'ARE YOU ...?' – MAKING QUESTIONS WITH THE VERB 'TO BE'

For questions using the verb *to be*, the adjective or noun does not change and the personal endings are added to the **mı-, mi-, mu-, mü-** question words which you learnt in Unit 4. When written, the two words are separate but when they are spoken they are said as one word.

| | | | |
|---|---|---|---|
| Ben **mi?** | *Is it me?* | Biz **mi?** | *Is it us?* |
| Sen **mi?** | *Is it you?* | Siz **mi?** | *Is it you?* |
| O **mu?** | *Is it him/her/it?* | Onlar **mı?** | *Is it them?* |

| | |
|---|---|
| Sekreter **miyim?** | *Am I a secretary?* |
| Öğretmen **misin?** | *Are you a teacher?* |
| Doktor **mu?** | *Is she/he a doctor?* |
| İngiliz **miyiz?** | *Are we English?* |
| İspanyol **musunuz?** | *Are you Spanish?* |
| Türk **mü?**/(Türk **müler?**) | *Are they Turks/Turkish?* |

Note: The word **miyim** in **Sekreter miyim?** is made from **mi** and **im** coming together. You need a 'buffer y' as explained earlier. Can you spot another 'buffer y' in the examples above? Yes, it is the 'buffer y' in İngiliz miyiz?

## MORE ABOUT ADJECTIVES

One of the great features of the Turkish language is that a few adjectives and nouns can get you a long way, providing you learn some word endings! Here are a few more ways of extending your word power by adding some endings.

As you saw earlier in the unit, Turkish adjectives can take personal endings.

**güzel** *beautiful* **güzeller** *they are beautiful* **güzelim** *I am beautiful*

It is also possible to make adjectives from some nouns. For example, by adding -lı, -li, -lu or -lü to the name of many countries or cities, you change the word from a noun naming a place to an adjective or noun indicating a person from that country or city.

| | | | |
|---|---|---|---|
| **Kanada** | *Canada* | **Kanadalı** | *from Canada* |
| **İzmir** | *Izmir* | **İzmirli** | *from Izmir* |
| **İstanbul** | *Istanbul* | **İstanbullu** | *from Istanbul* |
| **Ürgüp** | *Ürgüp* | **Ürgüplü** | *from Ürgüp* |

Words indicating nationality which are formed in this way can be nouns or adjectives. So **Danimarkalı** can be translated as *Danish* (adjective) or a *Dane* (noun).

Some nationality words do not take the -lı, -li, -lu, -lü endings, for example, **Türk, İngiliz, Fransız, Alman.**

### MORE WAYS OF USING THE LI, Lİ, LU, LÜ ENDINGS

The endings **lı, li, lu** and **lü** are added to the singular of nouns to make nouns or adjectives with the following meanings:

**a** *Added to the name of a quality, they mean someone or something possessing that quality:*

| | | | |
|---|---|---|---|
| şeker | *sugar* | şekerli | *sweet* |
| akıl | *intelligence* | akıllı | *intelligent* |
| bulut | *cloud* | bulutlu | *cloudy* |

**b** *Possessing that quality to a higher degree:*

| | | | |
|---|---|---|---|
| sevgi | *affection* | sevgili | *beloved* |
| yaş | *age* | yaşlı | *aged, old* |

**c** *Added to the name of a colour, they form an adjective or noun meaning dressed in that colour:*

| | | | |
|---|---|---|---|
| beyaz | *white* | beyazlı | *dressed in white* |
| mavi | *blue* | mavili | *dressed in blue* |

**d** *These endings may be added to a phrase to extend its meaning, so:*

| | | | |
|---|---|---|---|
| uzun boy | *long stature* | uzun boylu | *tall* |
| kısa saç | *short hair* | kısa saçlı | *short haired* |
| orta yaş | *middle age* | orta yaşlı | *middle aged* |
| mavi göz | *blue eyes* | mavi gözlü | *blue eyed* |

Now that you have learnt several word endings and some of the ways in which they build meaning from root words, you might start noticing that some words have combinations of these word parts:

**ev** *house*
**evli** *married* (lit. *with house*)
**evlilik** *marriage* (lit. *the state of being with a house*)

As you saw earlier in the unit, the ending -li means *with*, the ending -lik denotes the formation of an abstract noun. You will learn more about this later.

### WORD ORDER AND ADJECTIVES

Now that you know how to make more adjectives, you need to make sure you put them in the correct place in the sentence. In Turkish, adjectives come before nouns, as in English: **güzel kadın** (*beautiful woman*), **uzun saç** (*long hair*). The **bir**, which acts like the indefinite article (*a, an*), usually comes between the adjective and noun: **güzel bir kadın** (*beautiful a woman*) **yakışıklı bir erkek** (*handsome a man*).

### TAG QUESTIONS

**Soğuk, değil mi?**                *Cold, isn't it?*

Tag questions invite you to either agree or disagree, often very briefly with a 'yes' or 'no'. In English, tag questions are very difficult to form, as the tag (*wasn't it? aren't they? don't they? have you? did she?* etc.) changes according to the tenses, whether the sentence is positive or negative, and the personal pronoun. The good news is that in Turkish, question tags are very straightforward: they always stay the same!

| | |
|---|---|
| **Sen akıllısın, değil mi?** | *You are clever, aren't you?* |
| **Evet, akıllıyım.** | *Yes, I am.* |
| **O akıllı değil, değil mi?** | *He is not clever, is he?* |
| **Hayır, değil. (Evet, değil.)** | *No, he isn't. (Yes, he isn't.)* |

In the last example, there are two ways of expressing the same answer, but both answers show agreement that he is not clever. **Evet** or **Hayır** would be the informal short answer.

........................................................................................

## Addressing people correctly

In Turkey, only people who are very close call each other by their first names (see Unit 1), and then only if they are more

*(Contd)*

or less the same age. In the case of an age gap, the younger person will use an additional polite address form when speaking to the older person. For an older woman this would be **Hanım**, as in **Gül Hanım**, or just **Hanımefendi**. For an older man, this would be **Bey** as in **Ahmet Bey** or just **Beyefendi**. If you are addressing an older person who also has a professional title, the professional title comes first, as in **Doktor Bahadır Bey** or just **Doktor Bey, Profesör Hanım, Garson Bey. Hanım** is the equivalent of *Ms, Miss,* or *Mrs* and **Bey** is the equivalent of *Mr.* The important thing to remember, though, is that they are used with the first name, not the surname (surnames were only introduced during Atatürk's reforms).

## Insight
### Dialogue 1

The endings -ice and -ca are used to denote languages:

| | |
|---|---|
| **İngiliz** *English* (nationality) | **İngilizce** *English* (language) |
| **Alman** *German* (nationality) | **Almanca** *German* (language) |
| **Fransız** *French* (nationality) | **Fransızca** *French* (language) |
| **Türk** *Turkish* (nationality) | **Türkçe** *Turkish* (language) |
| **Rus** *Russian* (nationality) | **Rusça** *Russian* (language) |

## Practice

**1** *Translate these sentences into English.*
   **a** *Tarkan çok yakışıklı bir erkek.*
   **b** *Sezen Aksu çok güzel bir kadın.*
   **c** *Öğretmenler çok akıllı mı?*
   **d** *Çalışkan bir öğrencisin.*
   **e** *Türkçe çok ilginç.*
   **f** *Türkiye hem tarihi hem modern bir ülke.*
   **g** *Türkiye'de çok işsiz var.*
   **h** *Türkçe çok kolay.*

**i** İngilizce zengin bir dil, değil mi?

**j** Almanca ve Fransızca gramer zor.

**2** Match the following famous people with their nationality and their native language. The first one has been done for you.

| Person | Nationality | Language |
|---|---|---|
| **a** Atatürk _____ | **A** Türk _____ | **i** Türkçe |
| **b** Napoleon | **B** Alman | **ii** Fransızca |
| **c** Hemingway | **C** İspanyol | **iii** İspanyolca |
| **d** Shakespeare | **D** Rus | **iv** Almanca |
| **e** Goya | **E** Fransız | **v** Rusça |
| **f** M.Gandhi | **F** Amerikalı | **vi** İngilizce |
| **g** Tchaikovsky | **G** İngiliz | **vii** Hintçe |
| **h** Bach | **H** Hintli | **viii** İngilizce |

**3** Match the sentences (a–i) with the pictures (1–9).

**a** Çok güzel bir film, değil mi?
**b** Siz, Timur'sunuz, değil mi? Ben, Ahmet.
**c** Yiyecekler çok lezzetli, değil mi?
**d** Bu program çok ilginç değil, değil mi?
**e** Bebek çok güzel, değil mi?
**f** Doğru değil, değil mi?
**g** Burası biraz soğuk, değil mi?
**h** Çiçekler çok güzel, değil mi?
**i** Tarkan iyi bir şarkıcı, değil mi?

◀) CD2, TR 2, 05:00

**4** Andy and Ayşegül are having a party at their house in
Birmingham. The guests mingle and chat to each other. Choose
an answer from the box below to complete the following
conversations, then check your answers on the recording.
(They're also given in the Key at the back of the book.)

**a** Ben İstanbullu, yum.
İstanbul'un neresinden?

..................................

**b** Bu tatilde Türkiye'deyiz.
Türkiye'nin neresinde?

..................................

**c** Bu Türkçe'de ne demek?

..................................

**d** Bu İngilizce'de ne demek?

..................................

**e** Siz manken misiniz?
Hayır, sekreterim. Ya siz?

..................................

**f** Ben 45 yaşındayım.

..................................

**g** Bu telefon numaram
595 33 22.
Bu da benim telefon
numaram 454 78 81.

..................................

**h** Ben İngilizim.
Gerçekten mi?

..................................

**i** Ben bekarım. Ya, siz?

..................................

*neresinde? whereabouts?

**j** Tarkan, Alman mı?

..................................

| | | | |
|---|---|---|---|
| **i** | Ben evliyim. Eşim orada. | **vi** | Harita demek. |
| **ii** | Evet, Londralı yım. | **vii** | Ben 23 yaşındayım. |
| **iii** | Ben öğrenciyim. | **viii** | Map demek. |
| **iv** | Hayır, Türk. | **ix** | Güneyde, Alanya'da. |
| **v** | Teşekkürler. | **x** | Ataköy |

**5** *Match the questions in the left-hand column with their corresponding answer from the right-hand column.*

**a** *Ankara nerede?*
**b** *Paris nerede?*
**c** *Londra, İngiltere'de mi?*
**d** *New York nerede?*
**e** *Barselona, İtalya'da mı?*
**f** *Roma nerede?*
**g** *Moskova Rusya'da, değil mi?*
**h** *Samsun nerede?*
**i** *Tokyo, Japonya'da, değil mi?*
**j** *Brüksel nerede?*

**i** *Türkiye'de.*
**ii** *Brüksel, Belçika'da.*
**iii** *Paris, Fransa'da.*
**iv** *Evet, Japonya'da.*
**v** *Evet, İngiltere'de.*
**vi** *New York, Amerika'da.*
**vii** *Hayır, Barselona İspanya'da.*
**viii** *Roma, İtalya'da.*
**ix** *Evet, Rusya'da.*
**x** *Samsun, kuzey Türkiye'de.*

◀ **CD2, TR 2, 06:30**

**6** *Listen to the recording, then complete the following table. The first line has been done for you.*

| Name | Nationality | Job | Marital status | Age | Home town |
|------|-------------|-----|----------------|-----|-----------|
| Bülent | Turkish | doctor | __ | __ | Izmir |
| Lucy | | | | | |
| Trish Webb | | | | | |
| Phillipe | | | | | |
| Ülkü Gezer | | | | | |
| June | | | | | |

◀ **CD2, TR 2, 07:50**

**7** **Pronunciation: ö, p, r.** *Listen to the following sounds on the recording and copy until you are confident with your pronunciation.*

| ö | p | r |
|------|------|------|
| öç | ip | ar |
| ön | pil | er |
| çöp | çap | re |
| yön | pat | kar |

## Role play

### *TALKING ABOUT ONESELF AND DESCRIBING OTHER PEOPLE*

A Turkish woman engages you in conversation. Play your part in the conversation, according to the prompts.

| Turk | Merhaba. |
|------|----------|
| You | *[Say 'hello']* |
| Turk | Ben Türküm, siz Amerikalı mısınız? |
| You | *[Say no, you're not American, you're English]* |
| Turk | Aaa! Ben bekarım. Siz evlisiniz, değil mi? |
| You | *[Say yes, you're married to a Turk]* |
| Turk | Gerçekten mi? Çok ilginç. Ben öğretmenim. |
| You | *[Say you're an engineer]* |
| Turk | Çok akıllısınız. |
| You | *[Return the compliment. Say she's very clever, too]* |

## Mini-test

◀) **CD2, TR 2, 09:19**

Well done; you have now completed Unit 7! Give yourself a point for each of the following questions that you answer correctly in Turkish without looking at the book.

1 *Ask someone if they are from America (if they are American).*
2 *Ask someone how old they are.*
3 *Ask someone what nationality they are.*
4 *Say you are married.*
5 *Ask someone if they are single.*
6 *What are the appropriate ways of addressing someone older than you and someone younger than you?*
7 *Say 'you are English, aren't you?'*
8 *Ask someone if she/he is from Turkey.*
9 *Ask someone 'what does it mean?' in Turkish.*
10 *Ask someone if she/he is a Turk.*

*Points:_____/10*

# 8

# Shopping

In this unit you will learn
- *How to shop for presents*
- *How to say what is happening*
- *How to talk about your daily routine*
- *How to talk about what will happen shortly*
- *Pronunciation: s, ş, t*

## Dialogue 1 Planning the day

Listen to the recording several times before answering the following questions.

Questions
1 *What do they want to do today?*
2 *Where are they going to go?*

Laura and Ben are talking about what they are going to do.

| Ben | Bugün ne yapıyoruz? |
|---|---|
| **Laura** | Bilmiyorum. Ben hediye almak istiyorum. |
| **Ben** | Ben de deri ceket, ayakkabı ve lokum almak istiyorum. |
| **Laura** | Kapalı Çarşı'ya gidelim mi? *(Laura looks at her shopping list.)* Bluz, çanta, baharat, ayakkabı ve hediyelik şeyler. |
| **Ben** | Nereye gidelim? |

| **bugün** | *today* |
| **yapmak** | *to do* |
| **hediye** | *present* |
| **almak** | *to buy* |
| **istemek** | *to want* |
| **deri** | *leather* |
| **ceket** | *jacket* |
| **ayakkabı** | *shoes* |
| **Kapalı Çarşı** | *Grand Bazaar* |
| **bluz** | *blouse* |
| **çanta** | *bag* |
| **baharat** | *spices* |
| **hediyelik şeyler** | *presents* |
| **nereye gidelim?** | *where shall we go?* |

QUICK VOCAB

Shopping in Turkey is an experience in itself, whether you are bargaining for a kilim in the bustling **Kapalı Çarşı** *Grand Bazaar* in Istanbul, choosing clothes in a smart boutique or buying local produce in a country market. Don't be surprised if you are offered a glass of tea as you view a range of carpets or leather jackets!

Many big towns and cities have permanent covered markets and spice markets. In Istanbul, the historic **Kapalı Çarşı** is an indoor maze of over 4,000 shops, selling carpets, antiques, jewellery, leather goods, clothing and textiles. Its vaulted stone passages also house banks, restaurants, Turkish baths, cafés and mosques.

The **Mısır Çarşısı** *Egyptian Bazaar* gets its name from the ancient tradition of trade with Egypt in coffee, rice, incense and henna. Today you can still buy coffee, spices, fruit and herb teas, nuts and dried fruit – as well as aphrodisiacs!

## Dialogue 2 Buying bags

Later on, in Istanbul's Grand Bazaar ...

| | |
|---|---|
| **Laura** | Merhaba. |
| **Salesperson** | İyi günler. Buyrun, efendim. |
| **Laura** | Deri çantalar kaç lira? |
| **Salesperson** | Büyük 15, orta 10 ve küçükler de 5 milyon lira. |
| **Laura** | Şu orta boy, lütfen. 10 milyon çok pahalı, 4 milyon olur mu? |
| **Salesperson** | Ne renk? |
| **Laura** | Siyah, lütfen. |
| **Salesperson** | Buyrun. Sizin için 5 milyon. |
| **Laura** | Tamam. (*Laura hands over the money.*) |
| **Salesperson** | Güle güle kullanın. |
| **Laura** | Teşekkür ederim. |

## Questions

1 *Laura ne renk çanta alıyor?*
2 *Laura pazarlık yapıyor mu?*

| | |
|---|---|
| **çanta** | *bag* |
| **büyük** | *big* |
| **orta** | *medium* |
| **küçük** | *small* |
| **orta boy** | *medium sized* |
| **sizin için** | *for you* |
| **Güle güle kullanın!** | *Enjoy using it!\** |

*This is a commonly used pleasantry. Its literal translation is *use in happy days*. It's said to people who have bought or who have been given something new. For clothes **Güle güle giy!** *enjoy wearing it*, would be used.

For an information guide to Turkish lira, visit www.tcmb.gov.tr.

## Dialogue 3 Buying spices

Listen to the recording several times – it will become clearer each time you listen to it.

Laura and Ben walk to the spice market to buy spices and dried fruit.

| | |
|---|---|
| **Stallholder** | Buyrun? |
| **Laura** | Baharat almak istiyoruz. |
| **Stallholder** | Neler almak istiyorsunuz? |
| **Laura** | Köftelik baharat, kimyon, sumak falan. |
| **Stallholder** | Ne kadar? |
| **Laura** | Yüz gramlık paketler. |
| **Stallholder** | Başka bir şey istiyor musunuz? |
| **Ben** | Bu ne? |
| **Stallholder** | Padişah macunu. |
| **Ben** | Padişah macunu ne demek? |
| **Stallholder** | Afrodizyak demek. |

*(Contd)*

| Ben | Benim için gerek yok. Ben istemiyorum. (*laughter*) Biraz kuru yemiş istiyorum. |
| --- | --- |
| **Stallholder** | Ne kadar? |
| **Ben** | Yarım kilo kayısı, yarım kilo incir. Fındık var mı? Güzel mi? |

*The stallholder offers them some nuts to try.*

| **Ben** | Evet! Yarım kilo karışık fıstık, lütfen. Hepsi bu kadar. Kaç lira? |
| --- | --- |
| **Stallholder** | 10 milyon. Sudan ucuz! |

## Questions

**1** *Kim baharat alıyor?*
**2** *Ben afrodizyak istiyor mu?*
**3** *Ben ne kadar fıstık alıyor?*

| | |
| --- | --- |
| **baharat** | *spices* |
| **köftelik** | *for meatballs* |
| **kimyon** | *cumin* |
| **sumak** | *sumac* |
| **falan** | *and such like, etc.* |
| **gramlık** | *gram* |
| **paket** | *packet* |
| **başka bir şey** | *anything else* |
| **padişah macunu** | *aphrodisiacs* |
| **gerek** | *necessary* |
| **kuru yemiş** | *dried fruit* |
| **kayısı** | *apricot* |
| **yarım** | *half* |
| **incir** | *fig* |
| **fındık** | *hazelnuts* |
| **fıstık** | *nuts* |
| **hepsi bu kadar** | *that's all* |
| **sudan ucuz*** | *very cheap* |

QUICK VOCAB

***Sudan ucuz** is an expression meaning *very cheap*. Literally, it means *even cheaper than water.*

Turkish delight is called **lokum** in Turkish. It was invented by Ali Muhiddin Hacı Bekir in the 16th century. He came up with a translucent jelly-like sweet made from a mixture of refined sugar, lemon juice and cornflour, which tastes heavenly. The new sweet came to the attention of Sultan Abdulhamid and he liked it so much that Hacı Bekir became confectioner to the court. The story goes that the name 'Turkish delight' was coined when an English traveller took some **lokum** home to a friend who was 'delighted' by it!

Hacı Bekir's shop was established in 1777 and is still run by his family. It can be found at 81–3 Hamidiye Caddesi, the street which runs between Istanbul's main railway station and the Egyptian Bazaar. Here you will find all kinds of **lokum** and various sweets stored in big jars and laid out on trays. You will also find a more modern shop in Taksim, in Istanbul.

**Lokum** comes in various flavours: rosewater, fruit or peppermint, and it is sometimes filled with pistachios, hazelnuts or ground apricots. **Lokum** remains popular among Turks and tourists alike. It tends to be eaten on special occasions, holidays and birthdays. It also makes an ideal gift if you are invited to someone's house. There is an old Turkish saying: **Tatlı yiyelim, tatlı konuşalım** *eat sweetly and you shall speak sweetly*.

## Dialogue 4 Buying Turkish delight

Listen to the recording a couple of times and look at the book if you need to, then answer the following questions.

Having bought their spices, Laura and Ben want to buy Turkish delight from the famous Hacı Bekir Turkish delight and sweet shop.

## Questions

**1** *Do Laura and Ben haggle?*

**2** *Do they get the recipe for Turkish delight?*

| | |
|---|---|
| **Laura** | Afedersiniz, Hacı Bekir Lokumcusu nerede? |
| **Stallholder** | Düz gidin, sağa dönün solda. |
| **Laura** | Teşekkürler. |
| **Stallholder** | Rica ederim. |

*They go into the Hacı Bekir sweet shop.*

| | |
|---|---|
| **Shop assistant** | Buyrun, efendim. |
| **Laura** | Lokum almak istiyoruz, kaç lira? |
| **Shop assistant** | Hangi çeşit? |
| **Ben** | Neler var? |

*The assistant holds out a tray of free samples, pointing out the different types.*

| | |
|---|---|
| **Shop assistant** | Bu naneli, bu gül, bu sade, bu da fıstıklı. Buyrun. Tatlı yiyelim, tatlı konuşalım. Tatlı yerken biz her zaman böyle diyoruz. |
| **Laura and Ben** | Mmmm. |

*Laura and Ben both love the Turkish delight and they decide to buy some of their presents from here.*

| | |
|---|---|
| **Shop assistant** | Yarım kilo karışık – 3 milyon lira. |
| **Laura** | Yarım kiloluk dört kutu karışık, lütfen. |

*While their Turkish delight is being put into special boxes, wrapped and sealed, Ben asks some questions.*

| | |
|---|---|
| **Ben** | Dükkan yeni mi? |
| **Shop assistant** | Hayır, biz 1777'den beri lokum yapıyoruz. Lokumlarımız çok taze. Her gün yeni lokum geliyor. Bugün tüm dünyaya satıyoruz. Her hafta değişik bir çeşit yapıyoruz. |
| **Ben** | Nasıl yapıyorsunuz? |
| **Shop assistant** | Şeker, fıstık ve ... koyuyoruz ama tarifi bizim sırrımız. |
| **Ben** | Lokumu daha çok turistlere mi satıyorsunuz? |
| **Shop assistant** | Hayır, biz Türkler özel günlerde ve ziyaretlerde birbirimize hep hediye olarak lokum veriyoruz. |

| | |
|---|---|
| **lokumcu** | *Turkish delight shop* |
| **rica ederim** | *not at all* |
| **lokum** | *Turkish delight* |
| **çeşit** | *kind, type* |
| **naneli** | *peppermint-flavoured* |
| **gül** | *rose-flavoured* |
| **sade** | *plain* |
| **fıstıklı** | *nutty* |
| **Tatlı yiyelim, tatlı** | *Let's eat sweet, speak sweet.* (a common |
| **konuşalım** | saying when offering sweets) |
| **yerken** | *while eating* |
| **her zaman** | *always* |
| **kiloluk** | *for a kilo* |
| **kutu** | *box* |
| **1777'den beri** | *since 1777* |
| **taze** | *fresh* |
| **her** | *every* |
| **tüm** | *all* |
| **dünya** | *world* |
| **satmak** | *to sell* |
| **değişik** | *different* |
| **koymak** | *to put* |
| **tarif** | *recipe* |
| **sırrımız** | *our secret* |
| **turist** | *tourist* |
| **özel** | *special* |
| **ziyaret** | *visit* |
| **birbirimiz** | *each other* |
| **hep** | *all* |
| **olarak** | *as* |
| **vermek** | *to give* |

QUICK VOCAB

Questions
  **3** *Kaç kutu lokum alıyorlar?*
  **4** *Dükkan yeni mi?*
  **5** *Lokumlar çok taze, değil mi?*

## Dialogue 5 Buying clothes

Later that afternoon, Laura goes to a clothes shop to buy a blouse.

◀ CD2, TR 3, 05:03

| | |
|---|---|
| **Shop assistant** | Buyrun, efendim. |
| **Laura** | Bir bluz bakıyorum. |
| **Shop assistant** | Kaç beden? |
| **Laura** | 38. |
| **Shop assistant** | Buyrun. Bu bluz çok güzel. |
| **Laura** | Yeşil bana yakışmıyor. Mavi veya beyaz var mı? |
| **Shop assistant** | Buyrun. Bir mavi, bir beyaz, 38 beden. |
| **Laura** | Kaç lira? |
| **Shop assistant** | 58 milyon. |
| **Laura** | Denemek istiyorum. |
| **Shop assistant** | Tabii. |
| *Laura tries on the blouse.* | |
| **Laura** | Bunu alıyorum. Kaç lira? |
| **Shop assistant** | 58 milyon. |
| **Laura** | Çok pahalı. 40 milyon veriyorum. |
| **Shop assistant** | Burada pazarlık yapmıyoruz. Sizin için 50 milyon lira. |
| **Laura** | Tamam, alıyorum. |

Questions
1 *Laura kaç beden giyiyor?*
2 *Yeşil Laura'ya yakışmıyor mu?*

QUICK VOCAB

| | |
|---|---|
| **bluz** | *blouse* |
| **bakmak** | *to look* |
| **kaç beden?** | *what size?* |
| **yakışmak** | *to suit* |
| **denemek** | *to try on* |
| **pazarlık** | *bargain* |
| **pazarlık yapmak** | *to bargain, haggle* |
| **sizin için** | *for you* |

Turkish sizes for clothing and shoes are the same as European sizes.

| Women's clothes | | | | | | | | Men's clothes | | | | |
|---|---|---|---|---|---|---|---|---|---|---|---|---|
| British | 10 | 12 | 14 | 16 | 18 | 20 | 22 | British | 37–8 | 39–40 | 41–2 | 43–4 |
| European | 38 | 40 | 42 | 44 | 46 | 48 | 50 | European | 94–7 | 99–102 | 104–107 | 109–112 |
| American | 8 | 10 | 12 | 14 | 16 | 18 | 20 | American | 38 | 40 | 42 | 44 |

| Women's shoes | | | | | | | | Men's shoes | | | | | | |
|---|---|---|---|---|---|---|---|---|---|---|---|---|---|---|
| British | 3 | 4 | 5 | 6 | 7 | 8 | 9 | British | 7 | 8 | 9 | 10 | 11 | 12 | 13 |
| European | 35 | 36 | 38 | 39 | 40 | 42 | 43 | European | 41 | 42 | 43 | 44 | 45 | 46 | 47 |
| American | 4 | 5 | 6 | 7 | 8 | 9 | 10 | American | 8 | 9 | 10 | 11 | 12 | 13 | 14 |

## Language points

### USING THE -IYOR PRESENT TENSE

In the dialogues, you will notice that we have introduced a new tense, the **-iyor** present tense. For example, in Dialogue 5, Laura says, '**Bunu alıyorum**' '*I'll take it*'. This literally means '*I'm taking it.*'

The **-iyor** tense has several purposes. These are shown in the following table.

| Purpose | Example | Translation |
|---|---|---|
| Describing something happening now | Alışveriş yapıyoruz. | *We're shopping.* |
| Stating an unchanging fact | Alkol kullanmıyorum. | *I don't drink alcohol.* |
| Describing a habitual repeated action | Türkler sık sık çay içiyorlar. | *Turks often drink tea.* |
| Describing something that will happen soon | Bugün alışveriş yapıyoruz. | *We're shopping today.* |
| Stating how long you have been doing something | 1777'den beri lokum yapıyoruz/satıyoruz. | *We've been making/ selling Turkish delight since 1777.* |

The -iyor present tense is also used to express senses and emotions which in English are expressed in the simple present tense: **Biliyorum.** *I know.* (lit. *I'm knowing.*) **Seviyorum.** *I love.* (lit. *I'm loving.*) **Görüyorum.** *I see/I can see.* (lit. *I'm seeing.*) **İşitiyorum.** *I hear/I can hear.* (lit. *I'm hearing.*) **Hissediyorum.** *I feel.* (lit. *I'm feeling.*)

To use this tense, you need to remember to add two verb endings: the tense ending and the correct personal ending.

For the present -iyor tense, the endings are:

**1** *for the tense:*
   -ıyor, -iyor, -uyor, -üyor *(according to the rules of vowel harmony), or simply* -yor *after a verb ending in a vowel. If the verb stem ends in* a *or* e *then these vowels are replaced by* ı *and* i *respectively.*

**2** *personal endings:*

| -um | I | -uz | we |
|-----|-----|-----|-----|
| -sun | You | -sunuz | you |
| (none) | He/she/it | -ler/lar | they |

For example, *to buy/take/get/receive* is **almak**.

| Stem | Tense ending | Personal ending |
|------|--------------|-----------------|
| al- | -ıyor | -um |

*I am buying.* Alıyorum.

The verb *want/would like* is **istemek**; the stem is **iste-** but the **e** changes to **i**:

| Stem | Tense ending | Personal ending |
|------|--------------|-----------------|
| isti- | -yor | -um |

*I want/would like* **istiyorum...**

Some sample verbs:

|  | **istemek**<br>*to want/would like* | **ödemek**<br>*to pay* | **almak**<br>*to buy/take/get/<br>receive* |
|---|---|---|---|
| I | istiyorum | ödüyorum | alıyorum |
| you | istiyorsun | ödüyorsun | alıyorsun |
| he/she/it | istiyor | ödüyor | alıyor |
| we | istiyoruz | ödüyoruz | alıyoruz |
| you | istiyorsunuz | ödüyorsunuz | alıyorsunuz |
| they | istiyorlar | ödüyorlar | alıyorlar |

## Negatives

If you want to make a verb negative in the **-iyor** present tense, you add **-m** to the stem before the **-iyor/-yor** ending:

| Onu al<u>m</u>ıyorum. | *I am not buying that.* |
|---|---|
| Pazarlık et<u>m</u>iyorum. | *I am not haggling.* |
| Şapka giy<u>m</u>iyorum. | *I am not wearing a hat.* |
| Anla<u>m</u>ıyorum. | *I don't understand.* |

## Questions

If you want to turn a statement into a question in the **–iyor** present tense, you add **mı-**, **mi-**, **mu-** or **mü-** before the personal ending. In the written form, the two parts of the verb are separate, though they are spoken as one word:

| Alıyor <u>mu</u>sun? | *Are you buying?* |
|---|---|
| Deniyor <u>mu</u>sun? | *Are you trying it on?* |
| Deri seviyor <u>mu</u>sunuz? | *Do you like leather?* |
| Kredi kartı alıyor <u>mu</u>sunuz? | *Do you take credit cards?* |

Note: When you make questions using question words such as **Ne?** *What?*, **Kaç?** *How much/many?*, **Kim?** *Who?*, **Nasıl?** *How is it?/What is it like?*, **Nerede?** *Where?*, **Neden?** *Why?*,

Niçin? *Why?*, etc. you don't use **mu-** or its variations – you use the question word instead:

| | |
|---|---|
| **Ne istiyorsunuz?** | *What would you like?* |
| **Kaç tane istiyorsunuz?** | *How many do you want?* |

### PAIRS

In English, some items of clothing are usually spoken of as being in a pair, such as a pair of shoes, socks, gloves or slippers. You can choose to translate this expression literally in Turkish: **Bir çift ayakkabı almak istiyorum.** *I'd like to buy a pair of shoes.* But if you say **Ayakkabı almak istiyorum** (*I'd like to buy shoes*) your listener will normally assume that you want a pair of shoes.

However, English also talks of pairs of trousers, spectacles, glasses and tights, referring to only one item! In these instances, you would never say **bir çift** in Turkish, you would always refer to **bir pantolon, külotlu çorap, gözlük**. If you asked for 'pantolonlar' in Turkey, the shopkeeper would think you wanted more than one pair!

| | |
|---|---|
| **bir pantolon** | *a pair of trousers* |
| **bir çift ayakkabı** | *a pair of shoes* |
| **bir gözlük** | *a pair of glasses* |
| **eldiven** | *a pair of gloves* |
| **Pantolon almak istiyorum.** | *I'd like to buy a pair of trousers.* |
| **(Bir çift) ayakkabı almak istiyorum.** | *I'd like to buy a pair of shoes.* |

### Insight

Dialogue 1

**İstemek** means *to want*; **İstiyorum** means *I want* (lit. *I am wanting*).

Dialogue 2

**Buyrun** in this dialogue means *here you are*, but it can also mean *go ahead, feel free* or *what can I do for you?*

## Practice

**1** *Picture dictation. Read or listen to the Turkish passage that follows, draw the scene on a piece of paper and then check it with the answer at the back of the book.*

Suzan deniz kenarında bir kafede oturuyor. Meyve suyu içerken plajda ve denizdeki insanlara bakıyor. Üç çocuk dondurma alıyor. Bir çift kumlarda yatıyor. Bikinili ve şapkalı kadın kitap okuyor. Şortlu ve gözlüklü erkek denize bakıyor. Denizde bir sandal ve bir yelkenli var. Yedi kişi yüzüyor.

| | |
|---|---|
| **oturuyor** | *sitting* (**oturmak** *to sit*) |
| **plaj** | *beach* |
| **insanlar** | *people* |
| **çift** | *couple* |
| **yatıyor** | *lying* (**yatmak** *to lie down*) |
| **okuyor** | *reading* (**okumak** *to read*) |
| **kitap** | *book* |
| **şort** | *shorts* |
| **sandal** | *rowing boat* |
| **yelkenli** | *sailing boat* |
| **kişi** | *person* |
| **yüzüyor** | *swimming* (**yüzmek** *to swim*) |

QUICK VOCAB

◄) **CD2, TR 3, 06:45**

**2** *A woman is in a clothes shop talking to the salesperson. Unscramble the following dialogue and check it at the back of the book or by listening to the recording.*

**3** *Here are some items that you may like to buy in Turkey.*
*Sort them into groups under the headings supplied:*

| Food | Clothes | Presents |
|------|---------|----------|

çerez    kilim    elma çay    lokum

fıstık    T-shirt

padişah macunu    CD    bluz

incir    pantalon    ceket

kaset    çanta    Türk kahvesi    halı

ayakkabı    bal    cüzdan    baharat

| | |
|--------|-------------|
| **elma çay** | *apple tea* |
| **kaset** | *tape* |
| **halı** | *carpet* |
| **cüzdan** | *wallet, purse* |

qv

**4** *Wordsearch. Find ten items you can buy in Turkey.*

| A | G | L | O | K | U | M | K | D | N |
|---|---|---|---|---|---|---|---|---|---|
| B | S | T | O | B | P | H | R | E | F |
| A | Y | A | K | K | A | B | I | R | I |
| H | U | B | S | İ | T | Ş | Z | İ | S |
| A | V | L | M | L | R | A | E | G | T |
| R | T | U | E | İ | K | P | O | H | I |
| A | R | Z | P | M | T | K | H | E | K |
| T | O | P | A | N | T | O | L | O | N |
| I | E | T | R | B | R | P | A | Y | T |
| C | E | K | E | T | P | U | G | U | Z |

**5** **Pronunciation: s, ş, t.** *Listen several times and repeat until you are confident with your pronunciation.*

| s | ş | t |
|---|---|---|
| as | aş | at |
| es | eş | et |
| su | iş | ot |
| sis | şu | tüy |

---

## Role play

### *SHOPPING*

You are buying a leather jacket. Play your part in the conversation, according to the prompts.

| | |
|---|---|
| **Salesperson** | İyi günler. Buyrun, efendim. |
| **You** | *[Say 'hello' and ask how much the leather jackets are]* |
| **Salesperson** | Kaç beden? |
| **You** | *[Say 'size 40']* |
| **Salesperson** | Ne renk? |
| **You** | *[Say you would like to see a blue one]* |
| **Salesperson** | Sizin için 120 sterlin. |
| **You** | *[Tell her it is too expensive]* |
| **Salesperson** | Pazarlık yapmıyoruz, ama sizin için 100 sterlin. Bu da son fiyat. |
| **You** | *[Say 'ok, I'll buy it']* |

## Mini-test

**CD2, TR 3, 09:10**

You have now completed Unit 8. Now you will be able to shop for presents and to haggle. You will also be able to talk about your daily routine and what will happen shortly. Give yourself a point for each of the following things you can say in Turkish without looking at the book.

1  *Ask for a blue jacket in size 40.*
2  *Ask for some peppermint-flavoured Turkish delight.*
3  *Ask for half a kilo of dried fruit.*
4  *Buy a packet of cumin.*
5  *Say 'I don't drink wine' in Turkish.*
6  *Ask for a pair of shoes, size 41.*
7  *Ask for a pair of blue trousers.*
8  *Say 'red doesn't suit you'.*
9  *Say 'blue suits me'.*
10  *Say 'I would like to try it on' in Turkish.*

Points:____/10

# 9

## Where shall we go?

In this unit you will learn
- *How to make arrangements to go out or suggest doing something*
- *How to tell the time*
- *How to book a seat at the theatre*
- *How to buy tickets for public transport*
- *How to make, accept or refuse an invitation*
- *Pronunciation: u, ü, v*

### Dialogue 1 What shall we do at the weekend?

Listen to the dialogue a few times before answering Questions 1 and 2. Listen to the dialogue again, read it, then answer Questions 3–7.

**Questions**
1 *What are Şafak and Banu going to do at the weekend?*
2 *How do they find out what's on?*

Banu and Şafak are talking about what to do at the weekend.

◆ CD2, TR 4

| | |
|---|---|
| **Şafak** | Hafta sonunda ne yapalım? |
| **Banu** | Tiyatroya gidelim mi? Kenterler'de çok güzel bir oyun var. |
| **Şafak** | Ne oynuyor? |
| **Banu** | Bakalım. Galiba *Hep Aşk Vardı* oynuyor. |

> *They look at the Kenter Theatre's schedule.*
> **Şafak**   *Hep Aşk Vardı* oynuyor, saat 8.30'da.
> **Banu**   Evet, harika. Ben *Hamam*'ı da görmek istiyorum ama.
> **Şafak**   *Hamam*'ı ben de görmek istiyorum.
> **Banu**   Önce Kenterler'i arayayım mı?
> **Şafak**   Hadi, arayalım.
> *The telephone rings, but there is no reply.*
> **Şafak**   Saat kaç?
> **Banu**   Yarım. Öğle tatili.
> **Şafak**   Bir buçukta tekrar arayalım.
> **Banu**   Tamam.

Questions
**3** *Sinemaya mı, tiyatroya mı gitmek istiyorlar?*
**4** *Hangi tiyatroya gidiyorlar?*
**5** Hamam *film mi, oyun mu?*
**6** *Saat kaçta tiyatroya telefon ediyorlar?*
**7** *Bu hafta sonu siz ne yapıyorsunuz?*

| | |
|---|---|
| **hafta** | *week* |
| **hafta sonu** | *weekend* |
| **ne yapalım?** | *what shall we do?* |
| **tiyatro** | *theatre* |
| **gidelim mi?** | *shall we go?* |
| **ne oynuyor?** | *what's on?* |
| **bakalım** | *let's have a look* |
| **galiba** | *I think, perhaps, maybe* |
| **Hep Aşk Vardı** | *There has always been Love* (the name of a play) |
| **Hamam** | *Turkish Bath* (the name of a Turkish film) |
| **da** | *also* |
| **görmek** | *to see* |
| **istiyorum** | *I want/I would like* |
| **aramak** | *to call* |
| **arayayım** | *let me call (I'll call)* |
| **hadi, arayalım** | *let's call* |
| **yarım** | *half past twelve* |
| **bir buçukta** | *at half past one* |
| **tamam** | *OK* |

QUICK VOCAB

## Kenterler

Müşfik and Yıldız Kenter are brother and sister. They established the first really successful private theatre company in modern Turkey, which is still famous for high-quality productions (see www.kentersinematiyatro.com).

## Hamam

The cinema is a very popular form of entertainment in Turkey. *Hamam The Turkish Bath* was released in 1997. It tells the story of an Italian who inherited a Turkish bath and leaves Italy to go to run it.

If you have the opportunity, it's worth watching a Turkish film as it will give you a greater insight into Turkish culture. If the film is subtitled you will also be able to hear Turkish being spoken and may even be able to understand some of it.

---

## Language points

### *TELLING THE TIME*

There are two ways of telling the time in Turkish: using the 24-hour clock or the 12-hour clock. The international 24-hour clock is very simple; all you need to do is revise the numbers you have already learnt! The 24-hour clock is used at airports and stations, and also on the radio and television. However, for everyday purposes most Turkish people use the 12-hour clock and you will need to learn a few more words. When you are talking about the time in Turkish, there is no distinction between a.m. or p.m. Usually, people will be able to tell if you are talking about morning, afternoon or evening by the context of the conversation. But just to make sure, you can add the Turkish for morning and say **sabah sekizde** *at eight in the morning*, **öğleden sonra üçte** *at three in the afternoon*, **akşam altıda** *at six in the evening*, **gece onda** *at ten at night*.

Here is some useful vocabulary about time:

| | |
|---|---|
| saat | time, hour or clock |
| saat kaç? | what time is it? |
| saat kaçta? | at what time? |
| kaç saat? | how many hours? |
| dakika | minutes |
| saniye | seconds |
| çeyrek | a quarter |
| buçuk | it's half past |
| buçukta | at half past |
| geçiyor (-ı, -i, -u, -ü) | past |
| var (-e, -a) | to |
| öğlen | midday |
| gece yarısı | midnight |

◀) CD2, TR 4, 02:00

*SAAT KAÇ? WHAT TIME IS IT?*

The 24-hour clock

| a | b | c | d | e |
|---|---|---|---|---|
| 12:00 | 12:10 | 12:15 | 12:30 | 12:40 |
| oniki | oniki on | oniki onbeş | oniki otuz (yarım) | oniki kırk |

| f | g | h | i | j |
|---|---|---|---|---|
| 14:00 | 18:10 | 19:20 | 20:35 | 21:45 |
| ondört | onsekiz on | ondokuz yirmi | yirmi otuzbeş | yirmibir kırkbeş |

## The 12-hour clock

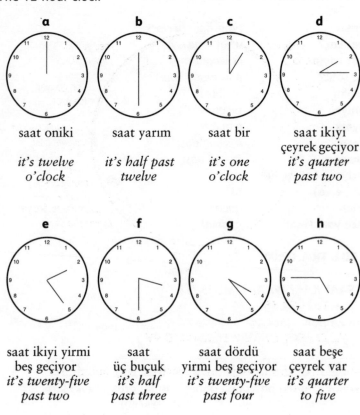

**a**
saat oniki

*it's twelve o'clock*

**b**
saat yarım

*it's half past twelve*

**c**
saat bir

*it's one o'clock*

**d**
saat ikiyi çeyrek geçiyor

*it's quarter past two*

**e**
saat ikiyi yirmi beş geçiyor

*it's twenty-five past two*

**f**
saat üç buçuk

*it's half past three*

**g**
saat dördü yirmi beş geçiyor

*it's twenty-five past four*

**h**
saat beşe çeyrek var

*it's quarter to five*

## Saat *Time, hour, clock*

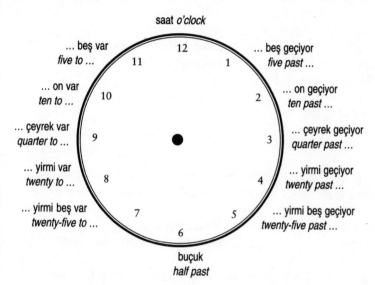

saat *o'clock*

... beş var
*five to ...*

... beş geçiyor
*five past ...*

... on var
*ten to ...*

... on geçiyor
*ten past ...*

... çeyrek var
*quarter to ...*

... çeyrek geçiyor
*quarter past ...*

... yirmi var
*twenty to ...*

... yirmi geçiyor
*twenty past ...*

... yirmi beş var
*twenty-five to ...*

... yirmi beş geçiyor
*twenty-five past ...*

buçuk
*half past*

◀) **CD2, TR 4, 02:55**

### *THE EFFECT OF VOWEL HARMONY*

Look at clock **d**: why **ikiyi çeyrek geçiyor**, why not just **iki çeyrek geçiyor**?

Look at clock **h**: why **beşe çeyrek var**, why not simply **beş çeyrek var**?

**Geçiyor** gives the hour **-ı** (**-i, -u, -ü**) endings according to vowel harmony:

| | |
|---|---|
| biri beş geçiyor *five past one* | yediyi beş geçiyor |
| ikiyi beş geçiyor | sekizi beş geçiyor |
| üçü beş geçiyor | dokuzu beş geçiyor |
| dördü beş geçiyor | onu beş geçiyor |
| beşi beş geçiyor | on biri beş geçiyor |
| altıyı beş geçiyor | on ikiyi beş geçiyor |

**Var** gives the hour the ending **-e** (**-a**) according to vowel harmony:

| | |
|---|---|
| bir<u>e</u> beş var *five to one* | yediy<u>e</u> beş var |
| ikiy<u>e</u> beş var | sekiz<u>e</u> beş var |
| üç<u>e</u> beş var | dokuz<u>a</u> beş var |
| dörd<u>e</u> beş var | on<u>a</u> beş var |
| beş<u>e</u> beş var | on bir<u>e</u> beş var |
| altıy<u>a</u> beş var | on ikiy<u>e</u> beş var |

### WORD ORDER

**Saat kaç?** or **Kaç saat?** Which is the correct answer? While both these questions relate to time, they have different meanings:

| | |
|---|---|
| **Saat kaç?** | *What time is it?* |
| **Kaç saat?** | *How many hours? How long?* |

Turkish word order is generally flexible, but, in this case, swapping the words around makes a difference to the meaning of the question. So both answers are actually correct but with different meanings.

---

## Dialogue 2 Booking seats at the theatre

Questions
1 *Are there any seats available for this Sunday?*
2 *How many tickets do they want to reserve?*

CD2, TR 4, 04:00

| | |
|---|---|
| **Receptionist** | Buyrun. 0212 246 35 89, Kenter Tiyatrosu. |
| **Şafak** | İyi günler. Bu pazar *Hep Aşk Vardı* için iki bilet ayırtmak istiyoruz. |
| **Receptionist** | İyi günler, efendim. Maalesef bu pazar için hiç bilet yok ama gelecek pazar için yer var. |
| **Şafak** | Fiyatlar nasıl acaba? |
| **Receptionist** | Tam 15 milyon lira, öğrenci 5 milyon lira, öğretmen ve emekli 12 milyon lira. |

| | |
|---|---|
| **Şafak** | İki bilet, bir tam ve bir öğrenci, lütfen. |
| **Receptionist** | Nasıl ödüyorsunuz? Kartla mı? |
| **Şafak** | Evet. |
| **Receptionist** | Kart numaranız, lütfen? |
| **Şafak** | 1234 1234 1234 1234. |

## Questions

Are Statements 3–6 true (**doğru**) or false (**yanlış**)?

3  *Kenter sinemasına gidiyorlar.*
4  *Bu pazar için bilet yok.*
5  *Öğrenci daha pahalı.*
6  *Kredi kartı ile ödüyorlar.*
7  *Siz tiyatro seviyor musunuz?*

| | |
|---|---|
| **buyrun** | *On the phone it means: Yes, I'm listening to you! How can I help you?* |
| **ayırtmak** | *to book, to reserve* |
| **maalesef** | *unfortunately* |
| **gelecek** | *next, coming* |
| **yer** | *place, seat* |
| **fiyatlar** | *prices* |
| **nasıl** | *how* |
| **tam** | *adult/full price* |
| **öğrenci** | *student* |
| **emekli** | *retired* |
| **ödemek** | *to pay* |
| **kartla** | *by card* |
| **kart/kredi kartı** | *card/credit card* |

QUICK VOCAB

---

## Dialogue 3 Choosing a film to watch

### Questions
1  *Where are Banu and Şafak going?*
2  *Are they going by car?*

| Şafak | Bu akşam sinemaya gidiyor muyuz? |
|-------|----------------------------------|
| Banu | Hadi *Hamam*'ı görelim. |
| Şafak | Bakalım sinemalarda hangi filmler var. |
| Banu | ABC'de *Vampirler* var. |
| Şafak | Ben korku filmi görmek istemiyorum. |
| Banu | Hisar'da *Şaban* oynuyor. |
| Şafak | O komedi değil mi? |
| Banu | Evet, ama ben *Hamam*'ı görmek istiyorum. |
| Şafak | Saat kaçta? |

*Banu looks at the newspaper.*

| Banu | Beşte, yedide ve dokuzda. |
|-------|----------------------------|
| Şafak | Yediye gidelim mi? |
| Banu | Tamam. Hadi şimdi çıkalım. |
| Şafak | Araba bozuk. Dolmuşla mı, otobüsle mi gidiyoruz? Otobüs daha ucuz, dolmuş daha rahat. |
| Banu | Fark etmez. |
| Şafak | Hadi otobüsle gidelim. |

## Questions

3 *Sinemalarda hangi filmler var?*
4 *Hangi filme gidiyorlar?*
5 *Saat kaçta?*
6 *Neyle gidiyorlar?*
7 *Niçin otobüsle gidiyorlar?*
8 *Siz hangi tür filmleri seviyorsunuz?*

QUICK VOCAB

| akşam | *evening* |
|-------|-----------|
| hadi | *let's* |
| korku | *horror* |
| komedi | *comedy* |
| dolmuşla | *by dolmuş (shared taxi)* |
| otobüsle | *by bus* |
| bozuk | *broken, not working* |
| rahat | *comfortable* |
| neyle | *by what (lit. how)* |

## Dolmuş

In some towns shared taxis called **dolmuş** operate on certain routes. **Dolmuş** only go when they are full (**dolmuş** means literally *it is filled up*). You can get on and off the **dolmuş** at any point along its route. **Dolmuş** are cheaper than ordinary taxis. The price is in proportion to the distance you travel. You can recognize a **dolmuş** by the sign on the roof or windscreen.

## Transportation

In Turkey, public transportation is very convenient and, as provided by coaches and the air-conditioned intercity coach services, also very comfortable. There is also a thriving minibus service and a lot of big cities have a subway system (only in and between major cities can you use airways or railways to travel around).

## Dialogue 4 Buying bus tickets

Şafak and Banu go to the nearest bus stop to buy tickets for the bus. In Istanbul, you need to buy your bus ticket before you get on a bus. This may differ from city to city or from town to town.

## Questions

**1** *Where are Banu and Şafak going to?*

**2** *Do they buy single or return tickets?*

CD2, TR 4, 08:02

| | |
|---|---|
| **Şafak** | Taksim'e iki bilet. |
| **Banu** | Dönüş için de al. |
| *At the ticket office.* | |
| **Şafak** | Dört bilet, lütfen. |
| **Clerk** | Dört milyon lira. |
| *Şafak hands over a 10-million lira note.* | |
| **Şafak** | Buyrun. |
| **Clerk** | Bozuk yok mu? |
| **Şafak** | Yok. |
| **Clerk** | (*handing over the change*) Buyrun. Altı milyon lira. |

## Questions

**3** *Otobüsle mi gidiyorlar?*

**4** *Dönüş bileti alıyorlar mı?*

**5** *Kart ile mi ödüyorlar?*

QUICK VOCAB

| | |
|---|---|
| **akşam** | *evening* |
| **hadi** | *let's/come on* |
| **korku** | *horror* |
| **komedi** | *comedy* |
| **dolmuşla** | *by dolmuş (shared taxi)* |
| **otobüsle** | *by bus* |
| **rahat** | *comfortable* |

---

## Language points

### İLE WITH/BY/BY MEANS OF TRANSPORT

The word **ile** means *with/by/by means* of transport.

| | |
|---|---|
| Kartla | *with a card/by card* |
| Neyle (ne + ile) gidiyorsun? | *How are you getting there? (lit. What are you going with/by?)* |

Otobüs ile gidiyorum.
Otobüs<u>le</u> gidiyorum.     }   *I'm going by* (lit. *with*) *bus.*
Vapur ile gidiyorum.
Vapur<u>la</u> gidiyorum.     }   *I'm going by boat.*

When **ile** is shortened to an ending, it becomes **-le** or **-la** and
follows the rules to vowel harmony, in the same way as the **-ler**
and **-lar** endings explained in Unit 2.

## COMMON FORMS OF TRANSPORT AND WHERE THEY STOP

| | |
|---|---|
| **otobüs** *bus* | **otobüs durağı** *bus stop* |
| **tren** *train* | **istasyon** *station* |
| **uçak** *aeroplane* | **havaalanı** *airport* |
| **vapur** *ferry* | **iskele** *port* |
| **dolmuş** *'shared' taxi* | **dolmuş durağı** *dolmuş stop* |
| **taksi** *taxi* | **taksi durağı** *taxi rank* |
| **metro** *underground* | **istasyon** *station* |
| **metrobüs** *tube bus* | **durak** *stop* |

## MAKING SUGGESTIONS, OFFERING HELP, ACCEPTING OR REFUSING AN OFFER

As explained earlier, Turkish adds endings to verb stems to change
meanings: here are some endings which show that someone is
making a suggestion, offering help, or expressing a hope. Not
all the examples have an exact translation in English, so in some
places we have tried to explain the sense, as well as giving a literal
translation. See if you can hear your Turkish friends use these
expressions. Gradually you will become more familiar with these
expressions and will feel confident enough to use them.

| | |
|---|---|
| **Taksim** | *Taksim Square in Istanbul* |
| **dönüş** | *return* |
| **bozuk** | *change* |

### The *let* forms of verbs

Look at the following examples, meaning let …:

Yapayım (*I*) — *let me do/make* or here *I'll do/make, I'd better do it*

Yapalım (*we*) — *let's do/make, we'd better do it*

Yapsın (*his/her*) — *let her/him do* or *she/he should do, he/she'd better do*

Yapsınlar (*they*) — *let them do/make* or *they should do/make, they'd better do*

**SUGGESTIONS OR POSITIVE OFFERS OF HELP WITH -EYİM**

Add **-eyim** onto the stem of a verb to give the meaning, *let me …*
You use it to offer help or make a suggestion. For example:

Tiyatroyu arayayım. — *Let me call the theatre./I'll call the theatre.*

Yardım edeyim. — *Let me help./I'll help.*

**SUGGESTIONS OR OFFERS OF HELP AS QUESTIONS WITH -EYİM**

Sinemayı arayayım mı? — *Shall I call the cinema?*

Yardım edeyim mi? — *Shall I help?*

**NEGATIVE SUGGESTIONS OR OFFERS OF HELP WITH -EYIM (-MEYEYİM)**

Şimdi aramayayım. — *I don't want to call now.* (lit. *Let me not call now.*)

Tiyatroyu aramayayım. — *I don't want to call the theatre.* (lit. *Let me not call the theatre.*)

Sinemayı aramayayım mı? — *Don't you want me to call the cinema?* (lit. *Shouldn't I call the cinema?*)

**POSITIVE SUGGESTIONS WITH -ELİM (-ELİM Mİ)**

Add **-elim** onto the stem of a verb to give the meaning *let's*. You use it for making suggestions. It behaves in the same way as **-eyim**. For example:

Bakalım. — *Let's have a look./Go on then.*

Gidelim. — *Let's go.*

**SUGGESTIONS IN QUESTION FORM WITH** *-ELIM*

| | |
|---|---|
| Bak<u>alım</u> <u>mı</u>? | *Shall we have a look?* |
| Gid<u>elim</u> <u>mi</u>? | *Shall we go?* |

**SUGGESTIONS AS NEGATIVE FORM WITH** *-ELIM (-MEYELIM)*

| | |
|---|---|
| Bak<u>mayalım</u>. | *Let's not look.* |
| Git<u>meyelim</u>. | *Let's not go.* |
| Bak<u>mayalım</u> mı? | *Shall we not have a look?* |

**POSITIVE REMARKS WITH** *-SIN*

Add **-sin** (-sın, -sun or sün, according to vowel harmony) to the verb stem to say what someone should do. You can also use it to express a hope that something will happen. It is frequently used in stock phrases. Turkish has many of these, and for a wider range of purposes than in English. Note that the third person singular (*he, she, it*) and plural (*them*) are not very common.

> **Şeker Bayrami** and **Kurban Bayramı** are both festive times when children are given new clothes, the poor are helped and family members are visited. It is usual to phone family or friends or send them **Bayram** cards.

**bayram**   *festivity, religious festival, national holiday, festival*

| İyi Bayramlar. | Bayramınız kutlu olsun. |
|---|---|

**QUESTIONS WITH** *-SIN (-SIN MI)*

| | |
|---|---|
| Üstü kal<u>sın</u> mı? | *Shall I/should I leave the change?* |

**NEGATIVE REMARKS WITH** *-SIN (MESİN OR MASIN)*

| | |
|---|---|
| Yap<u>masın</u>. | *Don't make him or her. (lit. Let him/ her not do.)* |

Although these forms are widely used in Turkish, in English they would be expressed very differently. So listen to your Turkish friends carefully. Try to get the gist of what is being said and try to get used to the Turkish way of thinking! All languages and all cultures have their differences. Just try to enjoy the differences!

### THE 'BUFFER Y' AND CONSONANT CHANGE

If there are two vowels next to each other you insert a connecting y to make it easier to say, e.g. bakmayalım, yardım edeyim. (For a fuller explanation see Unit 5.) In addition to the 'buffer y' there are also some consonant changes in Turkish if a word finishes with a hard consonant. The hard consonants are: ç, f, h, k, p, s, ş and t.

When a hard consonant is followed by an ending which usually starts with a d you must change the d to a t. This is similar to vowel harmony, but with consonants. At this stage do not worry about getting all these changes right. It is enough for you to recognize them. Even educated native speakers sometimes make mistakes.

Saat kaçda? *becomes* Saat kaçta?     *At what time?*
Saat ikide *remain* Saat ikide.        *At two o'clock.*

But

Saat üçte.                              *At three o'clock.*

........................................................................

### Insight
Dialogue 3

le means *by* when talking about means of transport:

otobüsle          *by bus*

See ile (in this unit), which means *with* or *by* in other circumstances.

Dialogues 3 and 4

**Bozuk** has two meanings:

**1** *out of order, not working*
**2** *change (money).*

Try not to get the two confused!

......................................................................................................

## Practice

**◄)) CD2, TR 4, 09:02**

**1** *Here is a list of leisure activities (shopping, cinema, theatre, museums, restaurant, etc.). First check their meanings in the vocabulary list.*

| | | | |
|---|---|---|---|
| **i** | *alışveriş yapmak* | **ii** | *sinemaya gitmek* |
| **iii** | *tiyatroya gitmek* | **iv** | *restorana gitmek* |
| **v** | *müzeye gitmek* | **vi** | *televizyon seyretmek* |
| **vii** | *müzik dinlemek* | **viii** | *yüzmek* |
| **ix** | *seyahat etmek* | | |

   **a** *Listen to the conversation between Yeşim and Ahmet in which they discuss their plans for the evening, and list the activities you hear mentioned.*
   **b** *What did they decide to do?*
   **c** *Listen again and write down the dialogue.*

| | |
|---|---|
| **rejimdeyim** | *I am on a diet* |
| **iyi fikir** | *good idea* |

**◄)) CD2, TR 4, 09:37**

**2** *Nesrin has a full week ahead of her. She goes through her diary and says what she has to do. Listen to the recording several times. Does she have any free days?*

| Ağustos | |
|---|---|
| **4 Pazartesi** <br> *8'de tiyatro Banu ile* | **8 Cuma** <br> *Boğaz Gezisi Yeşim ve Ahmet ile* |
| **5 Salı** | **9 Cumartesi** <br> *2'de Çemberlitaş Hamamı* |
| **6 Çarşamba** <br> *1.30'da öğle yemeği Gonca ile* | **10 Pazar** <br> *Vanessa ile Karagöz ve Hacivat* |
| **7 Perşembe** | |

*Now look at your diary and write out next week's entries in Turkish.*

## Karagöz ve Hacivat: puppets

*Karagöz*, a form of shadow puppet theatre, was introduced to the Ottoman Empire during the reign of Yavuz Sultan Selim in 1517. **Karagöz** and **Hacivat** are two main characters of the show.

**3** *Look at the following notes. Match up the invitations and replies.*

**a**

Suzan,

Dersten sonra
bira içelim mi?
Görüşürüz.

Gül

**b**

Sevgili Dave,

Bu yaz
İstanbul'a
gidelim mi?

Asu

**c**

Sevgili Ayşegül,

Yarın partiye
gidiyor muyuz?

Andy

**d**

Yeşim,

Bu pazar yüzmeye
gidelim mi?

Ahmet

**i**

Andy,

Yarın
meşgulüm
sevgilim.

Ayşegül

**ii**

İyi fikir.

Kafede
görüşürüz.

Suzan

**iii**

Sevgili Ahmet,

Harika bir fikir, gidelim.
Hava da çok sıcak.

Sevgiler

Yeşim

**iv**

Çok iyi fikir.

Cumartesi biletleri
alalım.

Dave

**4** *Write the following digital times in full, then convert them into 12-hour clock format. The first one has been done for you. Listen to them on the recording and repeat them out loud.*

| Saat kaç? | 24-hour clock | 12-hour clock |
|---|---|---|
| **a** *12.30* | on iki otuz | yarım |
| **b** *15.15* | .............. | .............. |
| **c** *08.50* | .............. | .............. |
| **d** *04.25* | .............. | .............. |
| **e** *18.45* | .............. | .............. |
| **f** *09.10* | .............. | .............. |
| **g** *24.00* | .............. | .............. |
| **h** *10.10* | .............. | .............. |
| **i** *05.05* , | .............. | .............. |
| **j** *13.02* | .............. | .............. |

**5** *Translate the following into Turkish.*
  **a** *It's five past two.*
  **b** *At twenty-five to three.*
  **c** *At a quarter past four.*
  **d** *It's a quarter to seven.*
  **e** *At half past twelve.*
  **f** *It's ten to eight.*
  **g** *At twenty-five past seven*
  **h** *It's a quarter past eleven.*
  **i** *It's a quarter to ten.*
  **j** *At five past nine.*

**6** *Add the -de/-da endings to the following words. Remember to use -de/-da according to the rules of vowel harmony and also to make any necessary consonant changes, e.g. d to t where necessary.*

  **a** *Sinema*          **g** *Vapur*
  **b** *Tiyatro*         **h** *Dolmuş*
  **c** *İş*              **i** *Uçak*
  **d** *Park*            **j** *Durak*
  **e** *Otobüs*          **k** *Otel*
  **f** *Tren*

**7** Write two short dialogues.

**a** You are going past a cinema. There is a very good film on, which you would like to see. Suggest to your friend that you go and see the film together. Your friend politely refuses the suggestion. Re-order the following sentences to form a meaningful dialogue.

  **i** Ne zaman?
  **ii** Bu cumartesi.
  **iii** Sinemaya gidelim mi?
  **iv** Özür dilerim. Meşgulüm.

**b** You are going past a tea garden in Turkey. It's hot and you are very thirsty. Suggest to your friend that you stop and have a drink. Your friend enthusiastically accepts the suggestion. Re-order the following sentences to form a meaningful dialogue.

  **i** Köşede. Kafede.
  **ii** Nerede?
  **iii** Çok iyi fikir. Hadi gidelim ve soğuk bir şey içelim.
  **iv** Çok sıcak, soğuk bir şey içelim mi?

**8** Reading passage

The Bosporus is the channel between the Black Sea and the Aegean and it also separates the two continents of Asia and Europe. If you take a boat tour along the Bosporus in Istanbul, you zigzag between continents!

Read the passage and timetable to get the gist of it. Don't worry if you don't understand every word. Read the passage a couple of times and try to answer the following questions.

  **a** Where do the boats leave from daily?
  **b** How many boats leave daily and at what time?
  **c** At how many places does the boat stop?
  **d** How long does it stop for at Anadolu Kavağı?

**Boğaz gezi vapuru** *Boat trips on the Bosporus*

Vapurumuz Eminönü'nden her gün saat 10.35, 12.00 ve 13.35'te kalkıyor. Özel Boğaz Gezisi Vapuru'muz sırasıyla, Barbaros Hayrettin Paşa, Kanlıca, Emirgan, Yeniköy, Sarıyer, Rumeli Kavağı iskelelerinde duruyor ve Anadolu Kavağı son iskeledir. Vapurumuz her seferinde Anadolu Kavağı'nda 2–3 saat kalmaktadır. Burada çok güzel balık lokantaları vardır.

Ayrıca, cumartesi, pazar ve bayram günleri saat 10.35 ile 13.35 vapurlarımızda canlı müzik vardır.

| GİDİŞ | | | | DÖNÜŞ | | | |
|---|---|---|---|---|---|---|---|
| EMİNÖNÜ Kalkış | 10.35 | 12.00 | 13.35 | A. KAVAĞI Kalkış | 15.00 | 16.15 | 17.00 |
| B. H. PAŞA | 10.50 | 12.15 | 13.50 | R. KAVAĞI | 15.10 | 16.00 | 17.10 |
| KANLICA | 11.15 | 12.40 | 14.15 | SARIYER | 15.20 | 16.25 | 17.20 |
| EMİRGAN | 11.25 | 12.50 | 14.25 | YENİKÖY | 15.35 | 16.40 | 17.35 |
| YENİKÖY | 11.40 | 13.05 | 14.40 | EMİRGAN | 15.50 | 16.50 | 17.50 |
| SARIYER | 11.55 | 13.20 | 14.55 | KANLICA | 16.00 | 17.00 | 18.00 |
| R. KAVAĞI | 12.05 | 13.45 | 15.05 | B. H. PAŞA | 16.25 | 17.25 | 18.25 |
| A. KAVAĞI Varış | 12.15 | 13.35 | 15.15 | EMİNÖNÜ Varış | 16.35 | 17.35 | 18.35 |

| | | | |
|---|---|---|---|
| **gidiş** | *going* | **kalkış** | *leaving* |
| **dönüş** | *return* | **varış** | *arriving/arrival* |

For more information go to the Turkish Maritime Organization (**Türkiye Denizcilik İşletmeleri A.Ş.**) website at: www.tdi.com.tr.

**9** *In the left-hand column someone is saying they have a problem, or need help. The right-hand column contains offers of help. Match the two together.*

| | | | |
|---|---|---|---|
| **a** | *Acıktım.* | **i** | *Ben taşıyayım mı?* |
| **b** | *Burası çok sıcak.* | **ii** | *Sana tost yapayım mı?* |
| **c** | *Program güzel değil.* | **iii** | *Televizyonu kapatayım mı?* |
| **d** | *Telefon çalıyor.* | **iv** | *Pencereyi açayım mı?* |
| **e** | *Sıkıldım.* | **v** | *Müzik koyayım mı?* |
| **f** | *Valiz çok ağır.* | **vi** | *Cevap vereyim mi?* |
| **g** | *Başım ağrıyor.* | **vii** | *Trenle gidelim.* |
| **h** | *Yağmur yağıyor.* | **viii** | *Sana Aspirin vereyim mi?* |
| **i** | *Çok güneş.* | **ix** | *Şemsiyeyi alalım.* |

| **j** | *Yorgunum.* | **x** | *Gölgede oturalım.* |
|---|---|---|---|
| **k** | *Program sıkıcı.* | **xi** | *Tatile gidelim.* |
| **l** | *Uçak pahalı.* | **xii** | *Televizyonu kapatalım mı?* |

**10** Here is an authentic environmental message taken from a Turkish newspaper. Translate it into English then check your answer at the back of the book. To help you find verbs in your dictionary:

▷ take the verb stem,
▷ add -**mek** or -**mak** to form the verb's dictionary form,
▷ now look it up in the dictionary.

> # Yeşili
> # sevelim,
> # ormanları
> # koruyalım.

◀) **CD2, TR 4, 11:41**

**11** Pronunciation: u, ü, v. First, listen to the recording, then listen while looking at the following sounds, finally listen and repeat.

| u | ü | v |
|---|---|---|
| uç | üç | av |
| ud | süt | ev |
| bu | güç | var |
| su | tüy | ver |

---

## Role play

### WHERE SHALL WE GO?

You and a friend are trying to decide what to do this evening. Play your part in the conversation, according to the prompts.

| Friend | Bu akşam ne yapalım? |
| You | [Suggest going to a pub] |
| Friend | Yarın çalışıyorum. |
| You | [Suggest that the two of you watch TV] |
| Friend | Güzel program yok. Lokantaya gidelim mi? |
| You | [Say 'It's a very good idea. Let's go'] |

## Mini-test

◆》 **CD2, TR 4, 13:16**

Well done; you have now completed Unit 9! Now you will be able to make arrangements to go out or suggest doing something, you'll be able to buy tickets for transport, you'll be able to tell the time, book a seat at a theatre or cinema and make and accept or refuse an invitation. Give yourself a point for each of the following things that you can say in Turkish without looking at the book.

1 Suggest going to the theatre as there's a good play on.
2 Ask for two return tickets to Istanbul.
3 Say and write out 15.15 in words using the 12-hour clock format.
4 Ask the time.
5 Book a seat at a cinema for this Sunday.
6 Ask what films are on at the cinemas.
7 Say you would like to go by bus or by dolmuş.
8 Say you like documentaries.
9 Ask 'what kind of films do you like?'
10 Say 'it is very sunny here, let's sit in the shade.'

Points:_____/10

# 10

## How was it?

In this unit you will learn
- *How to talk about the past, including your experiences and historical facts*
- *How to write a postcard*
- *How to have a social chat*
- *Pronunciation: y, z*

### Dialogue 1 The holiday was wonderful!

Yasemin's mother is Turkish, her father is English, she was born and brought up in England. She speaks very good Turkish. She is being interviewed by a Turkish TV presenter for a holiday programme.

◀ CD2, TR 5

| | |
|---|---|
| **Presenter** | İyi günler, Yasemin Hanım. |
| **Yasemin** | İyi günler. Bana Yasemin deyin, lütfen. |
| **Presenter** | Tatiliniz nasıldı? |
| **Yasemin** | Harikaydı. Her gün güneşliydi. Bütün hafta hiç yağmur yağmadı. |
| **Presenter** | Deniz? |
| **Yasemin** | Sakin ve masmaviydi. Su ılıktı. Her gün yüzdük, sandalda kürek çektik ve kumlarda yürüdük. |
| **Presenter** | Ya otel, otel nasıldı? |
| **Yasemin** | Çok rahattı, oda deniz manzaralıydı ve servis çok iyiydi. |

| Presenter | Yemekler? |
|---|---|
| Yasemin | Ah, yemekler harikaydı. Türk yemekleri yapmayı öğreniyorum. Çoban salatası çok yararlı ve lezzetli. Dün, Türk kahvesi yaptım ve arkadaşım fal baktı. Her şey çok güzeldi, gelecek tatil için odamı ayırttım bile. Ben burada bir ev almak istiyorum. |

Questions

1 *Tatil nasıldı?*
2 *Deniz nasıldı?*
3 *Tatilde ne yaptılar?*
4 *Otel nasıldı?*
5 *Yemekler nasıldı?*

QUICK VOCAB

| | |
|---|---|
| **bana Yasemin deyin** | *call me Yasemin* |
| **tatiliniz nasıldı?** | *how was your holiday?* |
| **harikaydı** | *it was wonderful* |
| **bütün** | *all* |
| **hiç** | *(not) at all* |
| **hiç yağmur yağmadı** | *it never rained* |
| **sakin** | *calm* |
| **masmavi** | *very blue, intense blue, crystal blue* |
| **ılıktı** | *it was warm* |
| **yüzmek** | *to swim* |
| **sandal** | *rowing boat* |
| **kürek çekmek** | *to row a boat* |
| **kumlar** | *sand* |
| **yürümek** | *to walk* |
| **servis** | *service* |
| **çoban salatası** | *mixed salad (lit. Shepherd's salad)* |
| **yararlı** | *good for you* |
| **yapmak** | *to make/to do* |
| **dün** | *yesterday* |
| **arkadaşım** | *my friend* |
| **fal bakmak** | *to read fortunes* |
| **gelecek** | *next* |
| **ayırtmak** | *to book* |
| **bile** | *even* |

## Language points

### THE PAST FORM OF VERBS

To talk about the past, you need to learn one simple past tense in Turkish. You use the same form of the verb to talk about things which happened and have happened.

You can spot the past tense by an ending which includes **-di**. To make a past tense form you put **-dı**, **-di**, **-du** or **-dü** endings after nouns, adjectives and verbs (or **-tı**, **-ti**, **-tu** or **-tü** after the hard consonants **ç, f, h, k, p, s, ş** or **t**). The good news is that almost all Turkish verbs follow these rules.

To make the simple past tense of a verb you take the following steps:

| | Action | | Example | |
|---|---|---|---|---|
| ▶ | take the infinitive of the verb, | | yürümek | to walk |
| ▶ | take the stem of the verb, | | yürü | walk |
| ▶ | add the past form of the verb to be. | | yürü**düm** | I walked |

Here are some more examples:

| | **sevmek** *to love* | **almak** *to buy/take* | **durmak** *to stop* | **yüzmek** *to swim* |
|---|---|---|---|---|
| ben | sev**dim** | al**dım** | dur**dum** | yüz**düm** |
| sen | sev**din** | al**dın** | dur**dun** | yüz**dün** |
| o | sev**di** | al**dı** | dur**du** | yüz**dü** |
| biz | sev**dik** | al**dık** | dur**duk** | yüz**dük** |
| siz | sev**diniz** | al**dınız** | dur**dunuz** | yüz**dünüz** |
| onlar | sev**diler** | al**dılar** | dur**dular** | yüz**düler** |

To make a verb in the past tense **negative** (*did not*), add **-me** or **-ma** onto the stem of the verb before the **-di** ending.

| ben | sevmedim | almadım | durmadım | yüzmedim |
|-----|----------|---------|----------|----------|
| sen | sevmedin | almadın | durmadın | yüzmedin |
| o | sevmedi | almadı | durmadı | yüzmedi |
| biz | sevmedik | almadık | durmadık | yüzmedik |
| siz | sevmediniz | almadınız | durmadınız | yüzmediniz |
| onlar | sevmediler | almadılar | durmadılar | yüzmediler |

To make a verb in the past tense into a question (*did I …?*) add
-mı, -mi, -mu or -mü after the -di and the personal endings.

| ben | sevdim mi? | aldım mı? | durdum mu? | yüzdüm mü? |
|-----|------------|-----------|------------|------------|
| sen | sevdin mi? | aldın mı? | durdun mu? | yüzdün mü? |
| o | sevdi mi? | aldı mı? | durdu mu? | yüzdü mü? |
| biz | sevdik mi? | aldık mı? | durduk mu? | yüzdük mü? |
| siz | sevdiniz mi? | aldınız mı? | durdunuz mu? | yüzdünüz mü? |
| onlar | sevdiler mi? | aldılar mı? | durdular mı? | yüzdüler mi? |

## Dialogue 2 The holiday was a disaster!

An unhappy holidaymaker is being interviewed by a Turkish TV
presenter for a holiday programme.

| | | |
|---|---|---|
| **Presenter** | Tatiliniz nasıldı? | |
| **Tourist** | Berbattı. Her şey her şey çok kötüydü. | |
| **Presenter** | Hava nasıldı? | |
| **Tourist** | Önce çok sıcaktı, sonra rüzgarlı ve yağmurluydu. | |
| **Presenter** | Ya deniz? | |
| **Tourist** | Berbattı. Deniz soğuk ve çok dalgalıydı. | |
| **Presenter** | Otel? Nerede kaldınız? Otel nasıldı? | |
| **Tourist** | Otel çok gürültülüydü. Önümüzde bir inşaat vardı, bütün manzarayı kapatıyordu. Açık disko çok yakındı ve müzik çok yüksekti. Yatak sertti, duş bozuktu. | |
| **Presenter** | Yemekleri sevdiniz mi? | |

*(Contd)*

CD2, TR 5, 01:50

> **Tourist**   Ah, yemekler berbattı, lezzetsizdi. Sebze ve meyveler taze değildi. Çatal, bıçak da hiç temiz değildi. Servis çok yavaştı. Her şey çok pahalıydı ve de çok kötüydü. Kız arkadaşım da beni bıraktı gitti. Tatilim berbat oldu.
>
> *During the interview the tourist is stung by a bee.*
>
> **Tourist**   Ahh! Arı soktu!

Questions

1 *Hava iyi miydi?*
2 *Deniz nasıldı?*
3 *Otel çok iyiydi, değil mi?*
4 *Yemekler nasıldı?*

| | |
|---|---|
| **berbat** | *terrible* |
| **her şey** | *everything* |
| **her şey her şey** | *absolutely everything* |
| **kötü** | *bad* |
| **önce** | *at first* |
| **sonra** | *later* |
| **dalgalı** | *rough* |
| **kalmak** | *to stay* |
| **gürültü** | *noise* |
| **gürültülüydü** | *it was noisy* |
| **önümüzde** | *in front of us* |
| **inşaat** | *building site* |
| **açık disko** | *open-air disco* |
| **sert** | *hard* |
| **bozuktu** | *out of order* |
| **çatal** | *fork* |
| **bıçak** | *knife* |
| **kötüydü** | *it was bad* |
| **berbat oldu** | *it is ruined* |
| **arı** | *bee* |
| **sokmak** | *to sting* |
| **arı soktu!** | *I've been stung by a bee! (lit. a bee has stung me!)* |

## Language points

### THE PAST FORM OF 'TO BE'

You can add the past tense endings of the verb *to be* to nouns, adjectives and adverbs to describe how things were. Here are some examples:

| Present tense | | Past tense | |
|---|---|---|---|
| ben | rahat**ım** *I am comfortable* | rahat**tım*** *I was comfortable* | |
| sen | rahat**sın** | rahat**tın** | |
| o | rahat | rahat**tı** | |
| biz | rahat**ız** | rahat**tık** | |
| siz | rahat**sınız** | rahat**tınız** | |
| onlar | rahat**lar** | rahat**tılar** or rahat**lardı** | |
| ben | iyi**yim**** *I'm fine/good* | iyi**ydim** *I was fine/good* | |
| sen | iyi**sin** | iyi**ydin** | |
| o | iyi | iyi**ydi** | |
| biz | iyi**yiz** | iyi**ydik** | |
| siz | iyi**siniz** | iyi**ydiniz** | |
| onlar | iyi**ler** | iyi**ydiler** or iyi**lerdi** | |

*Remember, **d** becomes **t** after **t** as in rahat**tım**.
**Connecting **y** used between vowels, as in **iyiyim** and **iyiydim**.

You say *was not* or *were not* by using the word **değil** with the endings used above. For example:

| Negatives in the present tense | Negatives in the past tense |
|---|---|
| ben iyi değil**im** *I'm not well* | ben iyi değil**dim** *I wasn't well* |
| sen iyi değil**sin** | sen iyi değil**din** |
| o iyi değil | o iyi değil**di** |
| biz iyi değil**iz** | biz iyi değil**dik** |
| siz iyi değil**siniz** | siz iyi değil**diniz** |
| onlar iyi değil**ler** | onlar iyi değil**lerdi** or değil**diler** |

You use **-mı, -mi, -mu,** or **-mü** to make the sentence a question.

| Questions in the present tense | Questions in the past tense |
|---|---|
| Harika **mıyım**? *Am I wonderful?* | Harika **mıydım**? *Was I wonderful?* |
| Harika **mısın**? | Harika **mıydın**? |
| Harika **mı**? | Harika **mıydı**? |
| Harika **mıyız**? | Harika **mıydık**? |
| Harika **mısınız**? | Harika **mıydınız**? |
| Harikalar **mı**?/Onlar harika **mı**? | Harikalar **mıydı**?/(Harika **mıydılar**?) |

## Reading comprehension: the postcard

Su is on holiday in Turkey. She stayed on the island for a week then came to Istanbul where she wrote this postcard. Pay particular attention to the use of tenses.

*Sevgili Anneciğim,*

*Tatil harika geçiyor. Her sabah simit yiyorum. Üç kere deveye bindim. Henüz rakı içmedim. Hava her gün güneşli. Bir hafta adada kaldık, şimdi İstanbul'dayız. Dün Topkapı'ya gittik ama henüz Ayasofya'yı gezmedik. Sana bir kilo lokum aldım. On gündür tavla öğreniyorum. Çok mutluyum. Yakında görüşürüz.*

*Sevgilerimle*

*Su*

*xx*

## Questions
Answer the questions and then check the answers at the back of the book.

**1** *Su hiç rakı içti mi?*
**2** *Su şimdi adada mı?*
**3** *Su, Ayasofya'yı gezdi mi?*

---

## Language points

### *USING THE PAST TENSE*

Turkish does not have an equivalent of the English tense *have done* (present perfect). Instead, you often use the past tense, for example:

| | |
|---|---|
| **Arı soktu!** | *A bee has stung me!* |
| **Hiç ayran içtin mi?** | *Have you ever drunk 'ayran'?* |
| **İstanbul'a hiç gitmedim.** | *I haven't been to Istanbul.* |
| **Ayasofya'ya gittin mi?** | *Have you been to St Sophia?* |

In some cases you use the Turkish **-iyor** tense to translate the English *have done* tense.

Where English uses a present tense (something ongoing) note that Turks sometimes use the past tense. In conversations, you are likely to hear the following:

| Phrase | Literal translation | Meaning |
|---|---|---|
| **Efendim, anlamadım.** | *Pardon, I didn't understand you.* | *I don't understand you.* |
| **sıkıldım** | *I was bored* | *I'm bored* |
| **acıktım** | *I was hungry* | *I'm hungry* |
| **susadım** | *I was thirsty* | *I'm thirsty* |
| **yoruldum** | *I got tired* | *I'm tired* |
| **yolumu kaybettim** | *I lost my way* | *I'm lost* |
| **geç kaldım** | *I was late* | *I'm late* |
| **geldim** | *I came* | *I'm coming, I've come, I'll be right there* |
| **memnun oldum** | *I became glad* | *I'm glad, I'm pleased* |

## PAST TIME EXPRESSIONS

| | |
|---|---|
| **dün** | *yesterday* |
| **dün akşam** | *yesterday evening* |
| **dün gece** | *last night* |
| **geçen hafta** | *last week* |
| **geçen hafta sonu** | *last weekend* |
| **geçen ay** | *last month* |
| **iki saat önce** | *two hours ago* |
| **geçen yıl/sene** | *last year* |

---

## Listening comprehension: guess who?

◀) **CD2, TR 5, 03:44**

Listen to this biography of a famous American. It is written in the past tense. How many clues do you need to guess this person's identity? Listen as many times as you need before looking at the transcript in the back of the book. Then answer the questions.

1 *Kim?*
2 *Askerlik yaptı mı?*
3 *Kimle evlendi?*
4 *Yakışıklı mıydı?*
5 *Mesleği neydi?*
6 *Ünlü müydü?*
7 *Siz onu hiç dinlediniz mi?*

**QUICK VOCAB**

| | |
|---|---|
| **doğmak** | *to be born* |
| **ilk** | *first* |
| **kez** | *time* |
| **plak** | *record* |
| **anlaşmak** | *to sign a contract* |
| **TV'ye çıkmak** | *to be on TV* |
| **askerlik** | *military service* |
| **askerliğini yaptı** | *did his military service* |

| ... ile evlenmek | to get married to ... |
|---|---|
| boşanmak | to divorce |
| arası | between |
| konser vermek | to give a concert |
| ölmek | to die |
| ...'den fazla | more than ... |
| müzikal | musical |
| oynamak | to act |
| ödül | award |
| altın | gold |
| platin | platinum |
| kral | king |

## Atatürk, Mustafa Kemal

Mustafa Kemal Atatürk was the founder of the Turkish Republic and as such he is still a key figure in modern Turkey. Under his leadership, Turkish society was transformed radically. Today you will find his statue in every town square and his portrait in schools and offices and on banknotes and stamps.

When Mustafa Kemal was a young man, at the end of the 19th century, Turkey was part of the decaying Ottoman Empire, which had been ruled for 600 years as an Islamic state by autocratic sultans. Atatürk's vision was to modernize Turkey and he looked towards Western Europe for models of democratic, secular government.

After the First World War, and the abdication of the last Sultan, Turkey became an autonomous state in 1923 with Atatürk as its leader. Atatürk started his reforms by establishing a parliamentary democracy, then began a cultural revolution. He wanted to abolish the culture and customs of the Islamic Ottoman society. He replaced the Arabic alphabet with the Roman alphabet; the Islamic calendar with the western calendar; the Friday 'day of rest'

*(Contd)*

was moved to Sunday. He reformed the dress code for men and women, outlawing the veil and the fez. He reformed the Turkish language. He promoted equality of the sexes, wanting men and women to socialize together. He separated religious affairs from politics, replacing Islamic law with a civil code, while upholding the right of the individual to follow their religion of choice.

Today Turkey is a member of NATO, and has for several years been seeking entry to the European Union. Following Atatürk's cultural and political revolution, Turkey is unique in being a secular Islamic country.

## Turkish writers

Some contemporary Turkish writers, including Ayşe Kulin, Buket Uzuner and Orhan Pamuk, are prolific and popular. Books by all three have been translated into English.

## Reading comprehension

Read the brief passage about Turkish history below and answer the questions. You do not need to know every word to be able to understand the passage. However, you will find key words in the vocabulary box and a translation of the passage at the back of the book. To reinforce the words and their past tense forms try Question 4 in the **Practice** section.

### *TÜRK TARİHİ TURKISH HISTORY*

Türkler, Anadolu'ya Orta Asya'dan geldiler. Selçuk Türkleri 1071'de doğuda Malazgirt'ten Anadolu'ya girdi ve batıya yayıldı. Osman Bey, Bursa'ya kadar geldi, sonra Bursa başkent oldu. 1453'te Fatih Sultan Mehmet, Konstantinapol'u aldı ve Osmanlı başkenti yaptı. Osmanlılar, Orta Avrupa'da Viyana'da durdular.

Osmanlılar, Avrupa ve Anadolu'da çok güzel camiler, köprüler ve kervansaraylar yaptılar. Birinci Dünya Savaşı'ndan sonra İngiliz, Fransız, İtalyan ve Yunanlılar Türkiye'yi işgal ettiler. Atatürk, Kurtuluş Savaş'ını kazandı. Türkiye, Cumhuriyet oldu. Ankara, başkent oldu. Atatürk ilk Türk Cumhurbaşkanı oldu ve çok devrimler yaptı.

Questions

1  *Why is Sultan Mehmet important?*
2  *What is the Ottomans' contribution to the architecture of Europe and Anatolia?*
3  *According to the passage, in which three ways did Atatürk contribute to the history of Turkey?*

| | |
|---|---|
| **tarih** | *history* |
| **Türk tarihi** | *Turkish history* |
| **Anadolu** | *Anatolia* |
| **Orta Asya** | *Central Asia* |
| **Selçuk Türkleri** | *Seljuk* |
| **Malazgirt** | *Manzikert* (the name of a town) |
| **girdi** | *entered* |
| **yayıldı** | *spread* |
| **Osman Bey** | *Osman* (the head of the Ottoman clan) |
| **Bursa'ya kadar** | *as far as Bursa* |
| **Fatih Sultan Mehmet** | *Sultan Mehmet the conqueror* |
| **aldı** | *conquered, took* |
| **Osmanlılar** | *Ottomans* |
| **Orta Avrupa'da** | *Central Asia* |
| **durdular** | *stopped* |
| **köprüler** | *bridges* |
| **kervansaraylar** | *caravanserai* (inns with large courtyards) |
| **Birinci Dünya Savaşı** | *First World War* |
| **...'dan sonra** | *after...* |
| **işgal ettiler** | *they occupied* |
| **Kurtuluş Savaşı** | *War of Independence* |
| **kazandı** | *won* |
| **devrimler** | *reforms* |

QUICK VOCAB

---

## Practice

🔊 **CD2, TR 5, 04:50**

**1** *You are a TV presenter who asked two holidaymakers (one happy, one unhappy) the same questions. Their answers got muddled up by the computer. Try to work out the answer each gave to each question.*

| | | | |
|---|---|---|---|
| **a** | *İyi günler.* | **i** | *İyi günler.* |
| **b** | *Tatiliniz nasıldı?* | **ii** | *Çok iyiydi.* |
| **c** | *Hava nasıldı?* | **iii** | *Yemekler berbattı, lezzetsizdi.* |
| **d** | *Otel nasıldı?* | **iv** | *Otel çok gürültülüydü.* |
| **e** | *Yemekler nasıldı?* | **v** | *Çok rüzgarlı ve yağmurluydu.* |
| | | **vi** | *Her gün güneşliydi.* |
| | | **vii** | *Çok rahattı, oda deniz manzaralıydı.* |
| | | **viii** | *Çok kötüydü.* |
| | | **ix** | *Yemekler harikaydı.* |
| | | **x** | *İyi günler.* |

**2** *Here are four situations where A says what he/she did and B asks questions about it. Match the statements with the questions.*

| | | |
|---|---|---|
| **i** | **A** Dün akşam sinemaya gittim. | **iii** **A** Geçen hafta kitap aldım. |
| | **B** ........................... | **B** ........................... |

**ii A** Geçen pazar pideciye gittik.

**B** ...........................

**iv A** Hafta sonunda yüzdüm.

**B** ...........................

| | |
|---|---|
| **a** | *Denizde mi, havuzda mı?* |
| **b** | *Hangi filmi gördün?* |
| **c** | *Hangi kitabı aldın?* |
| **d** | *Kimle gittin?* |

**3** *The verbs in the following vocabulary box are in the dictionary (infinitive) form. Give their past forms. The first one has been done for you.*

| | ben | sen | o |
|---|---|---|---|
| doğmak | doğdum | doğdun | doğdu |
| anlaşmak | | | |
| TV'ye çıkmak | | | |
| plak yapmak | | | |
| evlenmek | | | |
| boşanmak | | | |
| konser vermek | | | |
| oynamak | | | |
| ödül almak | | | |
| ölmek | | | |

**4** *Fill in the gaps. The following passage, taken from earlier in the unit, needs to have the correct verb endings inserted. They should all be in the past tense.*

**Türk tarihi**
Türkler, Anadolu'ya Orta Asya'dan 1 gel___. Selçuk Türkleri 1071'de doğuda Malazgirt'ten Anadolu'ya 2 gir___ ve batıya 3 yayıl___. Osman Bey, Bursa'ya kadar 4 gel___, sonra Bursa başkent 5 ol___. 1453'te Fatih Sultan Mehmet, Konstantinapol'u 6 al___ ve Osmanlı başkenti 7 yap___. Osmanlılar, Orta Avrupa'da Viyana'da 8 dur___. Osmanlılar, Avrupa ve Anadolu'da çok güzel camiler, köprüler ve

kervansaraylar 9 yap___. Birinci Dünya Savaşı'ndan sonra İngiliz, Fransız, İtalyan ve Yunanlılar Türkiye'yi işgal 10 et___. Atatürk, Kurtuluş Savaş,ını 11 kazan___. Türkiye Cumhuriyet 12 ol___. Ankara, başkent 13 ol___. Atatürk ilk Türk Cumhurbaşkanı 14 ol___ ve çok devrimler 15 yap___.

**5** *Things you have or you haven't done.*

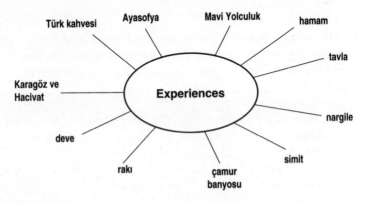

| QUICK VOCAB | |
|---|---|
| **tavla oynamak** | *to play backgammon* |
| **nargile içmek** | *to smoke a hookah* |
| **simit yemek** | *to eat simit* (bread in the shape of a ring) |
| **deveye binmek** | *to ride a camel* |
| **çamur banyosu yapmak** | *to have a mud bath* |
| **Ayasofya'yı gezmek** | *to visit St Sophia* |
| **hamama gitmek** | *to go to a Turkish bath* |
| **Karagöz ve Hacivat'ı seyretmek** | *to watch Karagöz and Hacivat* (traditional puppet show) |

Make up eleven questions, using these words, to ask about things which you have/have not done. Use the present perfect tense.

*Example:* Hiç rakı içtin mi? *Have you ever drunk raki?*

**6** Pronunciation: y, z. *Listen to the recording and repeat the following sounds until you feel comfortable with them.*

| y | z |
|---|---|
| ay | az |
| ye | iz |
| oy | oz |
| yi | zil |
| yıl | bizzz |

**7** *Wordsearch. There are ten adjectives (describing words) for you to find.*

| H | A | R | İ | K | A | G | M | O | D |
|---|---|---|---|---|---|---|---|---|---|
| F | B | A | Y | S | T | Ü | A | P | A |
| R | E | H | İ | Z | H | R | S | E | L |
| K | C | A | L | S | K | Ü | M | K | G |
| B | M | T | I | E | T | L | A | P | A |
| E | H | K | B | R | D | T | V | A | L |
| R | M | R | N | T | A | Ü | İ | H | I |
| B | A | İ | H | İ | N | L | F | A | M |
| A | K | I | Ü | M | T | Ü | J | L | K |
| T | R | B | O | Z | U | K | B | I | Ü |

## Role play

### HOW WAS IT?

You are talking with a friend about what you did yesterday. Play your part in the conversation, according to the prompts.

| Friend | Dün ne yaptın? |
| You | *[Say that you went to the beach]* |
| Friend | Deniz nasıldı? Burada yağmur yağdı. |
| You | *[Say the weather and the sea were very good. Ask what he/she did]* |
| Friend | Çalıştım. |

## Mini-test

**◄) CD2, TR 5, 07:02**

Well done. You have completed Unit 10. Now you will be able to talk about the past, past experiences and historical facts. You will also be able to write a postcard and have a short social chat. Give yourself a point for each of these things you can say in Turkish without looking at the book.

1 *Ask someone how their holiday was.*
2 *Explain that your holiday was awful and everything went wrong.*
3 *Say that you have been to a Turkish bath.*
4 *Say that you have not had a mud bath.*
5 *Ask someone if they have ridden a camel.*
6 *Ask someone how the food was.*
7 *Say the hotel was noisy.*
8 *Explain that the shower was out of order.*
9 *Say the weather was sunny every day.*
10 *Say you are very happy here.*

*Points:_____/10*

Congratulations! You have completed *Get started in Turkish* and are now a competent speaker of basic Turkish. You should be able to handle most everyday situations on a visit to Turkey and to communicate with Turkish people sufficiently to make friends. If you would like to extend your ability so that you can develop your confidence, fluency and cope in the language, whether for social or business purposes, why not take your Turkish a step further with the **Complete Turkish** course?

I hope that working your way through *Get started in Turkish* has been both a learning and enjoyable experience. If the course has provided you with what you wanted why don't you contact me and let me know what has worked well for you. If you think that the course could be improved I shall also be pleased to hear from you. All constructive comments and suggestions will be carefully looked at, and incorporated if possible into later editions.

You can contact me through the publishers at: Teach Yourself Books, Hodder Headline Ltd, 338 Euston Road, London NW1 3BH, UK

Good luck!

Asuman Çelen Pollard

# Taking it further

History, culture and literature
- *Harem: The World Behind the Veil*, A. L. Croutier (*1998*).
- *Culture Shock! Turkey: A Guide to Customs and Etiquette*, A. Bayraktaroğlu (*2000*).
- *Atatürk*, Andrew Mango (*2001*).
- *Mevlana – An Anthology of Translations of Mevlana Jalaluddin Rumi*, J. Rumi, K. Helminski (*2000*).
- *Turkish Delights*, P. Scott (*2001*).
- *Süleyman The Magnificent And His Age*, edited M. Kunt, C. Woodhead (*1995*).
- *The Book of Dede Korkut*, G. Lewis (*2001*).
- *Inside the Seraglio*, J. Freely (*2000*).
- *The Tales of Nasreddin Hodja*, Aziz Nesin (*1996*).

Websites
- http://mailgazete.com/turkharita/turkiye.htm (map of Turkey, city by city)
- http://www.gototurkey.co.uk
- http://www.meteor.gov.tr/webler/tahmin/tahminmaster.htm
- http://www.milliyet.com.tr
- www.mymerhaba.com
- http://www.osmanlı.org.tr/
- http://www.paltalk.com/www.sabah.com.tr
- http://www.radikal.com.tr
- http://www.sabah.com.tr
- http://www.turizm.gov.tr
- http://www.Turkishdailynews.com (a good English-language newspaper)
- www.thy.com.tr

# Translations

Dialogue 1 Good evening

| | |
|---|---|
| **Hüseyin** | Good evening, I'm Hüseyin. And you? |
| **Ülkü** | Good evening, I'm Ülkü. |
| **Hüseyin** | How are you, (Mrs) Ülkü? [**Hanım** is used after female names.] |
| **Ülkü** | Thanks, (Mr) Hüseyin. I'm fine. [**Bey** is used after male names.] How are you? |
| **Hüseyin** | I'm fine too. |
| **Hüseyin** | Wine? |
| **Ülkü** | Yes, please. |

Dialogue 2 Hi, how are you?

| | |
|---|---|
| **Bahadır** | Hello Ülkü, how are you? |
| **Ülkü** | I'm fine, thanks. How are you? |
| **Bahadır** | I'm fine too. |
| **Ülkü** | Beer? |
| **Bahadır** | Yes, please. |

Dialogue 3 It's a very nice party

| | |
|---|---|
| **Ülkü** | Good evening, I'm Ülkü. And you? |
| **Banu** | Good evening, I'm Banu. |
| **Ülkü** | How are you, Banu? |
| **Banu** | Thanks, I'm fine. |
| **Ülkü** | It's a very good party, isn't it? |
| **Banu** | Yes, it is. |
| **Ülkü** | Banu, (this is) Doktor Bahadır Bey. |

## Dialogue 4 Goodbye

| Bahadır | Good evening. |
| --- | --- |
| Banu | Good evening, (Mr) Bahadır. |
| Bahadır | How are you, Banu? |
| Banu | Thanks, I'm fine. How are you? |
| Bahadır | I'm fine too. |
| Banu | Goodbye, (Mrs) Ülkü. Goodbye, (Mr) Bahadır. Goodnight. |
| Ülkü and Bahadır | Goodbye, Banu. |

## UNIT 2

### Dialogue 1 A glass of tea, please

| Waiter | How can I help you sir/madam? |
| --- | --- |
| Banu | A glass of tea, please. |
| Waiter | A glass of tea. For you, sir? |
| Şafak | A beer and a bottle of water, please. |
| Waiter | There isn't any beer, sir. |
| Şafak | What is there to drink? |
| Waiter | Here you are, the menu. |
| Şafak | Thanks. One coffee, please. |
| Waiter | Milk? |
| Şafak | Yes, with milk. |
| Waiter | A tea and a coffee with milk? |
| Şafak | Yes, OK. |
| Waiter | Tea, coffee, milk and sugar. |
| Banu and Şafak | Thanks. |
| Waiter | Enjoy your drinks, sir/madam. |
| Şafak | Waiter! |
| Waiter | Yes, sir. |
| Şafak | The bill, please. |
| Şafak | Keep the change. |
| Waiter | Thank you, sir. |

## Dialogue 2 The coffee is very good here

| | |
|---|---|
| **Waiter** | Yes, sir/madam. |
| **Mother** | One sweet coffee. |
| **Father** | A coffee for me too, without sugar. |
| **Mother** | You (my child) sweetheart? [**Yavrum** is a term of endearment used with a child.] Still lemonade? |
| **Child** | No, ayran. |
| **Mother** | OK. |
| **Father** | Two coffees, one with sugar, one without and an ayran. |
| **Waiter** | Yes, sir. |
| **Waiter** | Here you are, your drinks. |
| **Everyone** | Thanks. |
| **Waiter** | Enjoy your drinks. |
| **Mother** | The coffee is good, isn't it? |
| **Father** | Yes, very good. |
| **Child** | I'm hungry. |
| **Mother** | Me too. A toasted sandwich? |
| **Child** | Yes, a toasted cheese sandwich and an ayran. |
| **Father** | Waiter, please. |
| **Waiter** | Yes? |
| **Father** | Three toasted cheese sandwiches and three ayrans. |
| **Mother** | The view is beautiful, isn't it? |
| **Father** | Yes, very beautiful. |

## Dialogue 3 One red wine, please

| | |
|---|---|
| **Şafak** | Good evening. |
| **Waiter** | Good evening, sir/madam. How can I help you? |
| **Banu** | A glass of wine, please. |
| **Şafak** | Red or white? |
| **Banu** | Red, please. |
| **Şafak** | A glass of red wine and a glass of raki, please. |
| **Waiter** | Of course, sir. Snacks? |
| **Şafak** | Yes, nuts and some mixed fruit and white cheese, please. |
| **Waiter** | Of course, sir. |

## UNIT 3

Dialogue 1 Which hotel?

| Ben | Hello. |
|---|---|
| **Clerk** | Hello, sir. |
| **Ben** | Have you got an accommodation list, please? |
| **Clerk** | Hotels, guest houses or campsites? |
| **Ben** | Hotels, please. |
| **Clerk** | Here you are. |
| **Ben** | Which hotel is near by? |
| **Clerk** | Yeşil Ev is very near. |
| **Ben** | How do you spell it, please? |
| **Clerk** | Y–e–ş–i–l E–v. |
| **Ben** | Thanks. |
| **Clerk** | Here is the map, this is the information office and this is 'Yeşil Ev.' |
| **Ben** | Oh! Wonderful, thank you very much. |
| **Ben** | I wonder which building it is. |
| **Laura** | I think it's that building. |
| **Ben** | Yes, that's the building. |

Dialogue 2 Do you have a vacant room?

| Ben | Good evening. |
|---|---|
| **Receptionist** | Good evening, sir, madam. |
| **Ben** | Do you have a vacant room? |
| **Receptionist** | For how many people? |
| **Ben** | Me and my sister, two single rooms. |
| **Receptionist** | Unfortunately, we do not have two single rooms. But we do have one big room with two single beds. |
| **Receptionist** | There is a balcony and a sea view. |
| **Laura** | Is there a bath and hot water? |
| **Receptionist** | Yes. There is both a bath and a shower. There is hot water 24 hours. |
| **Ben** | This room is beautiful, isn't it? |
| **Laura** | Yes. How much? |
| **Receptionist** | $120. |
| **Laura** | Is breakfast included? |

| | |
|---|---|
| **Receptionist** | Yes, it is included. |
| **Laura** | Yes. Fine. |
| **Receptionist** | How many nights? |
| **Ben** | Three nights. |
| **Receptionist** | Passports, please? |
| **Ben** | Of course, here they are. |
| **Receptionist** | Thanks. |
| **Receptionist** | Place of birth … date of birth … nationality … passport number … Room number 24 |
| **Receptionist** | Here is the key. |
| **Laura** | Suitcases? |
| **Receptionist** | Mehmet! |

## Dialogue 3 There are lots of good campsites

| | |
|---|---|
| **Şafak** | Hi. |
| **Clerk** | Good morning. (Good day.) |
| **Şafak** | Have you got a list of hotels and campsites? |
| **Clerk** | Yes. This is the hotel list. |
| **Banu** | The hotels are a bit expensive. |
| **Clerk** | There are lots of good campsites and they are very cheap. Here is the list with the addresses and the telephone numbers. |
| **Banu** | Is there a public phone near here? |
| **Clerk** | Yes. There is one over there. |
| **Şafak** | Have you got any telephone cards? |
| **Clerk** | Yes, 10 million lira. |
| **Şafak** | One card, please. |
| **Kamp** | Hello … 752 52 06 Truva campsite. Yes? |
| **Şafak** | Hello. This is Şafak Gezer. Have you got a tent for two? |
| **Kamp** | Yes, we have. For how many days? |
| **Şafak** | Five days. |
| **Kamp** | Fine. |
| **Şafak** | What facilities does the campsite have? Is there any electricity? |
| **Kamp** | Certainly. There is electricity, water and hot water all the time. There is a restaurant, swimming pool, beach, showers, a play area for children, first aid post and also a public telephone. |

*(Contd)*

| Şafak | Fine. See you tomorrow morning. |
|---|---|
| Kamp | OK. Your name, please? |
| Şafak | My first name is Şafak, surname Gezer. |
| Kamp | Pardon? How do you spell it? |
| Şafak | Ş – a – f – a – k  G – e – z – e – r. |

Dialogue 4 This is your tent

| Ayşegül | I'm Ayşegül. Welcome. |
|---|---|
| Banu | I'm Banu. This is Şafak. |
| Banu and Şafak | Hoş bulduk. (The set reply to 'Welcome'.) |
| Ayşegül | How are you? |
| Banu | We're fine, thanks. How are you? |
| Ayşegül | Very busy. |
| Ayşegül | This is your tent, here is the car park, this is the telephone, that (place) is the swimming pool and that is the restaurant, these are the toilets, those are the showers, this is the first aid post. |
| Ayşegül | And that is our dog, 'Karabaş'. |

### UNIT 4

Dialogue 1 Ordering breakfast

| Laura | Breakfast in the garden is very pleasant. |
|---|---|
| Ben | Yes. What beautiful weather! |
| Waiter | Good morning, sir, madam. |
| Ben | Good morning. We'd like Turkish breakfast, please. |
| Waiter | Of course, sir. |
| Laura | What is there for breakfast? |
| Waiter | Butter, honey, marmalade, jam, cheese, olives, sausages. |
| Ben | Have you got any Turkish sausages? |
| Waiter | We do, sir. We also have salami, tomatoes, cucumber, pepper. And fresh bread of course. |
| Ben | Do you have tea? |
| Waiter | Of course. |
| Laura | Thanks. |
| Laura | The tea is delicious (very tasty). |

| Waiter | Enjoy your meal. |
|--------|------------------|
| Waiter | Egg? |
| Laura | No, thanks. |
| Ben | Yes, soft boiled for me, please. |
| Waiter | Of course, sir. |
| Ben | The Turkish spicy sausage is very tasty. |
| Laura | Isn't there any salt? |
| Ben | Here it is on the table, dear. |
| Waiter | Here is the toast. Enjoy your meal. Anything else? |
| Laura | No, thanks. |

## Dialogue 2 At a fish restaurant

| Ahmet | Waiter, please. |
|-------|-----------------|
| Waiter | Yes, sir. |
| Ahmet | What wines do you suggest (are there)? |
| Waiter | Çankaya and Kutman are very good. |
| Yeşim | Çankaya, please. |
| Asuman | For me white Çankaya, please. |
| Ahmet | What about you, Vanessa? |
| Vanessa | (Sour) cherry juice, please. |
| Ahmet | One large, white Çankaya, one small rakı, one (sour) cherry juice. |
| Waiter | Straight away, sir. |
| Ahmet | And a bottle of water. |
| Ahmet | For me fried turbot and mixed salad, please. |
| Asuman | For me steamed bass and green salad, please. |
| Vanessa | For me fried mullet with sliced tomatoes, please. |
| Yeşim | For me grilled blue fish and rocket, please. |
| Waiter | Of course, sir. |
| Ahmet | Waiter, the bill, please. |
| Waiter | Here you are, the bill. |
| Ahmet | Thanks. Keep the change. |
| Waiter | Thank you, sir. |
| Ahmet | Where is the taxi? |
| Waiter | Here, on the right, sir. |

## Dialogue 3 At a *köfte* restaurant

| | |
|---|---|
| **Ben** | The pudding shop or the meatball restaurant? |
| **Laura** | Noon, meatball restaurant; evening, pudding shop. |
| **Ben** | OK. Come on. |
| **Ben** | Have you got meatballs? |
| **Waiter** | Yes, sir. How many portions? |
| **Laura** | Two portions, with cooked rice. |
| **Waiter** | Of course, madam. |
| **Laura to Ben** | Are you drinking beer, or ayran? |
| **Ben** | Is the beer cold? |
| **Waiter** | Yes, very cold. |
| **Ben** | For me, a cold beer. |
| **Laura** | And for me, chilled ayran. |
| **Waiter** | Anything else? (lit. What else?) |
| **Ben** | Have you got white bean salad? |
| **Waiter** | Yes, we have, sir. |
| **Ben** | I'll have the bean salad (lit. For me). |
| **Laura** | And for me a mixed salad. |
| **Waiter** | Enjoy your meals. |
| **Ben and Laura** | Thanks. |
| **Laura** | The meatballs are very very tasty, aren't they? |
| **Ben** | Yes, they are. |

### UNIT 5

Dialogue 1 At the airport

| | |
|---|---|
| **Bahadır** | Excuse me, where is the bank, please? [Using **siz** – polite – form.] |
| **Passer-by** | I am sorry. I don't know. Ask at the information desk. The information office is over there. |
| **Bahadır** | Thank you very much. |
| **Ülkü** | Excuse me, where is the bank, please? |
| **Clerk** | Go straight ahead, pass passport control and after customs turn right, go straight ahead again, it is on the left. |
| **Ülkü** | Ah, thank you very much. Where are the nearest toilets, please? |

184

| Clerk | Go straight ahead: there are two toilets before passport control, one on the right and one on the left. After passport control there are two more toilets. |
| --- | --- |
| Bahadır | Thank you very much. |
| Clerk | Not at all. |
| Bahadır | Where are the taxis, please? |
| Clerk | Go out of the door, cross the road, and they are there. |
| Driver | Where to, sir, madam? |
| Bahadır | Sultan Ahmet, please. Is Sultan Ahmet far? |
| Driver | Quite – 20 kilometres, approximately 40 minutes. |

## Dialogue 2 In Sultan Ahmet Square

| Ülkü | Excuse me, where is the Topkapı Museum, please? |
| --- | --- |
| Passer-by | Pardon? |
| Ülkü | Where is the Topkapı Museum, please? |
| Passer-by | I am sorry, I don't know. |
| Ülkü | Excuse me, where is the Topkapı, please? |
| Passer-by | Go straight on, turn right at the corner and it is right opposite you. |
| Ülkü | When are the museums open? |
| Passer-by | From 9 to 5 o'clock. |
| Ülkü | Thanks. |
| Passer-by | Not at all. |
| Bahadır | Two tickets, please. |
| Receptionist | Here you are. You can leave your bags here. |
| Bahadır | Thanks. Where is the Harem? |
| Receptionist | Go straight ahead. There are signs over there. |

## Dialogue 3 Blue Cruise

| Ülkü | Excuse me, are there Blue Cruises from Bodrum? |
| --- | --- |
| Clerk | Yes, there are. |
| Ülkü | Where do they go? (lit. Where to?) |
| Clerk | One goes from Bodrum to Ören, from Ören to Körmen, then from Körmen back to Bodrum. A second goes from Bodrum to Karaada, from Karaada to Cedre, from Cedre to Ballısu, from Ballısu to Bodrum. |

*(Contd)*

| Ülkü | Aaa! The first one sounds good. Where is the port? |
| Clerk | On the coast, in the centre (of the coast). |
| Ülkü | Thanks. |
| Clerk | Not at all. |

## UNIT 6

### Dialogue 1 At a travel agency

| Anne | What places are hot in Turkey? |
| Travel agent | The south is very hot in August and July. It's warm in spring, hot in June. |
| Anne | We like it very hot. We don't like rain. And (the) children like the sea and sand. |
| Travel agent | In July Alanya is 26°C, Antalya 28°C, Bodrum 27°C, Fethiye 27°C, Istanbul 23°C. In July, Antalya is the hottest. There is no rain in the summer in the south. The weather is sunny all the time. In the spring mostly there are spring rains and later (there is) a rainbow. In the countryside there is a variety of beautiful wild flowers. |
| Anne | Yes. Which days are there flights (lit. aeroplanes) to Antalya? |
| Travel agent | Monday, Wednesday, Friday there is a flight a day. Saturdays and Sundays there are two aeroplanes a day. |
| Anne | Are there seats Sunday 5th May? |
| Travel agent | Yes, there are. For how many people? |

### Dialogue 2 We like different things

| Cem | Gökhan and I like football, basketball, volleyball and tennis. |
| Gökhan | But we like football most. |
| Vanessa | We like the sea, dancing and day trips. What a nice day without rain and wind. |

| | |
|---|---|
| **Cem** | My parents like day trips, especially visiting ruins. Eating in restaurants is very enjoyable. Don't stand there, there is a lot of sun, come into the shade. Waiter, a chocolate ice cream for me. |
| **Vanessa** | Plain ice cream for me. |
| **Cem** | Fruit flavoured for me. |
| **Çiğdem** | Lemon flavoured for me. |
| **Gökhan** | Mixed for me. |
| **Waiter** | OK, sir/madam. |

Reading comprehension
**Seasons and climate in Turkey**

There are four seasons in Turkey: spring, summer, autumn and winter. The climate is different (in) each season.

In the Mediterranean, Aegean and Marmara regions summers are hot and dry, winters are warm and wet (rainy). There is snow on the very high mountains. The coasts are warmer in Turkey. In Istanbul and Marmara the average temperature (in winter) is 4°C, and in summer 27°C.

In the Black Sea region summers are hot. Winters are cooler in the south. Sometimes it is frosty and there is snow in every season. The average temperature in summer is 23°C and in winter 7°C. The most rainfall falls in Rize.

In Central Anatolia the difference in temperature between day and night is very great. Summers are less hot (cooler). In the summer the average temperature is 23°C, in winter −2°C. In the south-east of Anatolia summers are very hot, winters are less cold (warm).

In the south while you are on the sand (beach) there is snow on the Taurus Mountains.

Exercise 3
Ali is taller than Betül, but Ali is shorter than Can. Dursun is shorter than Can. Who is the shortest?

## UNIT 7

### Dialogue 1 Where are you from?

| | |
|---|---|
| **Woman** | Hello. |
| **Man** | Hello. |
| **Woman** | Where are you from? |
| **Man** | I'm from Leeds. Where are you from? |
| **Woman** | I'm German. From Bonn. |
| **Man** | I'm English but my wife (partner) is Turkish, from Istanbul. This book is for learning Turkish, *Teach Yourself Turkish*. I speak Turkish and German, French, Spanish, Italian, and a little Bulgarian. I like Turkish people, (the) language and Turkey very much. Our daughter Vanessa also speaks (lit. knows) Turkish. |
| **Woman** | Really? Very interesting. |
| **Man** | We love going (lit. It's very enjoyable to go) to Turkey for holidays. We are very lucky, Turks are very friendly and honest, aren't they? |
| **Woman** | Yes, you're right. |

### Dialogue 2 Are you Turkish?

| | |
|---|---|
| **Susie** | Hello, I'm Susie. And you? |
| **Ayda** | I'm Ayda. |
| **Susie** | Are you Turkish? |
| **Ayda** | Yes. And you? Are you American? |
| **Susie** | No. I'm English. I'm from London. |
| **Ayda** | Are you a model? |
| **Susie** | No, I'm a student. And you? |
| **Ayda** | I'm a doctor. |
| **Susie** | You must be (lit. are) very clever. |
| **Ayda** | I'm not very clever but I'm very hard working. |
| **Susie** | Are you married? |
| **Ayda** | No, I'm engaged. You? |
| **Susie** | I'm single, I'm only 23 years old. Is your fiancé handsome? |
| **Ayda** | Cem is tall, dark, black-haired, dark-brown eyed (lit. black eyed), and of course in my opinion very handsome. He is very clever and a very good person. He is an engineer and we're very good friends. |

## Dialogue 3 How are you?

| Ülkü | Hello! |
|------|--------|
| **Gonca** | Hello. Ülkü, is that you? |
| **Ülkü** | Yes, it's me. (Sister) Gonca, is that you? |
| **Gonca** | Yes, it's me, dear. How are you? |
| **Ülkü** | Thank you, I am fine. How are you? |
| **Gonca** | I'm fine. |

## Dialogue 4 Hello?

| **Banu** | Hello? |
|----------|--------|
| **Şafak** | Hello, Banuş, this is Şafak. |
| **Banu** | Hello, Şaf. How are you? |
| **Şafak** | I'm fine. |

## UNIT 8

### Dialogue 1 Planning the day

| **Ben** | What are we doing today? |
|---------|--------------------------|
| **Laura** | I don't know. I want to buy presents. |
| **Ben** | And I want to buy a leather jacket, shoes and Turkish delight. |
| **Laura** | Shall we go to the Grand Bazaar. Blouse, bag, spices, shoes and things for presents. |
| **Ben** | Where shall we go? |
| **Laura** | I want to go to the Grand Bazaar and Taksim. |
| **Ben** | OK. Let's go. |

### Dialogue 2 Buying bags

| **Laura** | Hello. |
|-----------|--------|
| **Salesperson** | Good day. Yes, madam. |
| **Laura** | How much are the leather bags? |
| **Salesperson** | The big one is 15, the medium-sized one is 10 and the small one 5 million lira. |

*(Contd)*

| Laura | That medium-sized one, please. 10 million is very expensive, is 4 million OK? |
|---|---|
| Salesperson | What colour? |
| Laura | Black, please. |
| Salesperson | Here you are. For you, 5 million lira. |
| Laura | OK. |
| Salesperson | Enjoy using it. (lit. use it in happy days.) |
| Laura | Thank you. |

## Dialogue 3 Buying spices

| Stallholder | How can I help you? |
|---|---|
| Laura | We want to buy spices. |
| Stallholder | What kinds would you like to buy? |
| Laura | Spices for meatballs, cumin, sumac and such like. |
| Stallholder | How much? |
| Laura | In 100 gram packets. |
| Stallholder | Would you like something else? |
| Ben | What's this? |
| Stallholder | Sultan's medicated taffy. |
| Ben | What is Sultan's medicated taffy really? |
| Stallholder | It is an aphrodisiac. |
| Ben | I don't need it. I don't want it. (laughter) I'd like some dried fruit. |
| Stallholder | How much? |
| Ben | Half a kilo of apricots, half a kilo of figs. Have you got any hazelnuts. Are they good? |
| Ben | Yes! Half a kilo of mixed nuts, please. That's all. How much? |
| Stallholder | 10 million. Very cheap. (lit. cheaper than water.) |

## Dialogue 4 Buying Turkish delight

| Laura | Where is the Haci Bekir Turkish delight shop, please? |
|---|---|
| Stallholder | Go straight ahead, turn right, it's on the left. |
| Laura | Thanks. |
| Stallholder | Not at all. |
| Shop assistant | How can I help you, madam? |

| Laura | We would like to buy some Turkish delight, how much is it? |
|---|---|
| Shop assistant | What kind? |
| Ben | What are there? |
| Shop assistant | This is mint flavoured, this is rose, this is plain, and this is nutty. Here you are. Let's 'eat sweet, talk sweet'. When we eat sweets we always say this. |
| Laura and Ben | Mmmm. |
| Shop assistant | Half a kilo mixed – 3 million liras. |
| Laura | Four half-kilo boxes of mixed, please. |
| Ben | Is the shop new? |
| Shop assistant | No, we have been making Turkish delight since 1777. Our Turkish delight is very fresh. We get fresh Turkish delight every day. Today we sell Turkish delight all over the world. We make different kinds every week. |
| Ben | How do you make it? |
| Shop assistant | We put sugar, nuts and … but the recipe is our secret. |
| Ben | Do you sell Turkish delight mostly to tourists? |
| Shop assistant | No, we Turks give Turkish delight as a present when we visit each other on special days. |

Dialogue 5 Buying clothes

| Shop assistant | Yes, madam. How can I help you? |
|---|---|
| Laura | I'm looking for a blouse. |
| Shop assistant | What size? |
| Laura | 38. |
| Shop assistant | Here you are. This blouse is very nice. |
| Laura | Green doesn't suit me. Do you have this in blue or white? |
| Shop assistant | Here you are. One blue, one white, size 38. |
| Laura | How much is it? |
| Shop assistant | 58 million. |
| Laura | I would like to try them on. |
| Shop assistant | Of course. |
| | *(Contd)* |

| Laura | I'll take this one. How much is it? |
| --- | --- |
| **Shop assistant** | 58 million. |
| Laura | That's very expensive. I'll give you 40 million. |
| **Shop assistant** | We do not haggle here. To you, 50 million lira. |
| Laura | OK, I'll take it. (I'll buy it.) |

## Picture dictation

Suzan is sitting at a seaside café. She is looking at the people on the beach and in the sea, while drinking fruit juice. Three children are buying ice-cream. A couple are lying on the sand. The woman is wearing a hat and a bikini, and is reading a book. The man is wearing glasses and shorts, looking at the sea. In the sea there are a rowing boat and a sailing boat. There are seven people swimming.

### UNIT 9

Dialogue 1 What shall we do at the weekend?

| Şafak | What shall we do at the weekend? |
| --- | --- |
| Banu | Shall we go to the theatre? There's a very good play on at (the) Kenterler. |
| Şafak | What's on? |
| Banu | Let's have a look. I think Hep Aşk Vardı (There has always been Love) is on. |
| Şafak | Hep Aşk Vardı is on at 8.30. |
| Banu | Yes, wonderful. But I want to go to the cinema to see Hamam as well. |
| Şafak | So do I. |
| Banu | Should I give the Kenter a ring first? |
| Şafak | Yes, let's call them. |
| Şafak | What time is it? |
| Banu | Half past twelve. It's lunchtime. |
| Şafak | Let's call them again at half past one. |
| Banu | OK. |

## Dialogue 2 Booking seats at the theatre

| | |
|---|---|
| **Receptionist** | How can I help you? 0212 246 35 89, the Kenter Theatre. |
| **Şafak** | Good day. I would like to book two seats for Hep Aşk Vardı for this Sunday. |
| **Receptionist** | Good day, madam. Unfortunately there are no tickets for this Sunday but there are seats for the following Sunday. |
| **Şafak** | What are the prices? |
| **Receptionist** | Adult 15 million lira, student 5 million lira, concessions (lit. teacher and retired) 12 million. |
| **Şafak** | Two tickets, one adult and one student, please. |
| **Receptionist** | How are you paying? By card? |
| **Şafak** | Yes. |
| **Receptionist** | Card number, please? |
| **Şafak** | 1234 1234 1234 1234. |

## Dialogue 3 Choosing a film to watch

| | |
|---|---|
| **Şafak** | Are we going to the cinema this evening? |
| **Banu** | Let's see Hamam. |
| **Şafak** | Let's have a look at which films are on at the cinemas. |
| **Banu** | Vampires is on at (the) ABC cinema. |
| **Şafak** | I don't want to see a horror film. |
| **Banu** | Şaban is on at the Hisar. |
| **Şafak** | Isn't it a comedy? |
| **Banu** | Yes, but I want to see Hamam. |
| **Şafak** | What time? |
| **Banu** | It's on at five, seven and nine. |
| **Şafak** | Shall we go to the 7 o'clock one? |
| **Banu** | OK. Let's go now. |
| **Şafak** | The car has broken down. Are we going by dolmuş (shared taxi) or by bus? The bus is cheaper but the dolmuş is more comfortable. |
| **Banu** | It doesn't matter. |
| **Şafak** | Let's go by bus. |

## Dialogue 4 Buying bus tickets

| | |
|---|---|
| **Şafak** | Two tickets to Taksim. |
| **Banu** | Buy them for the return journey as well. |
| **Şafak** | Four tickets, please. |
| **Clerk** | 4 million lira. |
| **Şafak** | Here you are. |
| **Clerk** | Have you got any change? |
| **Şafak** | No, I haven't. |
| **Clerk** | Here you are. 6 million lira. |

## Exercise 8
**Boat trips on the Bosporus**

Our boat leaves Eminönü every day at 10.35, 12.00 and 13.35.
The special Bosporus boat trip stops at the ports in this order:
Barbaros, Hayrettin, Paşa, Kanlıca, Emirgan, Yeniköy, Sarıyer,
Rumeli Kavağı; Anadolu Kavağı is the last port. Our boats stop
(each time) at Anadolu Kavağı for two hours. There are very good
fish restaurants there. And, on Saturdays, Sundays and Bayram
days at 10.35 and 13.35 we have live music on the boat.

## *UNIT 10*

### Dialogue 1 The holiday was wonderful!

| | |
|---|---|
| **Presenter** | Good day, (Ms) Yasemin. |
| **Yasemin** | Good day. Please call me Yasemin. |
| **Presenter** | How was your holiday? (lit. How has your holiday been?) |
| **Yasemin** | It was wonderful. It was sunny every day. It didn't rain all week. |
| **Presenter** | What about the sea? |
| **Yasemin** | It was calm and very blue. The water was warm. Every day we swam, we rowed in a rowing boat and we walked on the sand. |
| **Presenter** | And the hotel, what was the hotel like? |
| **Yasemin** | It was very comfortable, the room had a view of the sea and the service was very good. |

| Presenter | And the food? |
| --- | --- |
| Yasemin | Ah, the dishes were wonderful. I'm learning how to cook Turkish dishes. The mixed salad (lit. Shepherd's salad) is very good for you and very tasty. Yesterday, I made Turkish coffee and my friend read the coffee cup (lit. read fortunes). Everything was very good, I've already booked my room for my next holiday. I want to buy a house here. |

## Dialogue 2 The holiday was a disaster!

| Presenter | How was your holiday? |
| --- | --- |
| Tourist | Terrible. Absolutely everything went wrong (lit. was very bad). |
| Presenter | What was the weather like? |
| Tourist | At first it was too hot, later it was windy and rainy. |
| Presenter | What about the sea? |
| Tourist | It was terrible. The sea was cold and very rough. |
| Presenter | The hotel? Where did you stay? What was the hotel like? |
| Tourist | The hotel was very noisy. There was a building site in front of us, it blocked the whole view. An open-air disco was very near and the music was very loud. The bed was hard, the shower was broken. |
| Presenter | Did you like the food? |
| Tourist | Oh, the food was terrible, it was tasteless. The vegetables and fruit were not fresh. The forks and knives were not clean (at all). The service was very slow. Everything was very expensive and very bad. My girlfriend left me. My holiday was a disaster. |
| Tourist | Ah! I've been stung! |

Reading comprehension: the postcard

Dear Mum,

I'm having a wonderful holiday. I've been eating simit every morning. I've ridden a camel three times. I haven't drunk any raki yet.

The weather has been sunny every day. We stayed on the island for a week, now we are in Istanbul. We went to Topkapi yesterday but we haven't visited St. Sophia yet. I bought a kilo of Turkish delight for you. I've been learning backgammon for ten days. I'm very happy. See you soon. With (my) love.

## Listening comprehension: guess who?

He was born on 8 January 1935 in Mississippi, in Tupel.
He made his first record in 1954.
He signed a contract with RCA in 1955.
He was on TV for the first time in 1956.
He did his military service in Germany in 1958.
He married Priscilla Beaulieu in 1967.
Lisa Marie was born in 1968.
He got divorced in 1973.
He gave 300 concerts between 1970–7.
He died on 16 August 1977 in Memphis, Tennessee.
He made more than 900 records.
He acted in more than 31 musicals.
He had three Grammy awards, 37 gold and 26 platinum records.
He was the king of rock'n'roll.

## Reading comprehension: Turkish history

The Turks came to Anatolia from Central Asia. Seljuk Turks entered Anatolia through Manzikert (Malazgirt) in 1071 and spread westward. Osman Bey got as far as Bursa. Later Bursa became the Ottomans' capital. In 1453 the Conqueror Sultan Mehmet took Constantinople and made it the Ottomans' capital. The Ottoman Empire extended as far as Vienna in the centre of Europe. The Ottomans built beautiful mosques, bridges and inns in Europe and Anatolia. After the First World War the British, French, Italian and Greeks invaded Turkey. Atatürk won the War of Independence. Turkey became a Republic. Ankara became the capital city. Atatürk became the first President of the Republic and carried out many reforms.

# Transcripts

This section contains the transcripts of all the listening exercises in the book.

### UNIT 1
**Mini-test**
**1** Merhaba. **2** Hoşça kal. Hoşça kalın. **3** İyi geceler. **4** Nasılsınız?
**5** Nasılsın? **6** Teşekkürler. Sağol. **7** See the **Alphabet and pronunciation**
section in the **Introduction. 8** See Unit 1, Numbers. **9** Ben [*your name*].
**10** İyiyim. Teşekkürler. Siz nasılsınız?

### UNIT 2
**Exercise 2**
**a** Bira? **b** Çay? **c** Nescafé? **d** Ayran? **e** Şarap?

**Exercise 3**

| | |
|---|---|
| **a** çay | çaylar |
| **b** rakı | rakılar |
| **c** tost | tostlar |
| **d** teşekkür | teşekkürler |
| **e** bira | biralar |
| **f** içecek | içecekler |

**Mini-test**
**1** Garson. **2** Bir şekerli kahve, lütfen *or* Bir şekersiz kahve, lütfen *or* Bir
sade kahve, lütfen. **3** Sütlü Nescafé, lütfen. **4** Bir bardak çay, lütfen. **5** Bir
bardak kırmızı ve bir bardak beyaz şarap, lütfen. **6** Çerez, lütfen. **7** Afiyet
olsun. **8** Hesap, lütfen. **9** Üstü kalsın. **10** Elli, yetmiş, doksan, yüz.

### UNIT 3
**Exercise 1**
**a** İkiyüzkırkaltı elli otuzbeş. **b** İkiyüzaltmışiki sıfırbir otuzyedi.
**c** Altıyüzondört onüç otuzüç. **d** Yediyüzonyedi yirmiiki yirmidört.
**e** Sekizyüzdoksanaltı otuzaltı otuzaltı. **f** Üçyüzonbir kırksekiz elliyedi.

**Number and letter dictation**
This exercise is not in the book.

1 A 2 G 3 J 4 Ö 5 R 6 U 7 Ş 8 O 9 I 10 C 11 Ç 12 İ 13 K 14 S
15 Y 16 V 17 Ü 18 P 19 Ğ 20 E

## Mini-test

**1** Duşlu bir oda, lütfen. **2** Boş oda var mı? **3** Kahvaltı dahil mi? **4** ... nasıl yazılır? **5** Bu, şu, o. **6** Ben, sen, o, biz, siz, onlar. **7** İlk yardım. **8** Hoş geldin or hoş geldiniz. **9** Burası and şurası. **10** telefon, elektrik, su, sıcak su, restoran, yüzme havuzu, plaj, duş, çocuk oyun parkı, ilk yardım

### UNIT 4
## Mini-test

**1** Bir kahve, tereyağı, ekmek, sosis ve yumurta, lütfen. **2** Balik tava ve yeşil salata, lütfen. **3** Bir büyük beyaz şarap, lütfen. **4** İki porsiyon köfte ve pilav, lütfen. **5** Bira soğuk mu? **6** Vişne suyu lütfen. **7** Taksiler nerede? **8** Bir karışık salata, lütfen. **9** İki porsiyon pilav, lütfen. **10** Üstü kalsın.

### UNIT 5
## Exercise 5

**a** İstanbul'dan Ankara'ya 454 km. **b** İstanbul'dan Bodrum'a 815 km. **c** İstanbul'dan Çanakkale'ye 325 km. **d** İstanbul'dan Safranbolu'ya 404 km. **e** İstanbul'dan Pamukkale'ye 666 km. **f** İstanbul'dan Marmaris'e 814 km. **g** İstanbul'dan Göreme'ye 750 km. **h** İstanbul'dan İzmir'e 565 km. **i** İstanbul'dan Trabzon'a 1,079 km. **j** İstanbul'dan Fethiye'ye 926 km.

## Exercise 7

**a** Birinci gün: Marmaris'ten – Çiftlik'e. **b** İkinci gün: Çiftlik'ten – Bozukkale'ye. **c** Üçüncü gün: Bozukkale'den – Aktur'a ve Datça'ya. **d** Dördüncü gün: Datça'dan – Knidos'a. **e** Beşinci gün: Knidos'tan – Bodrum'a.

## Mini-test

**1** Afedersiniz, banka nerede acaba? **2** Afedersiniz, taksiler nerede acaba? **3** Düz gidin ve köşeden sağa dönün, lütfen. **4** Müze ne zaman açık? **5** iki bilet, lütfen. **6** Sultan Ahmet'e metro var mı? **7** İki bilet, lütfen? **8** Bodrum'dan Mavi Yolculuk var mı? **9** Liman nerede? **10** İstanbul'dan Ankara'ya kaç kilometre?

### UNIT 6

**1 a** İzmir nerede? Batıda. **b** İstanbul nerede? Kuzey batıda. **c** Ankara nerede? Ortada. **d** Van nerede? Doğuda. **e** Bodrum nerede? Güney batıda. **f** Samsun nerede? Kuzeyde. **g** Mersin nerede? Güneyde. **h** Alanya nerede? Güneyde. **i** Marmaris nerede? Güney batıda.

## Mini-test

**1** Yazın hiç yağmur yok. **2** İlkbaharda yağmur var/yağmurlu. **3** Temmuz, şubattan (daha) sıcaktır. **4** En çok dans etmeyi (*to dance*) ve voleybolu seviyorum. **5** Bodrum'a hangi günler uçak var? **6** Bir meyveli dondurma, lütfen. **7** Güneş seviyoruz *or* güneşi seviyoruz. **8** Bodrum'a hangi günler uçak var? **9** İstanbul, Ankara ve İzmir'den daha büyük *or* büyüktür. **10** Gölgeye gel.

## UNIT 7
### Exercise 4

**a** Ben İstanbullu, yum.
İstanbul'un neresinden?
Ataköy.
**b** Bu tatilde Türkiye'deyiz.
Türkiye'nin neresinde?
Güneyde, Alanya'da.
**c** Bu Türkçe'de ne demek?
Harita demek.
**d** Bu İngilizce'de ne demek?
Map demek.
**e** Siz manken misiniz?
Hayır, sekreterim. Ya siz?
Ben öğrenciyim.

**f** Ben 45 yaşındayım.
Ben 23 yaşındayım.
**g** Bu telefon numaram 595 33 22.
Bu da benim telefon
numaram 454 78 81.
Teşekkürler.
**h** Ben İngilizim.
Gerçekten mi?
Evet, Londralı, yım.
**i** Ben bekarım. Ya, siz?
Ben evliyim. Eşim orada.
**j** Tarkan Alman mı?
Hayır, Türk.

### Exercise 6

▶ Merhaba. Adım Bülent. Ben Türküm. Doktorum. İzmirli, yim.
▶ Manken. Amerikalı. Bekar. Adı Lucy. 24 yaşında.
▶ Trish Webb. Nerelisiniz Trish Hanım?
İngilizim. Birmingham'lıyım.
Evli misiniz?
Hayır, bekarım.
Öğretmensiniz, değil mi?
Evet, öğretmenim.
▶ Phillipe. Fransız. Bekar. Futbolcu. 21 yaşında. Parisli.
▶ Merhaba. Adım Ülkü Gezer. Fotoğrafçıyım. Türküm. Evliyim.
İstanbullu, yum. 43 yaşındayım.
▶ Merhaba, June Hanım.
Merhaba.
Sekreter misiniz?
Hayır, hostesim.
Amerikalı mısınız?

Hayır, Avustralyalı, yım. Sidney'liyim.
Evli misiniz?
Evet, evliyim. Eşim Türk.

## Mini-test
**1** Amerikalı mısınız? (= 'Are you American?') **2** Kaç yaşındasınız?
**3** Milliyetiniz ne? **4** Evliyim. **5** Bekar mısınız? **6** Siz (Hanım. Bey); sen.
**7** Sen İngilizsin, değil mi? *or* siz İngilizsiniz, değil mi? **8** Türk müsün?
*or* Türk müsünüz? **9** Bu Türkçe'de ne demek? **10** Türk müsün? *or* Türk
müsünüz?

## UNIT 8
### Exercise 2

Buyrun, efendim.
Bir pantolon bakıyorum.
Kaç beden?
40.
Buyrun, bu pantolon çok güzel.
Kahverengi bana yakışmıyor. Siyah veya gri var mı?
Buyrun bir siyah, bir gri. 40 beden.
Kaç lira?
80 milyon.
Denemek istiyorum, lütfen.
Tabii.

## Mini-test
**1** 40 beden, mavi bir ceket, istiyorum, lütfen. **2** Naneli lokum, lütfen.
**3** Yarım kilo kuruyemiş, lütfen. **4** Bir paket kimyon, lütfen. **5** Şarap
içmiyorum. **6** 41 numara, ayakkabı bakıyorum/istiyorum, lütfen. **7** Mavi
pantolon, bakıyorum/Mavi pantolon, istiyorum, lütfen. **8** Kırmızı sana *or*
size yakışmıyor. **9** Mavi bana yakışıyor. **10** Denemek istiyorum.

## UNIT 9
### Exercise 1

| Yeşim | Bu akşam ne yapalım? |
|-------|----------------------|
| Ahmet | Tiyatroya gidelim. |
| Yeşim | Çok pahalı. |
| Ahmet | Sinemaya gidelim mi? |

## Exercise 2

4 ağustos pazartesi günü saat 8'de Banu'yla tiyatroya gidiyorum.
6 ağustos çarşamba günü saat bir buçukta Gonca'yla öğle yemeği yiyoruz.
8 ağustos cuma günü Yeşim ve Ahmet'le Boğaz gezisi yapıyoruz.
9 ağustos cumartesi günü saat ikide Çemberlitaş Hamamı, na gidiyorum.
10 ağustos pazar günü Vanessa ile Karagöz ve Hacivat'a gidiyoruz.

## Exercise 4

a on iki otuz; yarım b on beş on beş; üçü çeyrek geçiyor c sekiz elli;
dokuza on var d dört yirmi beş; dördü yirmi beş geçiyor e on sekiz
kırkbeş; yediye çeyrek var f dokuz on; dokuzu on geçiyor g yirmi dört;
gece yarısı – on iki h on on; onu on geçiyor i beş beş; beşi beş geçiyor
j on üç iki; biri iki geçiyor

## Mini-test

1 Tiyatroya gidelim mi, iyi bir oyun var. 2 İstanbul'a iki gidiş dönüş bileti,
lütfen. 3 Üçü çeyrek geçiyor. 4 Saat kaç? 5 Bu pazar için bir bilet, lütfen.
6 Sinemalarda hangi filmler var? 7 Otobüs veya dolmuşla gitmek istiyorum.
8 Dokümanter filmler seviyorum. 9 Sen ne tür filmler seviyorsun? or Siz
ne tür filmler seviyorsunuz? 10 Burası çok güneşli, gölgede oturalım.

## UNIT 10

### Guess who?

8 Ocak 1935'te Mississippi, Tupel'de doğdu.
1954'te ilk kez plak yaptı.
1955'te RCA ile anlaştı.
1956'da ilk kez TV'ye çıktı.
1958'de askerliğini Almanya'da yaptı.
1967'de Priscilla Beaulieu ile evlendi.
1968'de Lisa Marie doğdu.
1973'te boşandı.
1970–77 arası 300 konser verdi.
16 Ağustos 1977'de Tennessee Memphis'te öldü.

900'den fazla plak yaptı.
31'den fazla müzikalde oynadı.
3 Grammy ödülü, 37 altın, 26 platin plak ödülü aldı.
Rock'n'roll kralıydı.

## Exercise 1
### Happy holidaymaker

| | |
|---|---|
| **You** | İyi günler. |
| **Tourist** | İyi günler. |
| **You** | Tatiliniz nasıldı? |
| **Tourist** | Çok iyiydi. |
| **You** | Hava nasıldı? |
| **Tourist** | Her gün güneşliydi. |
| **You** | Otel nasıldı? |
| **Tourist** | Çok rahattı, oda deniz manzaralıydı. |
| **You** | Yemekler nasıldı? |
| **Tourist** | Yemekler harikaydı. |

### Unhappy holidaymaker

| | |
|---|---|
| **You** | İyi günler. |
| **Tourist** | İyi günler. |
| **You** | Tatiliniz nasıldı? |
| **Tourist** | Çok kötüydü. |
| **You** | Hava nasıldı? |
| **Tourist** | Çok rüzgarlı ve yağmurluydu. |
| **You** | Otel nasıldı? |
| **Tourist** | Otel çok gürültülüydü. |
| **You** | Yemekler nasıldı? |
| **Tourist** | Yemekler, berbattı, lezzetsizdi. |

### Mini-test
**1** Tatilin(iz) nasıldı? **2** Berbattı. Her şey çok kötüydü. **3** Hamama gittim. **4** Çamur banyosu yapmadım. **5** Hiç deveye bindin mi? **6** Yemekler nasıldı? **7** Otel gürültülüydü. **8** Duş bozuktu. **9** Hava her gün güneşliydi. **10** Ben burada çok mutluyum.

# Key to the exercises

## UNIT 1 GREETINGS
**Dialogue 1**
Hayır. Bey.

**Dialogue 2**
**1** İyi. **2** İyi.

**Dialogue 3**
Çok güzel.

**Dialogue 4**
İyi.

**Practice**
**1 a** Merhaba. Selam. **b** Merhaba. Selam. İyi günler. **c** İyi günler.
Günaydın. **2** İyi geceler. **3** Hoşça kal/Hoşça kalın. **4** Hoşça kal/
Hoşça kalın/Güle güle. **5 a** Merhaba **b** ben. **6** e, c, b, d, a, f.
**7 a** 5, **b** 10, **c** 1, **d** 9, **e** 3, **f** 7, **g** 4, **h** 2, **i** 6, **j** 8, **k** 0. **8 a** yedi, **b** iki,
**c** altı, **d** dokuz, **e** sekiz, **f** iki, **g** üç, **h** dokuz, **i** sekiz **10** merhaba,
bir, nasılsın, hanım, bey, iki, sen, siz, iyiyim, on

**Mini-test**
**1** Merhaba. **2** Hoşça kal. Hoşça kalın. **3** İyi geceler. **4** Nasılsınız?
**5** Nasılsın? **6** Teşekkürler. Sağol. **7** See the **Alphabet and
pronunciation** section in the **Introduction**. **8** See Unit 1, Numbers.
**9** Ben [*your name*]. **10** İyiyim. Teşekkürler. Siz nasılsınız?

## UNIT 2 DRINKS
**Dialogue 1**
**1** Çay, Nescafé, su. **2** Sütlü.

**Dialogue 2**
**1** Şekerli ve şekersiz (sade)/Çok güzel. **2** Evet, çok güzel.

## Dialogue 3
1 Kırmızı. 2 Evet, beyaz peynir.

## Practice
a çay, b kahve, c bira, d şarap, e rakı. 2 a Bira? b Çay? c Nescafé?
d Ayran? e Şarap? 3 a çay<u>lar</u>, b rakı<u>lar</u>, c tost<u>lar</u>, d teşekkür<u>ler</u>,
e bira<u>lar</u>, f içecek<u>ler</u>. 4 a yeşil, b turuncu, c gri, d pembe, e mor.
6 a Yanlış, b Yanlış, c Doğru, d Doğru, e Yanlış. 7 a 0, b 57,
c 11, d 35, e 23, f 46, g 60. 8 Kahve, bira, süt, vişne suyu, şarap,
ayran, rakı, çay, su

## Mini-test
1 Garson. 2 Bir şekerli kahve, lütfen or Bir şekersiz kahve, lütfen
or Bir sade kahve, lütfen. 3 Sütlü Nescafé, lütfen. 4 Bir bardak çay,
lütfen. 5 Bir bardak kırmızı ve bir bardak beyaz şarap, lütfen.
6 Çerez, lütfen. 7 Afiyet olsun. 8 Hesap, lütfen. 9 Üstü kalsın.
10 Elli, yetmiş, doksan, yüz.

## UNIT 3 ACCOMMODATION
### Dialogue 1
1 Evet, var. 2 Yeşil Ev. 3 Y – e – ş – i – l E – v. 4 Otel.

### Dialogue 2
1 Var. 2 İki tek yataklı, büyük ve güzel (balkonlu, deniz
manzaralı). 3 Üç. 4 Evet.

### Dialogue 3
1 Evet, var. 2 Evet, var. 3 Elektrik, su, restoran, yüzme-havuzu,
plaj, duşlar, çocuk oyun parkı, ilkyardım, genel telefon.

### Dialogue 4
1 Evet, var. 2 Evet, var. 3 Ayşegül meşgul.

### Practice
1 a İkiyüzkırkaltı elli otuzbeş. b İkiyüzaltmışiki sıfırbir otuzyedi.
c Altıyüzondört onüç otuzüç. d Yediyüzyedi yirmiiki yirmidört.
e Sekizyüzdoksanaltı otuzaltı otuzaltı. f Üçyüzonbir kırksekiz
elliyedi. 2 a 531 b 444 c 6,755 d 1,001 e 3,033 f 916 g 7,814

**h** 4,000. **3 a** v, **b** i, **c** vi, **d** ii, **e** iii, **f** iv. **4 a** vii, **b** v, **c** iv, **d** i, **e** ii,
**f** iii, **g** vi. **6 a** ben, **b** sen, **c** o, **d** o, **e** o, **f** biz, **g** siz, **h** onlar **7** otel, duş,
anahtar, manzaralı, küvet, yatak, balkonlu, oda, kahvaltı, pansiyon

## Mini-test
**1** Duşlu bir oda, lütfen. **2** Boş oda var mı? **3** Kahvaltı dahil mi?
**4** ... nasıl yazılır? **5** Bu, şu, o. **6** Ben, sen, o, biz, siz, onlar.
**7** İlk yardım. **8** Hoş geldin or hoş geldiniz. **9** Burası and şurası.
**10** telefon, elektrik, su, sıcak su, restoran, yüzme-havuzu, plaj,
duş, çocuk oyun parkı, ilk yardım

### UNIT 4 EATING OUT
## Dialogue 1
**1** Doğru. **2** Doğru. **3** Çok güzel. **4** Tereyağı, bal, marmelat, reçel,
peynir, zeytin, sosis, sucuk, salam, domates, salatalık, biber,
ekmek. **5** Evet, var. **6** Masada.

## Dialogue 2
**1** Doğru. **2** Doğru. **3** Evet. **4** Evet. **5** Hayır, lüfer ızgara. **6** Hayır,
Asuman (Hanım) için.

## Dialogue 3
**1** Doğru. **2** Doğru. **3** İki porsiyon. **4** White bean salad. **5** Evet.

## Practice
**1** Çay, reçel, peynir, yumurta, zeytin, tereyağı, şeker. **2 a** mi?
**b** mi? **c** mi? **d** mu? **e** mu? **f** mü? **3** a, d, b, e, c, f. **4 a** çay **b** balık,
**c** salata, **d** ekmek. **5 a** Evet, Istanbul'da. **b** Evet, soğuk. **c** Evet, et.
**d** Evet, ucuz. **e** Hayır, meyve. **f** Evet, lezzetli. **g** Hayır, alkolsüz.
**h** Evet, tatlı. **i** Hayır, yeşil. **j** Evet, taze. **6 a** iv, **b** iii, **c** vi, **d** ii,
**e** i, **f** v.

## Mini-test
**1** Bir kahve, tereyağı, ekmek, sosis ve yumurta, lütfen. **2** Balık
tava ve yeşil salata, lütfen. **3** Bir büyük beyaz şarap, lütfen. **4** İki
porsiyon köfte ve pilav, lütfen. **5** Bira soğuk mu? **6** Vişne suyu
lütfen. **7** Taksiler nerede? **8** Bir karışık salata, lütfen. **9** İki porsiyon
pilav, lütfen. **10** Üstü kalsın.

## UNIT 5 DIRECTIONS
### Dialogue 1
**1** Evet. **2** Hayır. **3** Evet.

### Dialogue 2
**1** 9'dan 5'e kadar. **2** Topkapı'da. Düz gidin, işaretler var.

### Dialogue 3
**1** Evet, var. **2** Sahilde, merkezde.

### Practice
**1 a** iii, **b** iv, **c** i, **d** ii. **2 a** iii, **b** v, **c** ii, **d** iv, **e** i. **3 a** Here you are.
**b** On me. **c** Do not disturb! **d** Excuse me. **e** I am sorry. **f** I do not
know. **g** Thanks. **h** Not at all. **4 a** i/iii, **b** i/iii, **c** v, **d** vi, **e** iv,
**f** ii/iv. **5 a** 454 km **b** 815 km **c** 325 km **d** 404 km **e** 666 km **f** 814
km **g** 750 km **h** 565 km **i** 1,079 km **j** 926 km. **6 a** Where is the
information office? **b** Pass the traffic lights. **c** Go straight ahead,
take the first road on the right. **d** Go straight ahead, on the left, at
the corner. **7 a** Marmaris'ten Çiftlik'e. **b** Çiftlik'ten Bozukkale'ye.
**c** Bozukkale'den Aktur'a ve Datça'ya. **d** Datça'dan Knidos'a.
**e** Knidos'tan Bodrum'a.

### Mini-test
**1** Afedersiniz, banka nerede acaba? **2** Afedersiniz, taksiler nerede
acaba? **3** Düz gidin ve köşeden sağa dönün, lütfen. **4** Müze ne
zaman açık? **5** İki bilet, lütfen. **6** Sultan Ahmet'e metro var mı?
**7** Bir bilet, lütfen? **8** Bodrum'dan Mavi Yolculuk var mı? **9** Liman
nerede? **10** Istanbul'dan Ankara'ya kaç kilometre?

## UNIT 6 I LIKE THE WEATHER HERE!
### Dialogue 1
**1** Güney. **2** Antalya. **3** Pazartesi, çarşamba, cuma, cumartesi,
pazar.

### Dialogue 2
**1** football, basketball, volleyball, tennis. **2** the sea, dancing, ice
cream, day trips. **3** Yağmursuz ve rüzgarsız güzel bir gün. **4** Evet,
çok. **5** Beş çeşit.

## Reading comprehension
**1** Doğru. **2** Yanlış. **3** Doğru. **4** Yanlış. **5** Doğru. **6** Yanlış.

## Practice
**1 a** Batıda. **b** Kuzey batıda. **c** Ortada. **d** Doğuda. **e** Güney batıda.
**f** Kuzeyde. **g** Güneyde. **h** Güneyde. **i** Güney batıda. **2 a** iv, **b** ii,
**c** i, **d** iii, **e** vi, **f** viii, **g** v. **3** Dursun en kısa boylu. **4 a** ağus<u>to</u>s
**b** <u>eylül</u> **c** <u>ekim</u> **d** <u>haziran</u> **e** te<u>mmuz</u> **f** şu<u>bat</u> **5** hava, sisli, yağmurlu,
soğuk, sıcak, açık, karlı, bulutlu, güneşli, rüzgarlı

## Mini-test
**1** Yazın hiç yağmur yok. **2** İlkbaharda yağmur var/yağmurlu.
**3** Temmuz şubattan (daha) sıcaktır. **4** En çok dans etmeyi (*to dance*) ve voleybolu seviyorum. **5** Bodrum'a hangi günler uçak var? **6** Bir meyveli dondurma, lütfen. **7** Güneş seviyoruz or güneşi seviyoruz. **8** Bodrum'a hangi günler vapur var? **9** İstanbul, Ankara ve İzmir, den daha büyük or büyüktür. **10** Gölgeye gel.

## UNIT 7 TALKING ABOUT ONESELF AND DESCRIBING PEOPLE
### Dialogue 1
**1** Bonn. **2** Leeds. **3** İngiliz. **4** Türkçe, Almanca, Fransızca,
İspanyolca, İtalyanca, Bulgarca. **5** Erkek.

### Dialogue 2
**1** Turkish. **2** Nobody. **3** İngiliz. **4** Öğrenci. **5** Ayda, doktor. **6** Evet.
Cem uzun boylu, esmer, siyah saçlı, siyah gözlü, akıllı ve iyi bir insan.

### Dialogue 3
**1** İyi. **2** İyi.

### Dialogue 4
**1** İyi.

## Practice
**1 a** Tarkan is a very handsome man. **b** Sezen Aksu is a very
beautiful woman. **c** Are the teachers very clever? **d** You are a

hard-working student. **e** Turkish is very interesting. **f** Turkey is both an historic and a modern country. **g** There are a lot of unemployed in Turkey. **h** Turkish is very easy. **i** English is a very rich language, isn't it? **j** German and French grammar are very difficult. **2 a** A i, **b** E ii, **c** F vi, **d** G viii, **e** C iii, **f** H vii, **g** D v, **h** B iv. **3 a** 3, **b** 4, **c** 8, **d** 1, **e** 7, **f** 9, **g** 2, **h** 5, **i** 6. **4 a** x, **b** ix, **c** vi, **d** viii, **e** iii, **f** vii, **g** v, **h** ii, **i** i, **j** iv. **5 a** i, **b** iii, **c** v, **d** vi, **e** vii, **f** viii, **g** ix, **h** x, **i** iv, **j** ii.
**6**

| Name | Nationality | Job | Marital status | Age | Home town |
|------|-------------|-----|----------------|-----|-----------|
| Bülent | Turkish | doctor | ___ | __ | Izmir |
| Lucy | American | model | single | 24 | ___ |
| Trish Webb | English | teacher | single | __ | Birmingham |
| Phillipe | French | footballer | single | 21 | Paris |
| Ülkü Gezer | Turkish | photographer | married | 43 | Istanbul |
| June | Australian | air hostess | married | __ | Sydney |

Mini-test
**1** Amerikalı mısınız? (= 'Are you American?') **2** Kaç yaşındasınız? **3** Milliyetiniz ne? **4** Evliyim. **5** Bekar mısınız? **6** Siz (Hanım, Bey); sen. **7** Sen İngilizsin, değil mi? or Siz İngilizsiniz, değil mi? **8** Türk müsün? or Türk müsünüz? **9** Bu Türkçe'de ne demek? **10** Türk müsün? or Türk müsünüz?

### UNIT 8 SHOPPING
Dialogue 1
**1** Some shopping. **2** To the Grand Bazaar/Kapalı Çarşı.

Dialogue 2
**1** Siyah. **2** Evet.

Dialogue 3
**1** Laura. **2** Hayır, istemiyor. **3** Yarım kilo.

Dialogue 4
**1** No. **2** No. **3** Dört kutu. **4** Hayır, yeni değil. **5** Evet, çok taze.

Dialogue 5

**1** 38 beden. **2** Hayır, yakışmıyor.

Practice

**1**

**2** e, g, a, b, f, i, h, c, d, k, j. **3 Food:** Türk kahvesi; çerez; bal; elma çay; lokum; fıstık; incir; **Clothes:** T-shirt; bluz; ceket; ayakkabı; pantolon; çanta; **Presents:** padişah macunu; CD; kaset; halı; kilim; cüzdan; baharat **4** lokum, baharat, deri, ayakkabı, fıstık, şapka, kilim, bluz, pantolon, ceket

Mini-test

**1** 40 beden, mavi bir ceket, istiyorum, lütfen. **2** Naneli lokum, lütfen. **3** Yarım kilo kuru yemiş, lütfen. **4** Bir paket kimyon, lütfen. **5** Şarap içmiyorum. **6** 41 numara, ayakkabı bakıyorum/istiyorum, lütfen. **7** Mavi pantolon, bakıyorum/Mavi pantolon, istiyorum, lütfen. **8** Kırmızı sana or size yakışmıyor. **9** Mavi bana yakışıyor. **10** Denemek istiyorum.

### UNIT 9 WHERE SHALL WE GO?

Dialogue 1

**1** They're going to go to the theatre. **2** They look at the Kenter Theatre's schedule. **3** Tiyatroya. **4** Kenterler'e. **5** Film. **6** Yarımda. **7** (*Personal response.*)

Dialogue 2
**1** No, there aren't. **2** Two. **3** Yanlış. **4** Doğru. **5** Yanlış. **6** Doğru.
**7** (*Personal response.*)

Dialogue 3
**1** To the cinema. **2** No. **3** *Vampirler, Şaban, Hamam.* **4** *Hamam'a.*
**5** Yedide. **6** Otobüsle gidiyorlar. **7** Araba bozuk ve otobüs daha
ucuz. **8** (*Personal response.*)

Dialogue 4
**1** To Taksim. **2** Return. **3** Evet. **4** Evet. **5** Hayır.

Practice
**1 a** ii, iii, iv, vi. **b** Watch TV.
**c**

| | |
|---|---|
| **Yeşim** | Bu akşam ne yapalım? |
| **Ahmet** | Tiyatroya gidelim. |
| **Yeşim** | Çok pahalı. |
| **Ahmet** | Sinemaya gidelim mi? |
| **Yeşim** | Sinemalar çok uzak. |
| **Ahmet** | Restorana gidelim. |
| **Yeşim** | Ben rejimdeyim. |
| **Ahmet** | Ne yapalım? |
| **Yeşim** | Televizyon seyredelim, mi? |
| **Ahmet** | Çok iyi fikir. Gazeteye bakalım neler var. |

**2** Yes, Tuesday and Thursday **3 a** ii, **b** iv, **c** i, **d** iii. **4 a** on iki otuz;
yarım **b** on beş on beş; üçü çeyrek geçiyor **c** sekiz elli; dokuza on
var **d** dört yirmi beş; dördü yirmi beş geçiyor **e** on sekiz kırk beş;
yediye çeyrek var **f** dokuz on; dokuzu on geçiyor **g** yirmi dört;
gece yarısı – on iki **h** on on; onu on geçiyor **i** beş sıfır beş; beşi beş
geçiyor **j** on üç sıfır iki; biri iki geçiyor. **5 a** İkiyi beş geçiyor.
**b** Üçe yirmi beş kala. **c** Dördü çeyrek geçe. **d** Yediye çeyrek var.
**e** Yarımda. **f** Sekize on var. **g** Saat yediyi yirmi beş geçe. **h** On biri
çeyrek geçiyor. **i** Ona çeyrek var. **j** Dokuzu beş geçe. **6 a** Sinemada.
**b** Tiyatroda. **c** İşte. **d** Parkta. **e** Otobüste. **f** Trende. **g** Vapurda.

**h** Dolmuşta. **i** Uçakta. **j** Durakta. **k** Otelde. **7 a** iii, i, ii, iv. **b** iv, ii, i, iii or iv, iii, ii, i **8 a** From Eminönü. **b** Three boats at 10.35, 12.00 and 13.35. **c** At six places; the 7th place is the last stop. **d** For 2–3 hours. **9 a** ii, **b** iv, **c** iii, **d** vi, **e** v, **f** i, **g** viii, **h** ix, **i** x, **j** xi, **k** xii, **l** vii. **10** Let's love 'green' and protect the forests; or We should love 'green' and protect the forests.

## Mini-test
**1** Tiyatroya gidelim mi, iyi bir oyun var. **2** İstanbul'a iki gidiş dönüş bileti, lütfen. **3** Üçü çeyrek geçiyor. **4** Saat kaç? **5** Bu pazar için bir bilet, lütfen. **6** Sinemalarda hangi filmler var? **7** Otobüs veya dolmuşla gitmek istiyorum. **8** Dokümanter filmler seviyorum. **9** Sen ne tür filmler seviyorsun? or Siz ne tür filmler seviyorsunuz? **10** Burası çok güneşli, gölgede oturalım.

## *UNIT 10 HOW WAS IT?*
### Dialogue 1
**1** Harikaydı. **2** Sakin, masmavi ve ılıktı. **3** Yüzdüler, kürek çektiler ve kumlarda yürüdüler. **4** Rahattı, oda deniz manzaralıydı, servis iyiydi (ve yemekler harikaydı). **5** Harikaydı.

### Dialogue 2
**1** İyi değildi. Önce çok sıcaktı, sonra rüzgarlı ve yağmurluydu. **2** Berbattı. Deniz soğuk ve çok dalgalıydı. **3** Hayır, hiç iyi değildi. Gürültülüydü, hiç manzara yoktu, yatak sertti ve duş bozuktu. **4** Yemekler berbattı, lezzetsizdi. Sebze ve meyveler taze değildi.

### Reading comprehension: the postcard
**1** Hayır, içmedi. **2** Hayır, İstanbul'da. **3** Hayır, henüz gezmedi.

### Listening comprehension: guess who?
**1** Elvis Presley. **2** Evet, yaptı. **3** Priscilla Beaulieu ile evlendi. **4** Evet, yakışıklıydı. **5** Şarkıcı ve aktördü. **6** Evet, çok ünlüydü. **7** (*Personal response.*)

### Reading comprehension: Turkish history
**1** Sultan Mehmet took Constantinople and made it the capital of the Ottoman Empire. **2** The Ottomans built beautiful mosques,

bridges and inns in Europe and Anatolia. **3** Atatürk won the War of Independence, he became the first President of the Republic, and he carried out many reforms.

## Practice

**1** Happy holidaymaker: **a** i, **b** ii, **c** vi, **d** vii, **e** ix; unhappy holidaymaker: **a** x, **b** viii, **c** v, **d** iv, **e** iii. **2 i** b, **ii** d, **iii** c, **iv** a.

**3**

| | ben | sen | o |
|---|---|---|---|
| doğmak | doğdum | doğdun | doğdu |
| anlaşmak | anlaştım | anlaştın | anlaştı |
| TV'ye çıkmak | çıktım | çıktın | çıktı |
| plak yapmak | yaptım | yaptın | yaptı |
| evlenmek | evlendim | evlendin | evlendi |
| boşanmak | boşandım | boşandın | boşandı |
| konser vermek | verdim | verdin | verdi |
| oynamak | oynadım | oynadın | oynadı |
| ödül almak | aldım | aldın | aldı |
| ölmek | öldüm | öldün | öldü |

**4 1** geldi(ler) **2** girdi **3** yayıldı **4** geldi **5** oldu **6** aldı **7** yaptı **8** durdu(lar) **9** yaptı(lar) **10** etti(ler) **11** kazandı **12** oldu **13** oldu **14** oldu **15** yaptı. **5** Hiç tavla oynadın mı?/Hiç nargile içtin mi?/Hiç simit yedin mi?/Hiç deveye bindin mi?/Hiç çamur banyosu yaptın mı?/Hiç Ayasofya'yı gezdin mi?/Hiç hamama gittin mi?/Hiç Mavi Yolculuk yaptın mı?/Hiç Türk Kahvesi içtin mi?/Hiç Karagöz ve Hacivat seyrettin mi?/Hiç rakı içtin mi? **7** harika, bozuk, berbat, rahat, iyi, sert, gürültülü, masmavi, pahalı, dalgalı

## Mini-test

**1** Tatilin(iz) nasıldı? **2** Berbattı. Her şey çok kötüydü. **3** Hamama gittim. **4** Çamur banyosu yapmadım. **5** Hiç deveye bindin mi? **6** Yemekler nasıldı? **7** Otel gürültülüydü. **8** Duş bozuktu. **9** Hava her gün güneşliydi. **10** Ben burada çok mutluyum.

# Glossary of grammatical terms

**1** *THE ALPHABET*
The English alphabet has 26 letters: *Aa, Bb, Cc, Dd, Ee, Ff, Gg, Hh, Ii, Jj, Kk, Ll, Mm, Nn, Oo, Pp, Qq, Rr, Ss, Tt, Uu, Vv, Ww, Xx, Yy, Zz.*

The Turkish alphabet has 29 letters: **Aa, Bb, Cc, Çç, Dd, Ee, Ff, Gg, Ğğ, Hh, Iı, İi, Jj, Kk, Ll, Mm, Nn, Oo, Öö, Pp, Rr, Ss, Şş, Tt, Uu, Üü, Vv, Yy, Zz.**

Letters are divided into two groups called vowels and consonants.

For more information see Unit 3.

## 1.1 Vowels
The English vowels are: *a, e, i, o, u.*

The Turkish vowels are: **a, ı, o, u, e, i, ö, ü.**

## 1.2 Vowel harmony
Vowel harmony is used to harmonize Turkish vowels correctly.
Any vowels added to a word have to rhyme or 'harmonize' with the previous vowel in the word.

See Units 2, 4 and 5 and the **Appendix**.

## 1.3 Consonants
The English consonants are: *b, c, d, f, g, h, j, k, l, m, n, p, q, r, s, t, v, w, x, y, z.*

The Turkish consonants are: **b, c, ç, d, f, g, ğ, h, j, k, l, m, n, p, r, s, ş, t, v, y, z.**

For more information see Units 3–5.

## 2 ADJECTIVES

An adjective is a word that describes a noun or a pronoun, e.g. *good*, *beautiful*, *young*. Turkish adjectives, like other Turkish words, take endings.

### 2.1 Comparatives

Comparatives are used when comparing two people, animals, objects or groups. English uses the ending *-er* or *more* to compare: *Turkey is warmer than England*. In Turkish, **daha** is used for comparisons, e.g. **Türkiye İngiltere'den daha güneşli.** Not all English adjectives follow the rule but almost all Turkish adjectives do.

For more information see Unit 6.

### 2.2 Superlatives

Superlatives are used when comparing more than two people, animals, objects or groups. In English, *-est* is added to the end of the object or *most* is placed before the adjective, e.g. *prettiest*, *most expensive*. In Turkish, **en** means *the most* (*-est*). The word **en** is put before the adjective: **Ağustos en sıcak ay. En güneşli yer.**

For more information see Unit 6.

## 3 ARTICLES

*A*, *an*, *the* are called articles. In general, articles are not used in Turkish. As is mentioned in Unit 2 the equivalent of *a/an* is either **bir** or nothing. English uses *the* to talk about specific items. Likewise in Turkish, you use the *-i* ending if the direct object is a specific item. At this stage, don't worry about getting these endings right. People will understand you even if you do not use them. Just try to notice them when you hear or see them.

For more information see Units 2–5.

## 4 NOUNS

Words which name things (objects, ideas, people or places) are called nouns. *Woman*, *cinema*, *money* and *water* are all examples of nouns.

English nouns are divided into countable and uncountable nouns. Countable nouns can be singular or plural but uncountable nouns cannot. *Water*, *money* and *sugar* are examples of uncountable nouns. In English, you usually add *-s* or *-es* to the end of countable nouns. In English, some nouns are always plural, e.g. *jeans*, *trousers*, *glasses*. In Turkish, all nouns can be either singular or plural.

Use the singular noun if there is just one and add the plural ending if there is more than one. In Turkish, all nouns (names of things, opinions and feelings, etc.) can be made plural by adding **-ler** or **-lar**. Unlike English, however, there are no exceptions in Turkish. In Turkish, most greetings and wishes are in plural, e.g. **İyi akşamlar.** *Good evening.*

For more information see Unit 2.

### 4.1 Proper nouns
These are words that have their own special name, such as people's names, city names, countries, etc. All proper nouns begin with a capital letter, e.g. *Vanessa*, *Ayşegül*, *Paris*, *Istanbul*, *Turkey*.

### 4.2 Pronouns
Pronouns are short words, which are used instead of nouns to avoid repetition, e.g. *I*, *you*, *he*, *she*, *it*, *we*, *they*. The Turkish pronouns are: **ben, sen, o, biz, siz, onlar.**

For more information see Unit 3.

### 5 NEGATIVE
Negative means not, e.g. *He is not English.* In Turkish, **değil** is used to make a word or phrase negative, e.g. **O İngiliz değil.** For more information see Unit 1.

To tell people not to do things, add **-me** or **-ma** to the end of the main part of the verb, e.g. **Git*me*.** *Do **not** go.*

For more information see Unit 6.

### 6 WORD ORDER
Although Turkish word order is relatively free and flexible, it is best to follow the main principle that verbs go at the end of the sentence. The basic word order is subject – object – verb (SOV) (see Unit 7).

## 6.1 Subject
The subject in the sentence is the person or thing performing the action.

*Example*: The <u>cat</u> chased the mouse.

## 6.2 Object
The object of the sentence is the person or thing having the action done to it.

*Example*: The cat chased the mouse.

## 6.3 Verbs
Verbs are often called 'doing words'; they tell us what is happening, e.g. *go, do, walk, swim*. Remember *am, are, is, was* and *were* are verbs (verb *to be*). Verbs change according to who does something and/or when something happens. When you look up a word in an English dictionary (for the dictionary form) you see the main part of the verb with to in front of it, e.g. *to mean, to ask*.

### 6.3.1 INFINITIVE
The dictionary form of Turkish verbs is the stem plus the ending **-mek** or **-mak**. Dictionary forms are sometimes called 'the infinitive'. Sometimes the dictionary form is used as it stands, and sometimes you use it to make the correct form of the verb.

### 6.3.2 TENSE
The main tenses of verbs are present, past and future. Time is split into past, present and future. We can alter verbs (doing words) to show when the action is taking place.

In English, *I walk* is in the simple present tense and *I am walking* is in the continuous present tense. In Turkish, the **-er** ending is used in the present tense and **-iyor** is used for the present continuous tense.

In English, we add *-ed* to most verbs to show the past tense, e.g. *walked, talked*. Not all English verbs follow this rule so there are a lot of irregular past tense verbs, e.g. *go → went, swim → swam*. To make a past tense in Turkish, you almost always add the **-di** ending (according to vowel harmony), to the main part of the verb.

# Appendix: vowel harmony

### E-TYPE ENDINGS

For e-type endings, use this rule:

| e | goes after | e, i, ö, ü |
|---|------------|------------|
| a | goes after | a, ı, o, u |

The following are e-type endings:

| -ler | plural |
|------|--------|
| -de | 'at', 'on', 'in' |
| -mek | 'to' (infinitive) |
| -e | 'to', 'for' |
| -den | 'from' |
| -me | 'not' |
| -ce | makes a language word from a nationality word (adj.) |
| -elim | 'let's' |
| -le | 'by', 'with', 'using' |

### I-TYPE ENDINGS

For i-type endings, use this rule:

| i | goes after | e, i |
|---|------------|------|
| ı | goes after | a, ı |
| ü | goes after | ö, ü |
| u | goes after | o, u |

Here are some common i-type endings:

| -mı? | question word |
|------|---------------|
| -ı | Turkish equivalent of 'the' |
| -cı | denotes a person or occupation |
| -dır | 'is': very formal usage |
| -lı | 'with', 'containing', 'from' |
| -iyor | -ing (present tense) |
| -dı | past tense |
| -lık | '-ness' |
| -siz | 'without' |

# Turkish–English vocabulary

**ABD** *USA*
**acaba** *I wonder, please*
**acıkmak** *to get hungry*
**acıktım** *I'm hungry*
**açık** *open/light colour*
**açmak** *to open, to switch on*
**ad** *name*
**ada** *island*
**adres** *address*
**adım** *my name (first name)*
**adınız** *your name*
**afedersiniz** *excuse me*
**afiyet olsun** *enjoy your drinks!/*
  *enjoy your meal!*
**ağır** *heavy*
**ağrımak** *to ache*
**ağrıyor** *aching*
**ağustos** *August*
**Akdeniz** *Mediterranean*
**akıl** *intelligence*
**akıllı** *clever, intelligent*
**akılsız** *stupid, silly*
**akşam** *evening*
**akşamlar** *evenings*
**aktör** *actor*
**aldı** *conquered, took*
**alfabe** *alphabet*
**alışveriş** *shopping*
**almak** *to buy, to take*
**Alman** *German* (people)
**Almanca** *German* (language)
**Almanya** *Germany*
**alo** *hello* (on the phone)
**altın** *gold*
**ama** *but*
**Amerika** *America*

**Amerikalı** *American*
  (people)
**Anadolu** *Anatolia*
**anahtar** *key*
**anlamak** *to understand*
**anlaşmak** *to sign a contract*
**anne** *mother*
**annemler** *my parents* (lit.
  *my mothers*)
**ara sıra** *sometimes*
**araba** *car*
**aralık** *December*
**aramak** *to call*
**arası** *between*
**arasında** *in between*
**arayayım** *let me call (I'll call)*
**arkadaş** *friend*
**arkadaşım** *my friend*
**arı** *bee*
**arı soktu** *a bee has stung me*
**askerliğini yaptı** *did his military*
  *service*
**askerlik** *military service*
**aspirin** *aspirin*
**Asya** *Asia*
**Asyalı** *Asian*
**atmak** *to put*
**Avrupa** *Europe*
**Avrupalı** *European*
**Avustralyalı** *Australia*
**ayakkabı** *shoes*
**ayakkabıcı** *shoe shop*
**Ayasofya** *St. Sophia*
**ayırtmak** *to book, to reserve*
**ayran** *yogurt-based drink*
**ayrı** *separate*

**baba** *father*
**baharat** *spices*
**bahşiş** *tip*
**bakalım** *let's have a look*
**bakkal** *grocer/grocer's*
**baklava** *Turkish dessert*
**bakmak** *to look*
**bal** *honey*
**balık** *fish*
**balıkçı** *fishing/fisherman*
**balkon** *balcony*
**balkonlu** *with a balcony*
**bana** *me, for me*
**bana da** *for me too*
**bana Yasemin deyin** *call me Yasemin*
**banka** *bank*
**banyo** *bathroom*
**barbunya** *red mullet*
**bardak** *glass*
**basketbol** *basketball*
**baş** *head*
**Başbakan** *Prime Minister*
**başım ağrıyor** *I have a headache*
**başka** *what else*
**başka bir şey** *anything else*
**başkent** *capital*
**bekar** *single*
**Belçika** *Belgium*
**Belçikalı** *Belgian* (people)
**ben** *I*
**ben de** *me too, I too*
**bence** *in my opinion*
**benden** *on me*
**benim** *my, it's me*
**benim için** *for me*
**berbat** *terrible*
**bey** *Mr* (after first names only)
**beyaz** *white*
**beyazlı** *dressed in white*
**bıçak** *knife*

**bırak!** *leave!*
**bırakmak** *to leave*
**biber** *pepper*
**bikini** *bikini*
**bile** *even*
**bilet** *ticket*
**bilet gişesi** *ticket office*
**bilgisayar** *computer*
**biliyor** *he/she knows*
**biliyorum** *I know*
**bilmek** *to know*
**bilmiyorum** *I don't know*
**bina** *building*
**bir buçukta** *at half past one*
**bira** *beer*
**biraz** *a little*
**birbirimiz** *each other*
**birinci** *first*
**Birinci Dünya Savaşı** *First World War*
**biz** *we*
**bluz** *blouse*
**boş** *vacant/empty*
**boşanmak** *to get divorced*
**bozmak** *to break*
**bozuk** *change* (money); *broken, out of order*
**bölge** *region*
**börek** *pastry*
**börekçi** *pastry shop*
**Britanya** *Britain*
**bu** *this*
**buçuk** *it's half past*
**buçukta** *it's (at) half past*
**buğulama** *steamed*
**bugün** *today*
**Bulgar** *Bulgarian* (people)
**Bulgarca** *Bulgarian* (language)
**Bulgaristan** *Bulgaria* (country)
**bunlar** *these are*
**burada** *here*

**burası** *here, this place*
**buraya** *here* (shows movement)
**Bursa'ya kadar** *as far as Bursa*
**butik** *boutique*
**buyrun** *yes, I'm listening to you;*
  *here you are/do come in*
**buyrun, efendim?** *how can I help*
  *you, sir/madam?*
**büfe** *food stall*
**büro** *office*
**bütün** *all*
**büyük** *big*

**cadde** *street*
**cami** *mosque*
**canım** *my dear*
**canlı** *alive, live*
**ceket** *jacket*
**cevap** *answer*
**cevap vermek** *to answer*
**cezve** *Turkish coffee maker*
**cızbız** *sizzling/fried*
**ciddi** *serious*
**cuma** *Friday*
**cumartesi** *Saturday*
**cumhurbaşkanı** *President*
**cumhuriyet** *republic*
**cüzdan** *wallet, purse*
**çadır** *tent*
**çalmak** *to ring*
**çalışkan** *hard working*
**çamur** *mud*
**çamur banyosu** *mud bath*
**çanta** *bag*
**çarşamba** *Wednesday*
**çatal** *fork*
**çay** *tea*
**çek** *pull*
**çekmek** *to pull*
**çerez** *snacks*
**çeşit** *kind, type*
**çeşitli** *various*

**çeyrek** *a quarter*
**çık!** *come out/get out*
**çıkmak** *to come out/go up*
**çiçek** *flower*
**çift** *a pair*
**çikolatalı** *chocolate flavoured/*
  *with chocolate*
**çizme** *boots*
**çoban salatası** *mixed salad*
**çocuk** *child*
**çocuklar** *children*
**çok** *very*

**da** *also*
**dağ** *mountain*
**daha** *more (-er)*
**dahil** *included*
**dahil mi?** *is it included?*
**dakika** *minutes*
**dalgalı** *rough*
**dalmak** *to dive*
**-dan, (-den) sonra** *after*
**danışma** *information*
**dans** *dance*
**dantel** *lace*
**-de** *at, on, in*
**değil** *not*
**değil mi?** *Isn't it?*
**değişik** *different*
**-den beri** *since*
**-den -e kadar** *from ... to ....*
**-den önce** *before ....*
**-den sonra** *after .....*
**denemek** *to try on*
**deniz** *sea*
**deniz kenarları** *seaside*
**deri** *leather*
**ders** *lesson, class*
**dersten sonra** *after the class*
**devamlı** *continuous*
**deve** *camel*
**devrimler** *reforms*

**dikkat et!** *watch out! pay attention! be careful!*
**dil** *language, tongue*
**dilimlenmiş** *sliced*
**doğmak** *to be born*
**doğru** *right/true, straight*
**doğum tarihi** *date of birth*
**doğum yeri** *place of birth*
**doktor** *doctor*
**dolmuş** *sharing taxi*
**dolmuşla** *by sharing taxi*
**domates** *tomatoes*
**don** *frost*
**dondurma** *ice cream*
**dön** *turn!*
**döner** *doner*
**dönmek** *to turn/return/rotate* (takes **-e** or **-a** ending e.g. **sola dön**)
**dönüş** *return*
**durak** *stop, bus stop*
**durdular** *stopped*
**durmak** *to stop*
**duş** *shower*
**dut** *mulberry*
**dün** *yesterday*
**dünya** *world*
**dürüst** *honest*
**düz** *straight*

**-e, -a kadar** *as far as*
**eczane** *chemist's*
**efendim** *sir or madam, pardon*
**efendim?** *pardon?*
**Ege** *Aegean*
**ekim** *October*
**ekmek** *bread*
**elbise** *dress*
**eldiven** *gloves*
**elektrik** *electricity*
**elma** *apple*
**elma çay** *apple tea*
**emekli** *retired*

**en** *the most (-est \*)*
**en sıcak** *hottest*
**en yakın** *nearest*
**erkek** *man*
**eski** *old*
**esmer** *dark/olive skinned*
**es͵im** *my wife/my husband (my partner)*
**et** *meat*
**etek** *skirt*
**etli** *with meat*
**etsiz** *without meat*
**ev** *house, home*
**eve** *to the house*
**evet** *yes*
**evlenmek** *to get married to*
**evli** *married*
**eylül** *September*

**fal bakmak** *to read fortunes*
**falan** *roughly, or so, and such like*
**farklı** *different*
**farklıyız** *we are different*
**Fatih Sultan Mehmet** *Sultan Mehmet the Conqueror*
**fındık** *hazelnuts*
**fırın** *bakery/oven*
**fıstık** *nuts*
**fıstıklı** *nutty*
**fikir** *idea*
**film** *film*
**fiyatlar** *prices*
**Fransa** *France*
**Fransız** *French* (people)
**Fransızca** *French* (language)
**futbol** *football*

**galiba** *I think*
**garson** *waiter/waitress*
**gazete** *newspaper*
**gece** *night*
**gece yarısı** *midnight*

**geç** *cross! late*
**geç kaldım** *I'm late*
**geçen** *last*
**geçiyor** (-i) *past*
**geçmek** *to cross*
**geldim** *I've come/I came*
**gelecek** *next, coming*
**gelmek** *to come*
**genel telefon** *a public phone*
**genellikle** *generally*
**gerçekten** *really*
**gerek** *necessary*
**gezi** *trip/journey*
**gezmek** *travel/trip*
**gidelim mi?** *shall we go?*
**gidin** *go (please)*
**gir** *enter!*
**girdi** *entered*
**giriş** *entrance*
**girmek** *to enter*
**git** *go!*
**gitmek** *to go*
**gökkuşağı** *rainbow*
**gölge** *shade*
**gömlek** *shirt*
**görmek** (-i) *to see*
**görüşmek**(ile) *to see each other*
**görüşürüz** *see you*
**gözlük** *glasses*
**gramlık** *per gram*
**gri** *grey*
**gül** *rose*
**güle güle** *goodbye* (reply to **hoşça kal** or **hoşça kalın**)
**güle güle kullanın!** *enjoy using it*
**gümrük** *customs*
**gün** *day*
**güneş** *sun*
**güneşli** *sunny*
**güney** *south*
**günlük** *daily* (day)

**gürültü** *noise*
**gürültülüydü** *it was noisy*
**güzel** *beautiful, nice*

**hadi** *let's/come on*
**hadi, arayalım** *let's call*
**hafta** *week*
**hafta sonu** *weekend*
**haklısınız** *you are right*
**halı** *carpet*
**Hamam** *Turkish bath* (*Hamam* is also the name of a Turkish film)
**hangi?** *which?*
**Hanım** *Miss/Mrs/Ms* (after first names only)
**harabe** *ruin*
**harem** *harem*
**harika** *wonderful*
**harikaydı** *It was wonderful*
**harita** *map*
**hastahane** *hospital*
**hava** *air/weather*
**havaalanı** *airport*
**havlu** *towel*
**hayır** *no*
**haziran** *June*
**hediye** *present*
**hediyelik şeyler** *things for presents*
**hem ... hem** *both ... and*
**hemen** *straight away*
**henüz** *only, yet*
**hep** *all*
**hepsi bu kadar** *that's all*
**her** *every*
**her zaman** *always*
**her gün** *everyday*
**her şey** *everything*
**her șey her șey** *absolutely everything*
**hesap** *the bill*
**hızlı** *fast*

**hiç** *(not) at all, never*
**Hindistan** *India*
**Hintçe** *Hindi*
**Hintli** *Indian* (person)
**hisar** *fortress*
**hostes** *air hostess*
**hoş** *nice, pleasant*
**hoş bulduk** the standard reply to
  **hoş geldiniz** or **hoş geldin**
**hoş geldiniz** *welcome*
**hoşça kalın** *goodbye*

**ılık** *warm*
**ılıktı** *it was warm*
**ışıklar** *lights*
**ızgara** *grilled*
**içecek** *drink*
**içecekleriniz** *your drinks*
**içmek** *to drink*
**iken** *while/when*
**iklim** *climate*
**ilginç** *interesting*
**ilk** *first*
**ilkbahar** *spring*
**ilk yardım** *first aid post*
**incir** *fig*
**İngiliz** *English* (people)
**İngilizce** *English* (language)
**İngiltere** *England*
**insan** *person*
**inşaat** *building site*
**iskele** *port*
**İspanya** *Spain*
**İspanyol** *Spanish* (people)
**İspanyolca** *Spanish* (language)
**istasyon** *station*
**istemek** *to want*
**istiyorum** *I want/I would like*
**iş** *work, job*
**işaret** *sign*
**işgal etmek** *to occupy*

**işgal ettiler** *occupied*
**işsiz** *unemployed*
**işte** *here, here it is, there*
**it** *push*
**İtalyan** *Italian* (people)
**İtalyanca** *Italian* (language)
**itmek** *to push*
**iyi** *good*
**iyi akşamlar** *good evening*
**iyi geceler** *good night*
**iyiyim** *I am fine*
**iyiyiz** *we are well*

**Japon** *Japanese* (people)
**Japonca** *Japanese* (language)
**Japonya** *Japan*

**kabak** *courgette, pumpkin*
**kaç beden?** *what size?*
**kaç gün?** *how many days?*
**kaç günlük?** *for how many days?*
**kaç kişi?** *how many people?*
**kaç kişilik?** *for how many people?*
**kaç lira?** *how much?* (lira)
**kaç saat?** *how many hours?*
**kadın** *woman*
**kahvaltı** *breakfast*
**kahvaltıda** *at breakfast*
**kahve**(ler) *coffee(s)*
**kahveli** *coffee flavoured*
**kahverengi** *brown*
**kalacak yer listesi** *lists of
  accommodation*
**kalkan** *turbot*
**kalkış** *leaving*
**kalkmak** *to get up, to leave*
**kalmak** *to stay*
**kamp** *campsite*
**Kanada** *Canada*
**Kanadalı** *Canadian* (people)
**Kapalı Çarşı** *Grand Bazaar*

**kapatmak** to close, to switch off, to cover

**kar** snow

**Karadeniz** The Black Sea

**kardeş** sibling

**kardeşim** my sister/my brother

**karışık** mixed

**karışık meyve** mixed fruit

**karpuz** watermelon

**karşı** opposite

**kart** card

**kartla** by card (see **ile**)

**kaset** tape

**kasım** November

**kayısı** apricot

**kazak** jumper

**kazandı** won

**kazanmak** to win

**kemer** belt

**kere** times

**kervansaraylar** caravanserai (inns with large courtyards)

**keyif** pleasure, delight, joy, enjoyment

**keyifli** joyous, pleasurable, enjoyable

**kez** time

**Kıbrıs** Cyprus

**Kıbrıslı** Cypriot

**kır** countryside/wild

**kır çiçekleri** wildflowers

**kırmızı** red

**kış** winter

**kızarmış** toasted

**kızımız** our daughter

**kilim** woven rug

**kilise** church

**kilo** kg

**kiloluk** for a kilo

**kimyon** cumin

**kiremit** brick

**kiremitte** baked/roast on a tile in the oven

**kişi** person

**kolay** easy

**komedi** comedy

**komik** funny

**konser** concert

**kontrol** check in

**korku** horror

**korumak** to protect

**koymak** to put, to put … on

**köfte** Turkish meatballs

**köfteci** restaurant serving Turkish meatballs

**köftelik** for meatballs

**köpek** dog

**köprü** bridge

**köşe** corner

**kötü** bad

**kötüydü** it was bad

**köy** village

**kral** king

**kredi** credit

**kredi kartı** credit card

**kremrengi** beige

**kuaför** hairdresser

**kum** sand

**kumlar** sands

**kurak** dry

**Kurtuluş Savaşı** War of Independence

**kuru yemiş** dried fruit

**kutu** box

**küçük** small

**küpe** earrings

**kürek çekmek** to row a boat

**küvet** bath

**lahmacun** savoury pancake

**levrek** bass

**lezzetli** tasty

**likör** *liquor*
**liman** *port*
**limonata** *still lemonade*
**limonlu** *lemon flavoured*
**liste** *list*
**lokanta** *restaurant*
**lokum** *Turkish delight*
**lokumcu** *Turkish delight shop*
**lüfer** *blue fish*
**lüks** *luxury*
**lütfen** *please*

**maalesef** *unfortunately* (a polite remark)
**magazin** *magazine*
**Malazgirt** *town in southeast Turkey*
**manken** *model*
**manzara** *view*
**manzaralı** *with a view*
**Marmara** *Marmara* (the sea and region)
**mart** *March*
**masa** *table*
**masada** *on the table*
**masmavi** *very intense blue*
**mavi** *blue*
**Mavi Yolculuk** *Blue Cruise*
**mayıs** *May*
**mayo** *swimming costume*
**memnun oldum** *I'm glad*
**merhaba/selam** *hello/hi*
**merkez** *centre*
**mermer** *marble*
**meslek** *job, profession*
**meşgul** *busy*
**meşgulüm** *I am busy*
**meşgulüz** *we are busy*
**metal rengi** *metallic colour*
**mevsim** *season*
**meyve** *fruit*
**meyveli** *fruit flavoured/with fruit*

**meze** *starter*
**Mısır** *Egypt, corn*
**Mısırlı** *Egyptian* (people)
**milliyet** *nationality*
**modern** *modern*
**mor** *purple*
**mönü** *menu*
**muhteşem** *great*
**mutlu** *happy*
**mutsuz** *unhappy*
**mühendis** *engineer*
**müze** *museum*
**müzik** *music*
**müzikal** *musical*

**nane** *mint*
**naneli** *peppermint flavoured*
**nargile** *hookah*
**nasıl?** *how?*
**nasıl yazılır?** *how do you spell it?*
**nasılsın? (sen)** *how are you?*
**nasılsınız? (siz)** *how are you?*
**ne?** *what?*
**ne oynuyor?** *what's on?*
**ne yapalım?** *what shall we do?*
**neden?** *why?*
**neler?** *what are there?*
**nerede?** *where?*
**nereler?** *what places?*
**nerelisin?** *where are you from?*
**neresi?** *where/which place?*
**nereye?** *where to?* (shows movement)
**nereye gidelim?** *where shall we go?*
**Nescafé** *instant coffee*
**neyle (ne ile)?** *by what?/with what?/how* **(see ile)**
**niçin? (ne için)** *why?*
**nisan** *April*
**nişanlı** *engaged*
**nişanlın** *your fiancé*
**numara** *number*

**o** *that* (referring to something relatively far away)
**o** *he/she/it*
**ocak** *January*
**oda** *room*
**okumak** *to read*
**olarak** *as*
**onlar** *they*
**orada** *there*
**orman** *forest*
**orta** *medium*
**Orta Asya** *Central Asia*
**Orta Avrupa** *Central Europe*
**orta boy** *medium sized*
**ortada** *in the middle, centre*
**ortalama** *average*
**Osman Bey** Osman (the head of the Ottoman clan)
**Osmanlılar** *Ottomans*
**otel** *hotel*
**otobüs** *bus*
**otobüs bileti** *bus ticket*
**otobüs durağı** *bus stop*
**otobüsle** *by bus*
**otoyol** *motorway*
**oynamak** *to act, to play*
**oyun parkı** *play area*
**ödemek** *to pay*
**ödül** *award*
**öğlen** *noon*
**öğrenci** *student*
**öğrenmek** *to learn*
**öğretmek** *to teach*
**öğretmen** *teacher*
**ölmek** *to die*
**önce** *at first, ago*
**önümüzde** *in front of us*
**özel** *special*
**özellikle** *especially*
**özür dilemek** *to apologize*
**özür dilerim** *I'm sorry*

**padişah macunu** *aphrodisiacs*
**pahalı** *expensive*
**paket** *packet, parcel*
**pansiyon** *guest house*
**pantolon** *trousers*
**park** *park*
**parti** *party*
**pasaport** *passport*
**pasaport numarası** *passport number*
**pasta** *cake*
**pastahane** *cake shop*
**patates** *potatoes*
**patlıcan** *aubergine, egg plant*
**pazar** *Sunday*
**pazarlık** *bargain*
**pazarlık yapmak** *to bargain, haggle*
**pazartesi** *Monday*
**pembe** *pink* (colour)
**pencere** *window*
**perde** *curtain*
**perşembe** *Thursday*
**peynir** *cheese*
**pide** *Turkish pizza*
**pideci** *a Turkish pizza restaurant*
**pilav** *cooked rice*
**pilavlı** *with cooked rice*
**piliç** *chicken*
**piyaz** *white bean salad*
**plaj** *beach*
**plak** *record*
**platin** *platinum*
**popüler** *popular*
**porsiyon** *portion*
**portakalrengi** *orange* (colour)
**posta** *post*
**profesör** *professor*
**program** *programme*

**rafadan** *soft-boiled egg*
**rahat** *comfortable*

**rahatsız etmeyin!** *do not disturb!*
**rakı** *aniseed-flavoured spirit*
**reçel** *jam*
**rejimdeyim** *I'm on a diet*
**renk** *colour*
**renkler** *colours*
**resepsiyon memuru** *receptionist*
**restoran** *restaurant*
**rica ederim** *not at all*
**roka** *rocket leaves*
**Rus** *Russian* (people)
**Rusça** *Russian* (language)
**Rusya** *Russia*
**rüya** *dream*
**rüzgar** *wind*
**rüzgarlı** *windy*
**rüzgarsız** *without wind/windless*

**saat** *time, hour or clock*
**saat kaç?** *what time is it?*
**saat kaçta?** *at what time?*
**sabah** *morning*
**saç** *hair*
**sade** *plain/vanilla flavour, without sugar*
**sağ** *right*
**sağ olun/sağ ol** *thanks* (showing respect and gratitude)
**sağda** *on the right*
**sahil** *coast*
**sakin** *calm*
**salam** *salami*
**salatalık** *cucumber*
**salı** *Tuesday*
**samimi** *friendly*
**sana** *for you, to you*
**sandal** *rowing boat*
**sandalet** *sandals*
**saniye** *seconds*
**saray** *palace*
**sarı** *yellow*

**satmak** *to sell*
**sebze** *vegetables*
**sekreter** *secretary*
**Selçuk Türkleri** *Seljuk Turks*
**sen** *you* (singular)
**serin** *cool*
**sert** *hard*
**servis** *service*
**sevgi** *affection, love*
**sevgili** *beloved, dear*
**seviyorlar** *they love*
**seviyorum** *I like*
**seviyoruz** *we like/love*
**sevmek** *to love*
**sevmiyoruz** *we do not like/love*
**seyahat** *travel*
**seyahat acentası** *travel agency*
**seyretmek** *watch*
**sıcak** *hot*
**sıkıcı** *boring*
**sıkılmak** *to be bored*
**simit** *bread* (in the shape of a big ring)
**sinema** *cinema*
**sır** *secret*
**sırrımız** *our secret*
**sis** *fog*
**sisli** *foggy*
**siyah** *black*
**siyah gözlü** *dark-brown eyed* (lit. *black eyed*)
**siyah saçlı** *black haired*
**siz/sen** *you* (see Unit 1)
**sizin** *your*
**sizin için** *for you*
**sokmak** *to sting*
**sol** *left*
**sonbahar** *autumn/fall*
**sonra** *than, later*
**sor** *ask!*
**sormak** *to ask*

**sosis** sausage
**soyad** surname
**soyadım** my surname
**sözlük** dictionary
**spor** sport
**su** water
**sucuk** spicy Turkish sausage
**sudan ucuz** very cheap
**sumak** sumac
**susadım** I'm thirsty
**sür** drive
**sürmek** to drive
**süt** milk
**sütlü** with milk
**şampuan** shampoo
**şans** chance/luck
**şapka** hat
**şarap** wine
**şaraprengi** wine-coloured
**şarkıcı** singer
**şeker** sugar
**şekerli** with sugar, sweet
**şekersiz** without sugar
**şemsiye** umbrella
**şimdi** now
**şiş kebap** shish kebab
**şişe** bottle
**şoför** driver
**şu** that is, that
**şubat** February
**şunlar** these
**şurada** there
**şurası** there, that place

**tabii** of course
**takım elbise** suit
**taksi** taxi
**Taksim** Taksim Square in Istanbul
**tam** right, exactly, adult, full price
**tamam** OK
**tarif** recipe

**tarih** history, date
**tarihi** ancient, historic
**taşımak** to carry
**tatil** holiday
**tatiliniz** your holiday
**tatiller** holidays
**tatlı** dessert
**tatlı yiyelim, tatlı konuşalım** let's
    eat sweet, speak sweet (a common
    saying when offering sweet)
**tava** fried, frying pan
**tavla** backgammon
**taze** fresh
**tek kişilik** single room
**tek yataklı** single bed
**tekrar** again
**telefon numaraları** telephone
    numbers
**tembel** lazy
**temiz** clean
**temizlik yapmak** to do cleaning
**temmuz** July
**tenis** tennis
**tereyağı** butter
**teşekkür**(ler) thanks
**tık tık** knock knock
**tiyatro** theatre
**Topkapı Müzesi** Topkapı Museum
**tost (peynirli tost)** toasted
    sandwich (toasted cheese
    sandwich)
**tren** train
**turist** tourist
**turizm** tourism
**tüm** all
**turkuaz mavi** turquoise
**turuncu** orange
**tuvalet** toilet
**tuz** salt
**tür** kind
**Türk** Turkish (people)

**Türk kahvesi** Turkish coffee
**Türkçe** Turkish (language)
**Türkiye** Turkey
**TV'ye çıkmak** to be on TV

**ucuz** cheap
**uçak** aeroplane
**uzak** far
**uzun boylu** tall/long
**uzundur** it is long
**ülke** country
**üniversite** university
**ünlü** famous
**üstü kalsın** keep the change
**üzüm** grapes

**valiz** suitcase
**vapur** boat
**var** there is/are
**varış** arrival, arriving
**varmak (-e)** to arrive
**ve** and
**vermek** to give
**veya** or
**vişne suyu** sour cherry juice
**voleybol** volleyball

**ya siz?/ya sen?** and you?
**yaşındayım** I'm x years old
**yağıyor** it's raining
**yağmak** to rain
**yağmur** rain
**yağmurlu** rainy
**yağmursuz** without rain/rainless
**yakın** near
**yakında** soon
**yakışıklı** handsome
**yakışmak** to suit
**yalı** old wooden villa
**yanlış** wrong/false
**yapmak** to do

**yararlı** good for you
**yarım** half, half past twelve
**yarın** tomorrow
**yasak** forbidden
**yasaktır** it is forbidden
**yasaktır** forbidden
**yaş** age, old
**yaşlı** aged
**yatak** bed, mattress
**yavaş** slowly
**yavrum** my child (shows affection)
**yaya** pedestrian
**yayılmak** to spread
**yaz** summer
**yemek yemek** to eat food
**yer** place, seat
**yerken** while eating
**yeşil** green
**Yeşil Ev** Green House
**yok** there is none/we haven't got any
**yol** road
**yolcu** traveller
**yolcu vapuru** passenger boat
**yolculuk** journey
**yolumu kaybettim** I'm lost
**yorgun** tired
**yorgunum** I'm tired
**yoruldum** I'm tired
**yumurta** egg
**yüksek** high, loud
**yürümek** to walk
**yürüyerek** on foot
**yüzmek** to swim
**yüzme havuzu** swimming pool
**yüzük** ring

**zaman** time
**zengin** rich
**zeytin** olives
**zeytinyağlı** cooked with olive oil
**ziyaret** visit

# English–Turkish vocabulary

absolutely everything **her şey**
 **her şey**
ache, to **ağrımak**
aching **ağrıyor**
act, to **oynamak**
actor **aktör**
address **adres**
Aegean **Ege**
aeroplane **uçak**
affection **sevgi**
after **-dan, (-den) sonra**
after the class **dersten sonra**
again **tekrar**
age **yaş**
aged **yaşlı**
ago **önce**
air, weather **hava**
air hostess **hostes**
airport **havaalanı**
alive, live **canlı**
all **bütün, hep, tüm**
alphabet **alfabe**
also **da/de**
always **her zaman**
America **Amerika**
American (people) **Amerikalı**
Anatolia **Anadolu**
ancient, historic **tarihi**
and **ve**
and you? **ya siz?/ya sen?**
answer **cevap**
answer (to) **cevap vermek**
anything else **başka bir şey**
aphrodisiacs **padişah macunu**
apologize, to **özür dilemek**
apple **elma**

apple tea **elma çay**
apricot **kayısı**
April **nisan**
arrival, arriving **varış**
arrive, to **varmak (-e)**
as **olarak**
as far as; **Bursa -e, -a kadar;**
 **Bursa'ya kadar**
Asia **Asya**
Asian **Asyalı**
ask **sor**
ask, to **sormak**
aspirin **aspirin**
at **-de/-da**
at first **önce**
aubergine **patlıcan**
August **ağustos**
Australia **Avustralyalı**
autumn **sonbahar**
average **ortalama**
award **ödül**

backgammon **tavla**
bad **kötü**
bag **çanta**
bakery (oven) **fırın**
balcony; with a – **balkon; balkonlu**
bank **banka**
bargain **pazarlık**
bargain (to) (haggle) **pazarlık**
 **yapmak**
basketball **basketbol**
bass **levrek**
bath **küvet**
bath, bathroom **banyo**
beach **plaj**

*beautiful* **güzel**
*bed, mattress* **yatak**
*bee; a – has stung me* **arı; arı soktu**
*beer* **bira**
*before* ... **-den önce**
*Belgium* **Belçika**
*Belgian* (people) **Belçikalı**
*beloved* **sevgili**
*belt* **kemer**
*between* **arası**
*big* **büyük**
*bikini* **bikini**
*bill* **hesap**
*black; – haired; the – Sea* **siyah; siyah saçlı; Karadeniz**
*blouse* **bluz**
*blue* **mavi**; *very intense –* **masmavi**
*blue fish* **lüfer**
*Blue Cruise* **Mavi Yolculuk**
*boat; passenger –* **vapur; yolcu vapuru**
*book* (to) **ayırmak**
*boots* **çizme**
*bored* (to be) **sıkılmak**
*boring* **sıkıcı**
*born* (to be) **doğmak**
*both* ... *and* **hem** ... **hem**
*bottle* **şişe**
*boutique* **butik**
*box* **kutu**
*bread* **ekmek**
*break* (to) **bozmak**
*breakfast* **kahvaltı**
*brick* **kiremit, tuğla**
*bridge* **köprü**
*Britain* **Britanya**
*brother* (my) **kardeşim**
*brown* **kahverengi**
*building* **bina**
*building site* **inşaat**

*Bulgaria* (country) **Bulgaristan**
*Bulgarian* (language) **Bulgarca**
*Bulgarian* (people) **Bulgar**
*bus; by –; – stop; – ticket* **otobüs; otobüsle; otobüs durağı; otobüs bileti**
*busy; I'm busy* **meşgul; işim var, meşgulüm**
*but* **ama**
*butter* **tereyağ**

*cake; – shop* **pasta; pastahane**
*call* (to) (i.e. on the telephone) **aramak; arayayım**; *call me Yasemin* **bana Yasemin deyin**
*calm* **sakin**
*camel* **deve**
*campsite* **kamp**
*Canada* **Kanada**
*Canadian* (people) **Kanadalı**
*capital* **başkent**
*car* **araba**
*caravanserai* **kervansaray**
*card; by –* **kart; kartla**
*carpet* **halı**
*carry* (to) **taşımak**
*Central Asia* **Orta Asya**
*Central Europe* **Orta Avrupa**
*centre* **merkez**; *in the –* **ortada**
*chance* **şans**
*change; keep the –* **bozuk para; üstü kalsın**
*cheap* **ucuz**
*check in* **kontrol**
*cheese* **peynir**
*chemist's* **eczane**
*chicken* **piliç**
*child; my –* **çocuk; yavrum**
*chocolate flavoured/with chocolate* **çikolatalı**
*church* **kilise**

cinema **sinema**
class **ders**
clean **temiz**
clever **akıllı**
climate **iklim**
clock **saat**
coast **sahil**
close (to) **kapatmak**
coffee; – flavoured **kahve; kahveli**
colour **renk**
come, to **gelmek**
come on **hadi**
come out (to) **çıkmak**
comedy **komedi**
comfortable **rahat**
coming **gelecek**
computer **bilgisayar**
concert **konser**
conquered **aldı**
continuous **devamlı**
cooked with olive oil **zeytinyağlı**
cool **serin**
corner **köşe**
country **ülke**
countryside **kır**
courgette **kabak**
cover (to) **kapatmak**
credit; – card **kredi, kredi kartı**
cross (to) **geçmek**
cross **geç**
cucumber **salatalık**
cumin **kimyon**
curtain **perde**
customs **gümrük**
Cypriot **Kıbrıslı**
Cyprus **Kıbrıs**

daily (day) **günlük**
dance **dans**
dark-brown eyed (lit. black eyed)
 **siyah gözlü**

dark/olive skinned **esmer**
date of birth **doğum tarihi**
daughter; our – **kızımız**
day **gün**
dear; my – **sevgili; canım**
December **aralık**
dessert **tatlı**
dictionary **sözlük**
die (to) **ölmek**
diet; I'm on a – **rejim; rejimdeyim**
different **değişik, farklı**
disturb; do not – **rahatsız;**
 **rahatsız etmeyin**
dive (to) **dalmak**
do (to); cleaning **yapmak;**
 **temizlik yapmak**
doctor **doktor**
dog **köpek**
doner **döner**
dream **rüya**
dress **elbise**
dressed in white **beyazlı**
dried fruit **kuru yemiş**
drink **içecek**
drink (to) **içmek**
drive **sür**
drive (to) **sürmek**
driver **şoför**
dry **kurak, kuru**

each other **birbirimiz**
earrings **küpe**
easy **kolay**
eat food (to) **yemek yemek**
egg; soft-boiled – **yumurta;**
 **rafadan**
Egypt **Mısır**
Egyptian (people) **Mısırlı**
electricity **elektrik**
empty **boş**
engaged **nişanlı**

engineer **mühendis**
England **İngiltere**
English (language) **İngilizce**
English (people) **İngiliz**
enjoy (to); – using it; – your
  drinks; – your meal **güle güle
  kullanın; afiyet olsun**
enjoyable **keyifli**
enter (to) **girmek**
entrance **giriş**
especially **özellikle**
Europe **Avrupa**
European **Avrupalı**
even **bile**
evening **akşam**
every; – day; – thing **her; her gün;
  her şey**
excuse me **afedersiniz**
expensive **pahalı**

famous **ünlü**
far **uzak**
fast **hızlı**
father **baba**
February **şubat**
fiancé (your) **nişanlın**
fig **incir**
film **film**
fine; I'm – **iyi; iyiyim**
first **birinci**
first; – aid post **ilk; ilk yardım**
First World War **Birinci Dünya
  Savaşı**
fish **balık**
fisherman **balıkçı**
fishing **balıkçılık**
flower **çiçek**
fog **sis**
foggy **sisli**
foodstall **büfe**
foot; on – **yürüyerek**

football **futbol**
forbidden **yasak, yasaktır**
forest **orman**
fork **çatal**
fortress **hisar**
France **Fransa**
French (language) **Fransızca**
French (people) **Fransız**
fresh **taze**
Friday **cuma**
fried **tava, kızarmış**
friend; my – **arkadaş;
  arkadaşım**
friendly **samimi**
from ... to ... **-den -e kadar**
frost **don**
fruit; – flavoured/with – **meyve,
  yemiş; meyveli**
funny **komik**

generally **genellikle**
German (language) **Almanca**
German (people) **Alman**
Germany **Almanya**
get out **çık**
get up (to) **kalkmak**
give (to) **vermek**
glad; I'm – **memnun; memnun
  oldum**
glass **bardak**
glasses (spectacles) **gözlük**
gloves **eldiven**
go (to); please – **gitmek; gidin**
gold **altın**
good; – evening; – for you; – night
  **iyi; iyi akşamlar; yararlı; iyi
  geceler**
goodbye **hoşça kalın; güle güle**
  (reply to **hoşça kalın**)
Grand Bazaar **Kapalı Çarşı**
  (see Unit 8)

grapes **üzüm**
great **muhteşem**
green; – house **Yeşil; yeşil Ev**
grey **gri**
grilled **ızgara**
grocer/grocer's **bakkal**
guest house **pansiyon**

hair **saç**
hairdresser **kuaför**
half, half past twelve **yarım**
handsome **yakışıklı**
happy **mutlu**
hard; – working **sert, zor; çalışkan**
harem **harem**
hat **şapka**
hazelnuts **fındık**
he **o**
head; I have a –ache **baş; başım ağrıyor**
heavy **ağır**
hello; – (on the phone) **merhaba; alo**
here; – (shows movement); – you are; – it is; – this place **burada; buraya; buyurun; işte; burası**
Hindi **Hintçe**
hi **selam**
history **tarih**
holiday **tatil**
home **ev**
honest **dürüst**
honey **bal**
hookah **nargile**
horror **korku**
hospital **hastahane**
hot **sıcak**
hotel **otel**
hottest **en sıcak**
hour **saat**

house **ev**
how?; – (by –); – are you? – are you? … – can I help you sir/madam?; – do you spell it?; – many days?; – many hours?; – many people?; – much (lira)? **nasıl?; neyle (ne ile), nasıl; (see ile); nasılsın? (sen); nasılsınız (siz); buyrun, efendim; nasıl yazılır?; kaç gün?; kaç saat?; kaç kişi; kaç lira?**
hungry **aç**
hungry (to get) **acıkmak**

I **ben**
ice cream **dondurma**
idea **fikir**
in; – between; – front of us **-de; arasında; önümüzde**
include; is it included? **dahil; dahil mi?**
India **Hindistan**
Indian (person) **Hintli**
information **danışma**
instant coffee **Nescafé**
intelligence **akıl**
intelligent **akıllı**
interesting **ilginç**
island **ada**
isn't it? **değil mi?**
it **o**
Italian **İtalyanca**

jacket **ceket**
jam **reçel**
January **ocak**
Japan **Japonya**
Japanese (language) **Japonca**
Japanese (people) **Japon**
job, profession **meslek, iş**
journey **yolculuk**

joyous **keyifli**
July **temmuz**
jumper **kazak**
June **haziran**

keep the change **üstü kalsın**
key **anahtar**
kind **tür**
kind, type **çeşit**
king **kral**
knife **bıçak**
knock knock **tık tık**
know (to) **bilmek**

lace **dantel**
language **dil**
last **geçen**
late; I'm – **geç; geç kaldım**
later, than **sonra**
lazy **tembel**
leather **deri**
leave **bırak**
leave (to) **bırakmak**
leaving **kalkış**
left **sol**
lemon flavoured **limonlu**
lemonade (still) **limonata**
lesson **ders**
light (colour) **açık**
lights **ışıklar**
like (to) **sevmek**
liquor **likör**
list; lists of accommodation **liste; kalacak yer listesi**
little (a) **biraz**
long **uzun**
look (to) **bakmak**
lost; I'm – **kayıp; yolumu kaybettim**
loud **yüksek**
love (to) **sevmek**

luck **şans**
luxury **lüks**

magazine **magazin**
map **harita**
marble **mermer**
March **mart**
married; to get – to **evli; evlenmek**
mattress, bed **yatak**
May **mayıs**
me, for –; on –; – too **bana; benim için; benden; ben de**
meat; with –; without – **et; etli; etsiz**
Mediterranean **Akdeniz**
medium; – sized **orta; orta boy**
men **erkek**
menu **mönü**
middle; in the – **ortada**
midnight **gece yarısı**
military service **askerlik**
milk; with – **süt; sütlü**
mint **nane**
minutes **dakika**
Miss/Mrs/Ms (after first names only) **Hanım**
mixed; – fruit; – salad **karışık; karışık meyve; çoban-salatası**
model **manken**
modern **modern**
Monday **pazartesi**
more (comparative) **daha**
morning **sabah**
mosque **cami**
most (the) **en**
mother **anne**
motorway **otoyol**
mountain **dağ**
Mr (after first names only) **bey**
mud; – bath **çamur; çamur banyosu**

mulberry **dut**
museum **müze**
music **müzik**
musical **müzikal**
my, it's me **benim**

name **ad**
nationality **milliyet**
near **yakın**
nearest **en yakın**
necessary **gerek**
never **hiç**
newspaper **gazete**
next **gelecek**
nice **hoş**
night **gece**
no **hayır**
noise **gürültü**
noon **öğlen**
not; not at all **değil; rica ederim**
November **kasım**
now **şimdi**
number **numara**
nuts **fıstık**
nutty **fıstıkı**

occupy (to) **işgal etmek**
October **ekim**
office **büro**
OK **tamam**
old; – wooden villa **eski; yalı**
olives; – skinned **zeytin; esmer**
on; – foot; – me; – the right; – the
  table **yürüyerek; benden; sağda;**
  **masada**
only **henüz**
open **açık**
open (to) **açmak**
opinion; in my – **fikir; bence**
opposite **karşı**
or **veya**

orange **turuncu**
Ottomans **Osmanlılar**
oven **fırın**

packet **paket**
pair **çift**
palace **saray**
pardon? **efendim?**
parents, my – (lit. my mothers)
  **annemler**
park **park**
party **parti**
passport; – number **pasaport;**
  **pasaport numarası**
past **geçiyor (-i)**
pastry; – shop **börek; börekçi**
pay (to); – attention **ödemek;**
  **dikkat et**
pedestrian **yaya**
people **kişi, insanlar**
pepper **biber**
peppermint flavoured **naneli**
person **insan**
person **kişi**
pink (colour) **pembe**
place; – of birth **yer; doğum yeri**
plain/vanilla flavour **sade**
platinum **platin**
play area **oyun parkı**
please **lütfen**
pleasant **hoş**
pleasure **keyif**
popular **popüler**
port **iskele**
port **liman**
portion **porsiyon**
post **posta**
potatoes **patates**
present **hediye**
President **cumhurbaşkanı**
prices **fiyatlar**

Prime Minister **Başbakan**
profession, job **meslek**
professor **profesör**
programme **program**
protect (to) **korumak**
public phone **genel telefon**
pull (to) **çekmek**
purple **mor**
purse/wallet **cüzdan**
push **it**
push (to) **itmek**
put (to); to – ... on **atmak;
  koymak**

quarter **çeyrek**

rain; without – **yağmur;
  yağmursuz**
rain (to) **yağmak**
rainbow **gökkuşağı**
rainy **yağmurlu**
read (to); to – fortunes **okumak;
  fal bakmak**
really **gerçekten**
receptionist **resepsiyon memuru**
recipe **tarif**
record **plak**
red; – mullet **kırmızı; barbunya**
reforms **devrimler**
region **bölge**
republic **cumhuriyet**
reserve (to) **ayırmak**
restaurant **lokanta; restoran**
retired **emekli**
return **dönüş**
rice (cooked); with cooked – **pilav;
  pilavlı**
rich **zengin**
right; on the –; – (exactly); – (true);
  you are – **sağ; sağda; tam;
  doğru, haklısınız**

ring **yüzük**
ring (to) **çalmak**
road **yol**
rocket leaves **roka**
room **oda**
rose **gül**
rough **dalgalı**
roughly **falan**
row a boat (to) **kürek çekmek**
rowing boat **sandal**
ruin **harabe**
Russia **Rusya**
Russian (language) **Rusça**
Russian (people) **Rus**

salad **salata**
salami **salam**
salt **tuz**
sand **kum**
sandals **sandalet**
sands **kumlar**
Saturday **cumartesi**
sausage **sosis**
sea **deniz**
seaside **deniz kenarları**
season **mevsim**
seat **yer**
seconds **saniye**
secret **sır**
see (to); to – each other **görmek;
  görüşmek**
secretary **sekreter**
Seljuk Turks **Selçuk Türkleri**
sell (to) **satmak**
separate **ayrı**
September **eylül**
serious **ciddi**
service **servis**
shade **gölge**
shampoo **şampuan**
she **o**

shirt **gömlek**
shish kebab **şiş kebap**
shoes; – shop **ayakkabı;**
 **ayakkabıcı**
shopping **alışveriş**
shower **duş**
sibling **kardeş**
sign **işaret**
sign a contract (to) **anlaşmak**
since 1777 **1777'den beri**
singer **şarkıcı**
single; – bed; – ticket **bekar; tek**
 **yataklı; tek kişilik**
sister (my) **kız kardeşim**
size **beden, numara**
sizzling **cızbız**
skirt **etek**
sliced **dilimlenmiş**
slowly **yavaş**
small **küçük**
snacks **çerez**
snow **kar**
sometimes **ara sıra**
soon **yakında**
sorry (to be) **özür dilerim**
south **güney**
Spain **İspanya**
Spanish (language) **İspanyolca**
Spanish (people) **İspanyol**
special **özel**
spices **baharat**
sport **spor**
spread (to) **yayılmak**
spring **ilkbahar**
starter **meze**
station **istasyon**
stay (to) **kalmak**
steamed **buğulama**
sting (to) **sokmak**
stop (to) **durmak**
stop, bus – **durak**

straight; – away **düz; hemen**
street **cadde**
student **öğrenci**
stupid **akılsız**
sugar; with –; without – **şeker;**
 **şekerli; sade**
suit **takım elbise**
suit (to) **yakışmak**
suitcase **valiz**
sumac **sumak**
summer **yaz**
sun **güneş**
Sunday **pazar**
sunny **güneşli**
surname; my – **soyad; soyadım**
swim (to) **yüzmek**
swimming costume **mayo**
swimming pool **yüzme-havuzu**
switch off (to) **kapatmak**

table; on the – **masa; masada**
take (to) **almak**
tall **uzun boylu**
tape **kaset**
tasty **lezzetli**
taxi **taksi**
tea **çay**
teach (to) **öğretmek**
teacher **öğretmen**
telephone numbers **telefon**
 **numaraları**
tennis **tenis**
tent **çadır**
terrible **berbat**
than **sonra**
thanks; – (showing respect and
 gratitude) **teşekkür(ler); sağ olun**
that (referring to something
 relatively far way); – is; that's all
 **o; şu; hepsi bu kadar**
theatre **tiyatro**

*there* **orada**

*there; – is none; – is/are; – (that place)* **şurada; yok; var; şurası**

*these; – are* **şunlar; bunlar**

*they* **onlar**

*think (to); I –* **düşünmek; galiba**

*thirsty (to be); I'm thirsty* **susamak; susadım**

*this* **bu**

*Thursday* **perşembe**

*ticket; – office* **bilet; bilet gişesi**

*time* **kez**

*time* **zaman**

*time (hour); at what –?* **saat; saat kaçta?**

*times* **kere**

*tip* **bahşiş**

*tired* **yorgun**

*toast (to)* **kızarmış**

*toasted sandwich (toasted cheese sandwich)* **tost (peynirli tost)**

*today* **bugün**

*toilet* **tuvalet; 00**

*tomatoes* **domates**

*tomorrow* **yarın**

*took, conquered* **aldı**

*tourism* **turizm**

*tourist* **turist**

*towel* **havlu**

*train* **tren**

*travel; – agency* **seyahat; seyahat acentası**

*travel (to)* **gezmek**

*traveller* **yolcu**

*trip (journey)* **gezi**

*trousers* **pantolon**

*true* **doğru**

*try on (to)* **denemek**

*Tuesday* **salı**

*turbot* **kalkan**

*Turkey* **Türkiye**

*Turkish (language)* **Türkçe**

*Turkish (people); – Bath; – coffee; – coffee maker; – delight; – delight shop; – meatballs; – restaurant; – pizza* **Türk; Hamam; Türk kahvesi; cezve; lokum; lokumcu; köfte; köfteci; pide**

*Turkish pizza restaurant* **pideci**

*turn* **dön**

*turn (to)* **dönmek**

*turquoise* **turkuaz mavi**

*TV (to be on)* **TV, ye çıkmak**

*umbrella* **şemsiye**

*understand (to)* **anlamak**

*unemployed* **işsiz**

*unfortunately (a polite remark)* **maalesef**

*unhappy* **mutsuz**

*university* **üniversite**

*USA* **ABD**

*vacant* **boş**

*various* **çeşitli**

*vegetables* **sebze**

*very* **çok**

*view; with a –* **manzara; manzaralı**

*village* **köy**

*visit* **ziyaret**

*volleyball* **voleybol**

*waiter/waitress* **garson**

*walk (to)* **yürümek**

*wallet* **cüzdan**

*want (to)* **istemek**

*War of Independence* **Kurtuluş Savaşı**

*warm* **ılık**

*watch (to)* **seyretmek**

*watch out!* **dikkat et!**

*water* **su**
*watermelon* **karpuz**
*we* **biz**
*weather* **hava**
*Wednesday* **çarşamba**
*week* **hafta**
*weekend* **hafta sonu**
*welcome* **hoş geldiniz**
*what?; – are there?; –*
  *else; – places?; – shall we*
  *do?; – size?; – time is it?* **ne?;**
  **neler var?; başka ne?; nereler?;**
  **ne yapalım?; kaç beden?;**
  **saat kaç?**
*where?; – are you from?; – shall*
  *we go?; – (shows movement); –*
  *(which place)?* **nereye?; neresi?;**
  **nerelisin?; nereye gidelim?;**
  **nerede?;**
*which?* **hangi?**
*while* **iker -iken**
*white; – bean salad* **beyaz; piyaz**
*why?* **niçin? (ne için); neden?**
*wife* (my) **eşim; karım**

*wild; – countryside; – flowers* **kır;**
  **kır çiçekleri**
*win* (to) **kazanmak**
*wind; without –* **rüzgar;**
  **rüzgarsız**
*window* **pencere**
*windy* **rüzgarlı**
*wine* **şarap**
*wine* (colour) **şaraprengi**
*winter* **kış**
*woman* **kadın**
*wonderful* **harika**
*work* (job) **iş**
*world* **dünya**
*woven rug* **kilim**
*wrong* **yanlış**

*yellow* **sarı**
*yes* **evet**
*yesterday* **dün**
*yet* **henüz**
*you; for –; to –* **siz/sen; sana;**
  **senin için**
*your* **sizin**

# Index

The numbers refer to the units in which the information is to be found.